Understanding AI Decisions, Computer Vision, and Management Analytics

Mohit Mittal
Smart Lab AI GmbH, Germany

Swadha Gupta
CAI Conversational AI GmbH, Germany

IGI Global
Scientific Publishing
Publishing Tomorrow's Research Today

Vice President of Editorial	Melissa Wagner
Director of Acquisitions	Mikaela Felty
Director of Book Development	Jocelynn Hessler
Production Manager	Mike Brehm
Cover Design	Jose Rosado

Published in the United States of America by
IGI Global Scientific Publishing
701 East Chocolate Avenue
Hershey, PA, 17033, USA
Tel: 717-533-8845 | Fax: 717-533-7115
Website: https://www.igi-global.com E-mail: cust@igi-global.com

Library of Congress Cataloging-in-Publication Data

Names: Mittal, Mohit, 1988- editor http://id.loc.gov/rwo/agents/n2024049498 | Gupta, Swadha, 1991- editor http://id.loc.gov/rwo/agents/n2024062689
Title: Understanding AI decisions, computer vision, and management analytics / edited by Mohit Mittal, Swadha Gupta.
Other titles: Understanding artificial intelligence decisions, computer vision, and management analytics
Description: Hershey, PA : IGI Global, [2026] | Includes bibliographical references and index. | Summary: "The primary objective of this book is to provide an in-depth exploration of Artificial Intelligence (AI) with a specific focus on its capabilities in decision-making, computer vision, and management analytics"-- Provided by publisher.
Identifiers: LCCN 2024049795 (print) | LCCN 2024049796 (ebook) | ISBN 9798369383278 hardcover | ISBN 9798369383285 paperback | ISBN 9798369383292 ebook
Subjects: LCSH: Decision making--Data processing http://id.loc.gov/authorities/subjects/sh2008102118 | Computer vision http://id.loc.gov/authorities/subjects/sh85029549 | Artificial intelligence http://id.loc.gov/authorities/subjects/sh85008180 | Management--Data processiong
Classification: LCC HD30.23 .U56 2025 (print) | LCC HD30.23 (ebook) | DDC 658.4/030285--dc23/eng/20250106
LC record available at https://lccn.loc.gov/2024049795
LC ebook record available at https://lccn.loc.gov/2024049796
British Cataloguing in Publication Data
A Cataloguing in Publication record for this book is available from the British Library.

Table of Contents

Detailed Table of Contents

Natural Language Processing (NLP) is transforming the customer experience and transforming businesses into data-driven ones. NLP technologies enable personalized customer relations and machine-like service completion through chatbots and virtual assistants. These tools use artificial intelligence to provide timely and relevant help, enhancing service speed. NLP-based sentiment analysis helps businesses understand customer emotions from various platforms, improving products and marketing strategies. NLP also helps turn ill-structured textual data into useful insights, such as topic analysis, keyword extraction, and entity identification. This helps organizations analyze trends, consumer preferences, and emerging issues for strategic decision-making. NLP increases efficiency by saving time on repetitive data processing activities. Integrating NLP with data-driven methodologies enhances customer interaction and improves business performance in today's data-driven environment.

The main facets of digital transformation and their effects on the retail industry are covered in this chapter. Digital transformation and its significance in the current corporate environment are defined at the beginning of the chapter. It talks about how the retail industry is changing as a result of cutting-edge technology like artificial intelligence (AI), big data analytics, and the Internet of Things (IoT). The chapter looks at how merchants are using these tools to improve customer service, streamline processes, and obtain a competitive advantage. The significance of the customer experience in the digital era is one of the main topics discussed in this chapter. It explores how merchants are personalizing their goods, enhancing customer interaction,

This chapter explores the transformative impact of these systems on logistics, highlighting their role in optimizing operations, enhancing decision-making, and improving overall efficiency. The chapter also examines implementation strategies, including the integration of machine learning models, real-time data processing, and predictive analytics, to facilitate informed decision-making across various logistics functions such as inventory management, route optimization, and demand forecasting. Case studies of leading logistics companies are presented to illustrate successful applications and the tangible benefits achieved. Additionally, the chapter addresses challenges related to data security, scalability, and the need for continuous system updates to adapt to changing market conditions. By providing a comprehensive overview of the design and implementation processes, this chapter aims to guide logistics professionals and researchers in leveraging AI-driven DSS to create smarter, more responsive logistics networks..

PCOS is a condition which leads to growth of ovarian cysts and prevalent endocrine disorder in child bearing women which can lead to infertility during the upcoming years. It causes hormonal imbalance and issues with metabolism thereby affecting the overall health and appearance. Some of the common symptoms include oily skin, darkened acne marks, weight gain, hypertension and irregular menstrual cycle. According to that the proposed work discloses a novel method to predict the PCOS disease based on external symptoms like pigmentation, patches and hair growth in face using camera sensors. This model is implemented by getting face images using the camera sensor and predicting PCOS using machine learning and deep learning techniques. Currently, diagnosis of PCOS is done only using ultrasound scans, which are bound to produce several harmful effects on the internal organs. Moreover, many women are unaware of the presence of PCOS. As an alternative to the current method of diagnosis, this system will be an alternative to predict the PCOS based on external symptoms.

Brain tumor is one of the most fatal diseases in the world. As per the WHO cancer is the 2nd leading cause of death globally and around 9.6 million people died in 2018. Tumors are of 2 types: Benign and malignant. Benign tumors are usually not dangerous as they do not spread to other parts of the body but malignant tumors are dangerous as they are fast growing and spread to other body parts and can be life threatening. In order to quickly and effectively start the brain tumor treatment, it is really important for the doctor to diagnose the patient to correctly identify the type of tumor the patient has. But manual diagnosis by the doctor is not the best way to proceed with a disease fatal like tumors as manual diagnosis is prone to errors, time consuming and highly depends on the skill level of the doctor itself. In situations like this the deep learning models for Brain MRI image classification task can be quite useful as it gives better results with higher accuracy than the manual diagnosis and saves time. Prior researchers have done a lot of work in this field but still there is room for improvement. The proposed model utilize the dataset having 7022 Brain MRI images is a merger of 3 datasets: Br35H, figshare, SARTAJ which is publicly available on kaggle. The classification of the dataset is done into 4 categories namely: pituitary, no tumor, glioma and meningioma. The training and testing dataset comprises of 5712 and 1310 images respectively. The proposed Brain tumor classification model with test accuracy of 99.8% uses EfficientNetB3 pretrained model for extraction of powerful features and utilizes transfer learning in order to study the complex Brain MRI images patterns in depth. It is evident from the outcomes that the proposed method achieves higher accuracy compared with existing state of art techniques.

This chapter explains the significance of Underwater Target Recognition (UTR) for marine research, defence, and exploration, focusing on the challenges posed by the unique underwater environment. It begins by examining the difficulties of underwater sensing and introduces Reinforcement Learning (RL) as a promising approach to improve UTR systems. RL enhances decision-making in uncertain,

Preface

Artificial Intelligence is no longer a distant promise, it is an operational reality reshaping industries, redefining decision-making, and augmenting human capability across domains. From customer engagement and retail transformation to motorsports analytics, healthcare diagnostics, logistics optimization, underwater exploration, and blockchain security, AI systems are increasingly embedded in the fabric of modern society.

This volume, *Understanding AI Decisions, Computer Vision, and Management Analytics*, brings together diverse yet interconnected explorations of how intelligent systems interpret data, generate insights, and support strategic action. The chapters collectively highlight not only the technical sophistication of contemporary AI models—ranging from machine learning and deep learning to reinforcement learning—but also their managerial, ethical, and societal implications.

At its core, this book is about decision intelligence: how algorithms transform raw, structured, and unstructured data into actionable knowledge. Whether analyzing human language, interpreting medical imagery, predicting competitive performance, or detecting vulnerabilities in digital contracts, the contributions in this volume demonstrate how AI-driven analytics are evolving from supportive tools into central pillars of organizational and scientific progress.

CHAPTER OVERVIEW

Chapter 1: Applications of NLP in Customer Service, Sentiment Analysis, and Market Research

This chapter examines how Natural Language Processing (NLP) enhances customer engagement and business intelligence. It discusses applications such as chatbots, virtual assistants, sentiment analysis, topic modeling, and entity extraction. By transforming unstructured textual data into strategic insights, NLP enables organizations to improve personalization, operational efficiency, and data-driven decision-making.

Chapter 2: Applications of Sentiment Analysis in Customer Service through Market Research in the Horn of Africa

Focusing on retail digital transformation, this chapter explores how AI, big data analytics, and IoT technologies reshape customer experience and competitive positioning. It highlights how sentiment analysis supports market research, enabling retailers to personalize offerings, enhance engagement, and foster brand loyalty within emerging markets.

Chapter 3: Entertainment Revolution & Applications of Machine Learning Innovations

This chapter explores the transformative role of machine learning in the entertainment industry. From content creation to personalization and audience analytics, it discusses how AI expands creative possibilities while raising important economic, ethical, and authenticity debates. The chapter situates entertainment within broader interdisciplinary contexts, including psychology, human–computer interaction, and digital consumption behavior.

Chapter 4: Predictive Modeling of Drivers' Positions in Formula 1 Racing Using Machine Learning Techniques

Using the global motorsport platform of Formula 1 as a case study, this chapter demonstrates how machine learning models, such as Random Forest, Gradient Boosting, Support Vector Classifier, and Neural Networks, can forecast race outcomes. By analyzing historical data on driver performance, team dynamics, weather, and track conditions, the chapter illustrates how predictive analytics can inform competitive strategy and performance optimization.

Chapter 5: Smart Logistics: Designing and Implementing AI-Driven Decision Support Systems

This chapter presents frameworks for developing AI-powered decision support systems in logistics. It covers predictive analytics, route optimization, inventory management, and real-time data integration. Through case studies and implementation insights, the chapter provides guidance for building scalable, secure, and adaptive logistics networks.

Chapter 6: Deep Learning-Based Polycystic Ovarian Syndrome (PCOS) Disease Prediction

Addressing women's health, this chapter introduces a novel deep learning approach for predicting PCOS using facial image analysis and external symptom detection. By proposing a non-invasive alternative to traditional ultrasound diagnostics, the work highlights how computer vision can expand early detection capabilities and promote preventive healthcare.

Chapter 7: Deep Learning in Medical Imaging – Improving Diagnostics of Brain Tumors

This chapter explores neural network-based classification of brain MRI images using transfer learning and advanced pretrained architectures. By categorizing tumors into clinically relevant classes with high accuracy, the research demonstrates how AI-driven medical imaging can enhance diagnostic precision, reduce manual workload, and support clinical decision-making.

Chapter 8: Methodologies, Challenges, and Opportunities in Underwater Target Recognition

Focusing on marine and defense applications, this chapter investigates Underwater Target Recognition (UTR) through Reinforcement Learning (RL) and Deep RL frameworks. It addresses environmental sensing challenges and demonstrates how adaptive learning algorithms can improve decision-making in uncertain underwater conditions.

Chapter 9: Towards Secure Smart Contracts – An AI-Enhanced Framework for Vulnerability Detection

Centered on blockchain ecosystems such as Ethereum, this chapter proposes an AI-driven framework for detecting vulnerabilities in smart contracts. By integrating machine learning and deep learning techniques with security analysis, the work contributes to building more reliable and resilient decentralized systems.

Chapter 1
Applications of NLP in Customer Service, Sentiment Analysis, and Market Research

Piyal Roy
http://orcid.org/0009-0007-5378-2789
Brainware University, India

Rajat Pandit
West Bengal State University, India

Amitava Podder
http://orcid.org/0009-0004-9268-3781
Brainware University, India

ABSTRACT

Natural Language Processing (NLP) is transforming the customer experience and transforming businesses into data-driven ones. NLP technologies enable personalized customer relations and machine-like service completion through chatbots and virtual assistants. These tools use artificial intelligence to provide timely and relevant help, enhancing service speed. NLP-based sentiment analysis helps businesses understand customer emotions from various platforms, improving products and marketing strategies. NLP also helps turn ill-structured textual data into useful insights, such as topic analysis, keyword extraction, and entity identification. This helps organizations analyze trends, consumer preferences, and emerging issues for strategic decision-making. NLP increases efficiency by saving time on repetitive data

DOI: 10.4018/979-8-3693-8327-8.ch001

processing activities. Integrating NLP with data-driven methodologies enhances customer interaction and improves business performance in today's data-driven environment.

1. INTRODUCTION

Machine understanding of human language is as a result of Natural Language Processing (NLP) has greatly being enhanced. Due to the possibilities of translating the human language into something that computers can interpret, NLP remains one of the fundamental foundations of today's AI. The present chapter is devoted to the analysis of the relevance and application of NLP in customer service, analysis of customers' sentiment, and market research, which specify the importance of NLP in the present business environment.

1. 1 Overview of NLP

NLP is also stated as an important area of study within artificial intelligence that concerns with the communication between humans and computers using natural language information processing. NLP includes several subfields and algorithms that provide the ability to machines regarding the understanding, parsing, and creating natural languages. Its importance is based on the fact it enables humans to communicate with computers so that technology is easy to use.

1. 1. 1 Definition and Significance

Natural Language Processing entails the creating capability of algorithms as well as models that enable machines to deal with, scrutinize, as well as produce natural language text. This is for instance activities like speech recognition, text mining, machine translation as well as sentiment analysis. On this aspect, NLP empowers devices to understand and create human language; thus, building the interface or facilitation of interaction with machines. This capability is useful in such contexts as voice interfaces, computing assistants, and bots as well as customer support and data processing.

Precisely, one has to underline that the importance of NLP does not stop with the denial of plain text processing capacity. It is widely used for improving the interaction with users, managing numerous processes that are repetitive, and analyzing big volumes of information that is unstructured. Today, different applications in NLP are essentials for numerous industries such as healthcare, finances, e-commerce, and entertainment due to efficiency, novelty, and competitiveness.

1.1.2 Historical Context and Evolution

It has been quite a long trip for NLP starting its journey at the early dawn of the computer science world. The history of machine translation was kicked off in the 1950s and this was where experts started developing translation systems that could translate from one language to another at the click of a button. It also introduced the preliminary studies of what could be called computational linguistics, which dealt with the syntactic and semantic structure of language.

The two decades that ruled the NLP field were the 1960s and the 70s, where rule and based systems followed by symbolic approaches dominated this field. The former was based on an extraction of rules and knowledge of language using skilled manpower. Although within the framework of certain procedures they provided good results, artificial intelligence based on rules had shortcomings in terms of extensiveness and flexibility. The appearance of an adequate number of papers on statistical methods in the 1980s and 1990s made a great contribution to NLP. Early generations of Machine Learning used probabilistic models including Hidden Markov Models (HMMs) and early neural networks and this laid the foundation for the large corpora of text data used in today's Natural Language Processing systems.

However, the year 2000 marked the major shift in NLP due to modern methods of deep learning and neural network models. Models like Word2Vec and GloVe revolutionized the way machines dealt with words in the context of a Hilbert space. With the help of these embeddings, semantic connection between the words were captured, thus enhancing the depth and overall efficiency of language understanding.

New concepts like recurrent neural networks, long short-term memory networks, and transformers, including BERT and GPT, also progressed NLP solutions. These models proved to be very effective in capturing both future and past dependencies and also contextual information about the words in the text and outperformed most other models in a number of language tasks.

Present day NLP is again an active area of research and development with stimulations from developments in machine learning fields, computing power and accessibility of humongous corpora. The field has now encompassed aspects like conversational artificial intelligence, sentiment analysis, and machine translation and text summarization and is applied across different fields and domains.

1.2 Importance of NLP in Business

NLP as an important part of modern business functioning facilitates the improvement of the customer's experience, automates various processes, extracts significant information from the unstructured data. Learning from this criss-cross strategy and through the use of natural language processing technologies, possible new approaches of business challenges can be extended and future business models can be set up.

1. 2. 1 Enhancing Customer Experience

In the current world, customer experience has become the key competitive advantage among the players in industries. NLP hence is central to improving customer satisfaction since it aims at optimizing the interactions between institutions and customers. Most of the engagement models, including the chatbots and virtual assistants, apply NLP in real-time to meet customers' requirements. These agents can include quickly answering general questions, recommending products, and solving various types of technological problems.

Sentiment analysis tools derived from NLP help companies determine the feelings of customers through feedback in forms of reviews, social media activities, and feedback surveys. Customers' emotions and opinions about a certain product are significant factors that help organizations to improve on the delivery of the products and services and the way they are marketed. Further, NLP is useful in other customer care related activities such as handling most of the response frequently asked by the customers, thus cutting down on response time and at the same time, providing the customers with consistent service.

1. 2. 2 Driving Data-Driven Decisions

It remains a common fact in the age of big data that organizations and companies receive large volumes of textual data in the form of e-mails, reports, social media posts, and customer feedbacks. Analyzing this unstructured data through NLP helps to extract the data's value and convert it into useful information for use in decision making. Text analytics is one of the applications of NLP and comprises subject identification, text mining for keyword spotting and entity identification, among others; all of which assist firms to identify emerging trends, trends and problems.

For example, front-end companies such as market research organizations employ NLP to decipher consumer trends and his/her purchasing pattern from volatile sources like social calendar and feedbacks. This orientation allows the company to better analyse the market and its changes, competition, and customers' requirements for products and services, decisions on product launches, marketing strategies, and long-term strategies.

NLP as an important part of modern business functioning facilitates the improvement of the customer's experience, automates various processes, extracts significant information from the unstructured data. Learning from this criss-cross strategy and through the use of natural language processing technologies, possible new approaches of business challenges can be extended and future business models can be set up.

1. 2. 3 Enhancing Customer Experience

In the current world, customer experience has become the key competitive advantage among the players in industries. NLP hence is central to improving customer satisfaction since it aims at optimizing the interactions between institutions and customers. Most of the engagement models, including the chatbots and virtual assistants, apply NLP in real-time to meet customers' requirements. These agents can include quickly answering general questions, recommending products, and solving various types of technological problems.

Sentiment analysis tools derived from NLP help companies determine the feelings of customers through feedback in forms of reviews, social media activities, and feedback surveys (Roy et al., 2023). Customers' emotions and opinions about a certain product are significant factors that help organizations to improve on the delivery of the products and services and the way they are marketed. Further, NLP is useful in other customer care related activities such as handling most of the response frequently asked by the customers, thus cutting down on response time and at the same time, providing the customers with consistent service.

1. 2. 4 Driving Data-Driven Decisions

It remains a common fact in the age of big data that organizations and companies receive large volumes of textual data in the form of e-mails, reports, social media posts, and customer feedbacks. Analyzing this unstructured data through NLP helps to extract the data's value and convert it into useful information for use in decision making. Text analytics is one of the applications of NLP and comprises subject identification, text mining for keyword spotting and entity identification, among others; all of which assist firms to identify emerging trends, trends and problems.

For example, front-end companies such as market research organizations employ NLP to decipher consumer trends and his/her purchasing pattern from volatile sources like social calendar and feedbacks. This orientation allows the company to better analyse the market and its changes, competition, and customers' requirements for products and services, decisions on product launches, marketing strategies, and long-term strategies.

1.2.5 Sentiment Analysis

Positive and negative feedback analysis is made possible by using NLP at different customer touch points such as in reviews, social media posts, and feedback polls. Sentiment analysis is the process of mining and analyzing subjective information from text data that can shed a light on customers' attitudes toward a certain product or service. For instance, in customers' feedback, it is possible to make a distinction between positive, negative or neutral attitudes to this or that product or service, which will help business people to define the directions of its further development or, conversely, the aspects that are popular among consumers (Pang & Lee, 2008).

Thus, evaluation of customer's feelings and perceptions assists companies in making the necessary adjustments in their products, services, and marketing communication campaigns. Thus, if sentiment analysis shows that customers are constantly complaining concerning a certain aspect of a product, then the company can dedicate its effort in fixing this in the subsequent versions. On the other hand, positive attitude towards an element can be used in promotional strategies to bring in more consumers.

1. 2. 6 Automation and Efficiency

Automated requirements of customer care services are also critical functions of NLP. Applying NLP in the development of communication bots means the company can accommodate more than one person or organization's inquiries at one particular time, besides providing quality services at maximum feature. For instance, an automated ticketing system may sort and prioritize the customer's inquiry based on the words used in the message that such habitual ticketing systems as Zendesk, Freshdesk, help human operators to prioritize several messages by ticket content (Hirschberg & Manning, 2015).

Initially, it enhances operation efficiency, secondly, human call center agents are free to attend to other delicate and more socially related issues. Thus, cutting time on simple operations would improve overall service quality and guarantee a customer's timely and correct help.

1. 2. 7 Driving Data-Driven Decisions

In the current world of large data, the primary, though not exclusive, mode of communication is textual; businesses experience an overload of such textual information as emails, reports, social media, or customers' feedback. It plays a crucial role of making this unstructured data structural and useful for the organization's decision-making process.

1.2.8 Text Analytics

Some of the application of NLP include text analytics which includes; topic modeling, keyword extraction and entity recognition. The methods of topic modeling such as Latent Dirichlet Allocation (LDA) in fact let us determine and classify the topics in the large textual data sets to reveal hidden patterns and (Blei et al., 2003). Keyword extraction and entity recognition also help to extract terms and entities relevant for the analysis of the market and its trends, customers' preferences, and emerging issues.

For example, market research uses NLP to analyze the consumers' conversations in social media and their feedback on online reviews. It offers a more robust analysis of the market forces, competitors, and customers, enabling a firm to conceive its products and services, market in general, and its strategic directions in the best way possible. Studying 'What's hot,' helps to adjust a company's initiatives to existing conditions or clients' preferences.

1. 2. 9 Operational Efficiency

The use of NLP in automating data analysis also improves the tasks carried out in the operation as less manpower is needed in data processing. Routine data pre-processing, classification, and summarization are some of the activities that can be performed with the help of NLP algorithms and thus, save time that can be used for more important work. For example, text summarization can be helpful in quick analysis of large reports or clients' feedback, as an application can provide analysts with summaries of the main points, thus saving time (Nenkova & McKeown, 2011).

Besides, this automation enhances efficiency and quality in the execution of responsibilities, especially when it comes to analysing data. Using NLP for repetitive missions means that focus loads of businesses will be shifted to the priority tasks, increasing their overall efficiency and competitive edge.

1.3 Scope of the Chapter

This chapter aims to explore the multifaceted applications of NLP in three critical business areas: It will help in call center or customer relations, business intelligence with sentiment analysis, and in analyzing market trends and sentiments. Through these examples, the chapter offers a broad look at what NLP means for business and helps to understand how this field contributes to the transformation of the business world and the provision of innovative solutions for organizations today.

1. 3. 1 Customer Service

It will expand on how such key areas as NLP driven technologies including chatbots and virtual assistants are reshaping customer interaction, delivering real time support and increasing the level of customer satisfaction. Hence, the chapter will explore multiple application areas of NLP, approaches for their integration into the customer service processes, as well as advantages and drawbacks of using NLP in different scenarios.

1. 3. 2 Sentiment Analysis

The chapter will thereby focus on understanding the concepts of sentiment analysis, the approaches used on the analysis and its real life use on various fields. Sentiment analysis, based on the assessment of the positive, negative, or neutral attitudes customers' express machine learning, can show the overall sentiment, reveal shifts in opinions, and trends in brand perception from the textual data of the reviews, posts, and other sources. Specific examples and the use of case-studies will help explain how sentiment analysis works and what benefits it brings to the business world.

1. 3. 3 Market Research

In this subtopic, we will discuss how NLP applies itself to market researches with a specific emphasis on how it assists various organizations collect and analyze information with a view of making sense of consumer behavior, trends, and competition. In the given chapter, the author begins by outlining the array of NLP tools in market analysis, from topic modeling, creating entity recognizers, or classifying large corpora of text, and emphasize on their utility in understanding strategic markets.

The analysis of these applications will be helpful to understand how NLP changes business, creates new opportunities, and helps organizations to be on the pertinent trends in the world of big data.

2. NLP IN CUSTOMER SERVICE

NLP has emerged as one of the most important technologies when it comes to reinventing client experience. Applying NLP in operations of a business makes it possible to automate customer relations, support, and interaction to near perfection with added benefits of developing fully customized relations with them. This section widens on the aspects of NLP for the particular context of customer service, specifically on the distinct aspects of automatized assistance, interaction improvement, advantages and drawbacks pertained to such technologies.

2. 1 Automated Customer Support

2. 1. 1 Chatbot and Virtual Assistant

Of all the uses of NLP, chatbots and virtual assistants are the most prominent and frequently encountered by customers. These systems are designed to include natural language understanding for processing the user's query, and natural language generation for generating an appropriate response to the customer, thus making the customer service experience engaging and natural to the users. Chatbots can effectively and efficiently engage the customers through the provision of information and assistance to fulfill tasks including; appointment bookings and fixes of technical problems.

For example, IBM Watson Assistant is a complex platform that utilizes NLP to fulfill customers' search queries and give the relevant answers. It is easily adaptable to any form of media which includes the website, mobile application, or social media networks thus availing a homogenized customer experience.

Another good example in this respect is the application of the chatbots in the banking industry. Erica, which is the Virtual Assistant by Bank of America, offers the customers an assist by sharing data on their account balance, recent transactions and even tips. In essence, the repetitive communication that is evident in these instances is effectively handled by Erica, which frees up human customer care attendants for other.

2.1.2 Case Studies and Real-World Examples

One good example is the incorporation of chatbots into the Sephora business model for increasing its customers' engagement. Sephora, a worldwide chain of beauty stores and online retail, uses a chatbot to help consumers to select products, schedule appointments at the stores and answer frequently asked questions via Sephora's website and the Facebook Messenger. As a result, the consumption experience from customers via the chatbot is maximized due to natural language processing for proper query interpretation in providing optimal solutions. A case study done by Conversocial shows that Sephora chatbot not only helped to enhance the customer satisfaction, but also boosted the conversion rate.

In the telecom sector, Vodafone recently introduced a virtual assistant known as TOBi to respond to the clients' queries. As a virtual employee, TOBi can apply NLP on all sorts of customers' complaints ranging from bill payment to product malfunction. To this effect, TOBi was said to have dealt with 70% of, if not many more customer inquiries independently, cutting costs and enhancing service delivery at Vodafone.

These examples illustrate the automation of customer care support by using NLP-based chatbots and virtual assistants, productivity improvement, and, therefore, better customer service.

2. 2 Enhancing Customer Interaction

2. 2. 1 Natural Language Processing (NLP) and Generation (NLG)

As for NLP sub-discipline, both NLU and NLG are important in improving the relations with customers. NLU also helps in identifying the primary motive of customers, for which the systems understand the syntactical and semantical properties of the text. This understanding is very important as it ensures that the right and relevant information is produced. While, NLG is the opposite where text is written based on the understanding that the system has about the query.

Amazon's Alexa and Google Assistant are perfect instances of how NLU and NLG functions. These virtual assistants apply profound NLP elements to analyze user inputs and respond to them accordingly so they are friendly. For example, if a user says, "What's the weather like today?", the assistant first understands what the user said through NLU, then goes and fetch the weather details to finally use NLG to respond to the user.

2.2.2 Personalization Techniques

The aspect of personalization is one of the core elements that help to improve interactions with the customers. Having incorporated NLP into its operations, it becomes easier for companies to conform to the customer's wish, and this depends on their need. Communication customization or personalization means the process of studying the client in terms of previous communication, his/her previous or current purchase experience, and his/her browsing history, inter alia.

Netflix is perhaps the best example of NLP for personalization. This streaming service employs NLP for the identification of user reviews, viewing history, as well as searched terms for aiming to provide recommendations in the context of user's preferences. It also improves the perception of the technology and thus increases the users' interest in the service and their loyalty to it.

Likewise, other web-based applications such as the Amazon e-business employ NLP in customizing solutions to the consumers' needs. This way, the recommendation engine built into the service based on the data from customer feedbacks, searches for specific products, and purchasing behavior, offers the client the items that may be interesting for him or her, thus stimulating sales and increasing customer satisfaction.

Personalization methods based on NLP enhance the loyalty to a certain brand/ producer and augment the overall number of satisfied customers.

2. 3 Benefits and Challenges

2. 3. 1 Efficiency and Cost Savings

Another advantage of implementing NLP in customer services is the increase in the work's speed and a decrease in expenses. Chatbots and virtual assistant help to minimize workload in the community because many customers' inquiries can be addressed at once. Due to its flexibility, organisations are able to deliver round the clock service without necessarily increased their labour cost.

A report by Juniper Research shows that firms utilizing the services of chatbots will likely cut their expenses by $8bn a year by 2022, mainly because of the lower costs of managing customer relations and higher capacity. Thus, the opportunities to save on expenses in this sphere are significant, which makes the usage of NLP for automation of relevant customer service desirable for businesses.

2. 3. 2 Limitations and Ethical Considerations

However, like all good things, the integration of NLP in customer service also has the following drawbacks and limitations of its application.

Limitations

One of the key potential drawbacks is the existence of a large number of phenomena associated with the complexity of human speech. Challenges that are related to context, sarcasm, or lack of specificity in the question posed can pose as headaches for the NLP systems resulting in either wrong or suboptimal results. For instance, a customer may type, 'can I get assist with my order' and depending on the exact words and context in which it will be asked, the bots might not be able to capture it as intended.

Also, often, people come to the forum with specific questions, and, although chatbots can cope with ordinary requests, they can often fail with complex or delicate ones where it is important to take into account the individuality of the user or show certain sensitivity. Several clients may get annoyed with a bot that does not adapt to a new context or give them the proper solutions they need.

Ethical Considerations

Some of the ethical issues including in NLP are data privacy, Public transparency, and bias. NLP systems are otherwise data-dependent and questions can be raised on how customers' data is processed, analyzed, and protected. Meeting and exceeding customer expectations as well as the legal requirements as relates to data protection such as the GDPR is hence vital.

They also need to have high levels of ethical standards to put into consideration the following aspects: It is recommended that customers should be told when they are dealing with a bot rather than a real person. Sneaky approaches when the account is programmed to engage in natural-like conversation with the audience without stating the fact is detrimental to the company's reputation.

There are issues related to bias in models to NLP. Some of these models are trained with a set of information that includes bias hence arriving at biased results. For example, if a chatbot is programmed to learn from samples in customer relations conversations, and such relations are soaked in bias in a society in question, then the chatbot is likely to be biased in its recovery. Eradicating bias calls for a thorough consideration of the data used in the model's training process and subsequent checking for acts of bias.

3. SENTIMENT ANALYSIS

Business intelligence appraised as a beneficiary use of NLP entails a technique referred to as sentiment analysis or opinion mining. Sentiment analysis in particular converts the qualitative data received into understandable and relatively quantitative means, thus, offering an understanding of customers' opinions, brands' image, and trends. First, more details about the concept of sentiment analysis are provided, as well as types of industries that use it and the tools that help apply it.

3. 1 Fundamentals of Sentiment Analysis

3. 1. 1 Definition and Types

Bearing this in mind, and for the purpose of this paper, sentiment analysis can be described as the process of identifying the subjectivity being portrayed in a given text. It entails classifying text into positive, negative or neutral and, where further developed, the specifics of emotions like happiness, anger, or sadness.

Polarity Detection: This is the simplest form of analysis where the whole text is categorized as positive, negative or neutral in views. For instance, a product review such as - "The phone has excellent battery life" would be felt as positive while a review such as – "The phone keeps crashing" would be felt as negative.

Emotion Detection: This goes further than polarity to determine the actual emotions described in the text. Categorization of emotions also generalized which include joy, anger, sad, surprise, and fear emotions. For example, if a word is – 'I am so happy that I bought a new laptop,' then happiness is sensed, if the word is – 'I am unhappy with slow customer service,' then unhappiness is sensed.

3.1.2 Techniques and Algorithms

Both broaden and simple ML processes and new cutting-edge DL techniques are used in the sentiment analysis process.

Lexicon-Based Methods: These methods use so called lexicons – the set of words which can be linked to particular emotions. The text is analyzed in such a manner that each word is checked against the lexicon and depending on the sentiment scores of these words, general sentiment of the text is derived. In this case, words such as: great, wonderful could have positive scores, bad, terrible could have negative scores. The one of the frequently used is SentiWordNet that provides sentiment ratings of words from the WordNet vocabulary database.

Machine Learning-Based Methods: These methods involve the use of supervised learning algorithms to make a classification on texts depending on some training data. Some of the commonly used algorithms are based on whether it is a binary or multi-class classification problem and these are Naive Bayes, SVMs, and the Random Forest algorithms. The text features the units and they are Word Frequencies or n-grams which help in training of the model. For example, a Naive Bayes classifier might be trained on some training data set which contains or to classify in trending topics of tweets.

Deep Learning-Based Methods: Thankfully with the help of deep learning, there has been advancements in the process of sentiment analysis. Some of the approaches reported in the literature include CNNs, RNNs, LSTM networks, and transformer-based models, for instance, BERT (Bidirectional Encoder Representations from Transformers) that delivers near-perfect performance. These models can analyse the text for complicated patterns as well as the context, which help in giving better prediction of sentiment. For instance, BERT captures the relation of words with the rest of the words in a sentence, therefore has a better understanding of the sentiment behind the text.

3. 2 Applications in Various Industries

3. 2. 1 Product Reviews and Feedback Analysis

Indeed, one of the most popular approaches that employ sentiment analysis methods is the analysis of the product reviews and customers' feedback. Customer knowledge allows for the evaluation of the organisation's and competitor's strengths and limitations in providing goods and services, evaluation of new ideas, and improvement of customer satisfaction.

E-commerce: Companies such as Amazon take advantage of sentiment analysis by using it for consumers' review analyzing. Thus, the accumulation of sentiment data will enable them to find the most frequent complaints about them, enhance descriptions, and offer recommendations for what to consume. For instance, if several repetitions position a given aspect of a given product as positive, then the retailer may incorporate such aspect in the marketing strategy.

Consumer Electronics: Today's firms, such as Apple and Samsung, commit time to accumulate data about the perceptions and experience of their customers from sources including the World Wide Web and social media sites. Such companies benefit from sentiment analysis in that they are able to keep tabs with the latter from a competitor's perspective, where customers' needs are identified and instances of negativity are dealt with keenness.

3. 2. 2 Social Media Monitoring

The availability of social media presents loads of information in the form of user-generated content that depict public opinion. Businesses and organizations can use sentiment analysis to collect and analyze these discussions in order to grasp the public sentiment, changes in brand image and to respond to new trends.

Brand Monitoring: Some of the big players who have adopted sentiment analysis include Coca-Cola and Nike; they apply sentiment analysis to track the performance of their brands within social medial sites like Twitter, Facebook, and Instagram. They are able to determine and monitor the perception that different people have about their brands, measure and assess the impact of a particular marketing or advertising strategy, as well as address customers' complaints and issues as and when they arise. For instance, an increase in the level of negative perception could be a sign of an error on a recently launched product which the company can then look into.

Political Campaigns: Social media sentiment analysis is mainly applied in the analysis of the public opinion of various politics, the evaluation of political campaigns, and the subsequent adjustment of discourses. So, they can track social media topics of interest to voters and adapt the strategies according to the given issues.

For instance, in a campaign season a given candidate may use sentiment analysis to determine the views of the voters on policies on health and change their policy accordingly.

Crisis Management: Sentiment analysis is crucial during a crisis as it assists organizations in tracking the public's reaction and their response. For instance, in the case of a product recall, a company comes with sentimental analysis to monitor people's disposition toward them and modify what they say or do to counter controversies. During disaster, the government agency can use data mining to assess the needs and moods of the affected population from the posts on social networks.

3. 3 Tools and Technologies

There are many tools and technologies to carry out sentiment analysis and they have got different characteristics.

TextBlob: TextBlob is a straightforward and convenient library for the work with the textual information in the Python language. It offers primitive capability of sentiment analysis that enables users to perform polarity and subjectivity analysis of text. TextBlob is a library that is based on NLTK, and it is quite simple to work with so it can be used by beginners or when working on rather small project.

VADER: Valence Aware Dictionary and Sentiment Reasoner (VADER) is an example of lexicon and rule-based tool that was developed to handle sentiment analysis on social media text only. The type is capable of processing the positive and negative polarity of sentiments as well as the strength of these sentiments. VADER is especially appropriate for short texts, such as texts of tweets, and is located in the NLTK library.

NLTK: Natural Language Toolkit (NLTK) is Python based tool and is a suite of libraries for natural language processing in Python. They include basically different instruments and opportunities for text analysis, including sentiment analysis. As such, NLTK offers the analysts and developers a rich set of SA models and lexicons to work with.

SpaCy: SpaCy is a very powerful, effective and fast NLP library in Python. It also offers ready-made state of the art models for several NLP sub-problems such as sentiment analysis. All SpaCy's models are recognized for their efficiency and reliability, which makes the library suitable for use in production.

Stanford NLP: The Stanford NLP group provides the component that is developed as the set of tools for NLP as well as the Stanford CoreNLP library. CoreNLP also has superior features of sentiment analysis apart from the other NLP functionalities like POS tagging and NER. Academic programs and many commercial construction projects apply this form of construction.

Google Cloud Natural Language API: The cloud natural language processing program by Google which is known as the Google Cloud Natural Language API has robust sentiment analysis features. The tool can be used to determine the sentiment delivered from text in different languages and gives sentiment strength and intensity. The API is commercial and scalable with other products of Google Cloud platform.

IBM Watson Natural Language Understanding: IBM Watson comprises AI services, such as the Watson Natural Language Understanding API. This service comes with other extra features such as emotion detection, keyword extraction, and entity recognition in addition to the sentiment analysis feature. Another issue that many enterprises address with help of Watson is sentiment analysis that is considered rather accurate.

4. MARKET RESEARCH

Every business that wants to design products from the customers' perspective, identify shifts in customer behavior, or merely emerge in an industry with a strong contender needs market research. NLP has enriched the studies in the field of market research since it allows handling and comparing significantly larger textual data. This section focuses on the application of NLP to market research, the ways of data acquisition and analysis, and the utilization of NLP results in managerial planning.

4. 1. NLP Application in Market Research

4. 1. 1 Consumer Analysis

Knowledge concerning the consumer behavior and their preference is one of the critical aspects that must always be considered in market research. NLP helps in the processing of a large amount of textual information created by consumers, for example, a review, feedback, or posts on social media. Through such extraction and analysis of this data, various businesses can be capable of identifying the opinions of the customers, the kind of products that can be sold to them and the purchasing tendencies of the customers.

Sentiment Analysis: Sentiment analysis enables organisations to determine the perception that customers have with regards to the products and services of the firm. For instance, the sight of rooms, product reviews can be used to establish the sentiments of customers towards the product which can be used to determine satisfaction and dissatisfaction. Thus, the marketing strategies which correspond to different segments of sentiment data, which can be age, location, or gender, maximize the potential of the company's interaction with consumers.

Topic Modeling: Such approaches to text mining, as LDA, will find recurring topics and themes that are more dominantly discussed by the consumers. This gives business people a clue on which aspect of the product or service being offered by a particular business is more valuable. For instance, a car producing company may apply the topic modeling technique to determine that customers and prospects talk about aspects such as fuel economy and safety when giving their opinions.

4. 1. 2 Competitors & Market Trends and forecasts

NLP plays a pivotal role in performing competition analysis and calculating market trends. Here it should be mentioned that thanks to the analysis of competitors' data and tendencies, the businesses will be able to make the correct choices and build up the adequate strategies in order to hold the competitive advantage.

Competitor Analysis: This way, NLP is beneficial since it enables organizations to track the actions by competitors and the feedback given by clients on the products of the competitors. Competitive benchmarking can be done through reviewing restaurants' related reviews and posts on social media and articles that published in the newspapers. For example, a company can use NLP to monitor the customers' views on the newly released product of a competitor and potential flaws that can be capitalized on, or strengths where their product can give competition a run for their money.

Trend Prediction: As a result, the integration of predictive analytics and NLP can be used to forecast market trends to aid businesses. Looking at specific data and the flow of conversations in the market, NLP models can identify trends that might be on the rise soon. For instance, in the period of COVID-19, organizations applied NLP to assess social media and news data to forecast the use of home office devices and home fitness equipment.

4.2 Data Collection and Processing

4.2.1 Sources of Data

Organised information is collected from various sources to facilitate the process of market research based on NLP.

Surveys and Questionnaires: It was asserted that conventional questionnaires and surveys are still used to collect quantified, structured databases. Open-ended questions allow NLP to understand people's opinions by extracting hidden and latent themes and sentiments from their answers.

Social Media: It is essential to note that, through the use of applications such as Twitter, Facebook, and Instagram, users create copious amounts of content.

Social media listening tools are the NLP based tools that help in monitoring the brand name, Hashtags or topics of the interest to provide instant analysis of public sentiment and trending topics.

Customer Reviews and Feedback: Reviews left on the sites such as Amazon, Yelp, and TripAdvisor represent valuable information for carrying out the sentiment analysis and topic modeling. These remind businesses of the status of customer satisfaction and the frequent complaints raised.

News Articles and Blogs: Reading through the news articles and blogs allows for comprehension of a particular industry news and trends or perception. NLP can monitor discussion of companies, products, trends, etc. so business itself will remain updated with the market.

4. 2. 2 Preliminary Analysis Tools and Issues

Data preprocessing is one of the most vital stages in NLP since it forms the basis of the data analysis step. Preprocessing can be done on the raw data in a way that makes it fit for the analysis to be done on it.

Text Cleaning: The raw text data frequently comprise of noise in form of punctuations, special characters and unnecessary information. Removal of these elements is known as text cleaning that enhances the quality of the obtained data. They begin by stripping the resulting documents of HTML tags, symbols, and stop words – words that are not legally relevant such as 'and,' 'the,' 'is. '

Tokenization: Preprocessing makes use of tokenization which entails the splitting of text into individual words or phrases referred to as tokens. This is a crucial step for most of the NLP activities including sentiment analysis and topic modeling among others. Tokenization can prove to be harder for languages with a rich inflectional morphology or for texts with limited literacy and many contractions and user-generated content that use nonstandard abbreviations.

Lemmatization and Stemming: These techniques word base or root words reduces this helps in standardizing the text and also reduces the dimensionality. Lemmatization includes contextual analysis and converts a word to its simplest form, use (for example, 'running' to 'run'), while stemming removes the suffix to accomplish similar outcomes (for example, 'jumps,' 'jump'.

Handling Multilingual Data: In this case, the businesses end up dealing with data in at least two languages due to the global markets. NLP tools must also be usable with data from different languages, which can be tasking because of the differences in the language and its structure.

Sentiment Calibration: There could also be case-by-case or platform-based baseline of the extent to express sentiments. To overcome such variations, fat sentiment scores need to be adjusted for productive comparisons. Specifically, opinions proposed on social networks may differ from opinions given in questionnaires and polls, so they need to be standardized.

4. 3 Insights and Decision Making

4. 3. 1 Transforming Data into Actionable Insights

The end user of NLP in market research is the business organization whose main aim will be to use NLP to analyze and interpret data collected in a market so as to apply the insights gained in formulating its strategies.

Consumer Insights: Customers' experience and opinions can also be assessed based on the recurring factors analyzed from the feedback that they give. These help firms to be knowledgeable on matters to do with the customers, this is with regard to their wants, desires and areas that they consider challenging. For instance, if through sentiment analysis you find that clients have a negative attitude towards a given product aspect then the firm learns to enhance it in the following product version.

Market Segmentation: Market segmentation can also be assisted by NLP in terms of the customers' behavior and their inclination. When the society is segmented according to the customers' characteristics, it is easier for the businesses to address the related segments for more enhanced and effective targeting. For instance, a retail firm can apply NLP to create different groups of customers concerning their shopping habits to create campaigns properly.

Competitive Positioning: The data on competitors assists businesses to place themselves in the market based on the strengths and weaknesses of their rivals. With the identification of competitors' capabilities and susceptibility, companies can adjust their plans and align themselves with the appropriate opportunities. For instance, if there is positive feedback on a competitor's product due to a particular aspect, it may be necessary for the firm to integrate it.

4.3.2 Case Studies Demonstrating Impact

Several quite vivid examples demonstrate the positive shifts experienced by various companies through the application of NLP in the market research sphere.

Unilever: Naturally, the large multinationals such as Unilever, a consumer goods maker, has for example utilises NLP by searching for opinions and discussions on social media. By using SA and TM, Unilever arranges information on consumers' demands and ideas that can be implemented in the production of new goods. It facilitates the creation of product portfolios that are suitable to the market by employing proof from the field. For instance, analysis of the conversations carried out on the social media has showed an increasing concern of the customers towards natural and organic products this put pressure on Unilever and forced it to diversify on these product types.

Coca-Cola: NLP is used by Coca-Cola to track their brand=name and sentiment on the social media platforms. Through identifying more millions of shares in social platforms, it monitors consumer's attitude to products and the marketing strategies in real time. This makes it possible for Coca-Cola to make appropriate timely responses to any negative comments and alter its promotional techniques. To be specific, during the release of a new product, NLP was used to assess consumers' reactions to understand which marketing messages to employ.

Airbnb: The selective processing of customer feedback with the help of NLP is used in Airbnb. Airbnb through sentiment analysis of the reviews is therefore able to determine the problems that crops up most frequently and the opportunities for change. For instance, if many reviews point at the lack of cleanliness, Airbnb can resolve this problem by providing the managers with new guidelines concerning cleanness. Further, it also assists Airbnb in refining its recommendation services with respect to the visitors, thus improving guests' satisfaction.

These case studies show examples of how market research based on NLP offers invaluable information that may guide managerial decisions, turn consumers' and clients' discontent into the competitive advantage, and create a top-notch customer experience.

5. INTEGRATION AND IMPLEMENTATION

It is crucial to apply NLP in conjunction with other technologies to make the most of the mentioned approaches to the development of different applications, such as customer care and advanced market analysis. This section focuses on how is it possible to integrate NLP with AI, ML, big data, and real-time analytics along with depicting the methodologies concerning the efficient implementation of such technologies.

5.1 Combining NLP with Other Technologies

5.1.1 AI, ML, and Big Data

Integration of NLP with AI/ML and big data enables more capable and feature rich solutions to be created.

AI: AI can be defined in a very broad sense as the set of tools that aims at imitating human behaviour. Due to the fact that NLP is a subfield of AI, developments using AI are also beneficial – for instance, in algorithms and computational capabilities.

Neural networks like deep learning, reinforcement learning, and transfer learning improve the NLP models as they can learn from big data, learn in different domains, and learn from the previous learning. For example, GPT-4 is an AI language model for deep learning for natural language generation and is contextually consistent proving the combination of AI and NLP[1].

ML: The features of ML are particularly important for the development of NLP models that make it possible to recognize and produce human language. Classification and regression are used for learning based on labeled datasets while clustering and topic modeling are useful for learning features from the text data. Natural language processing often makes use of popular ML types; for instance, SVM, random forest, and neural treatments. For instance sentiment analysis when applied in natural language processing involves the employment of the ML algorithms to classify a text data into positive, negative or even neutral based on the training data (Manning et al., 2008).

Big Data: The main technologies enabling the utilization of big data technologies are big data and unstructured text data. Techniques like Apache Hadoop and Apache Spark are used to settle Big Data management issues and make it easier to process the data in the real-time. Large data systems enable NLP solutions through offering the means of handling and processing large amounts of textual information gathered from social media, customer reviews, and articles. For instance, one may use big data analytics to monitor the data collected from the social media sites to monitor the brand perception and identify new trends over the real time basis (Chen et al., 2014).

5.1.2 Real-Time Analytics and Dashboarding

The use of real-time analytics and permanent dashboarding expands the possibilities of the NLP by providing vivid and changing in time interrogative Data.

Real-Time Analytics: Real-time analytics implies the means of analyzing data as soon as they are produced. In the context of NLP, real-time analytics means that the organization is processing text data in real-time as it gets created. For example, real-time sentiment analysis can be used to conduct customers' feedback analysis during the product launch or to monitor the social media for trending topics. Such platforms as Apache Kafka and Apache Flink help in real-time data streaming and processing that can be beneficial for business decisions (Kreps et al., 2011).

Dashboarding: Dashboarding includes forming dynamic representations of KPIs and conclusions that are produced consequent to the examination of data. NLP dashboards give a general view of the text data and may include sentiment trends, topics in text, and frequency of specific words. Tableau, Power BI and Looker enables a user to design ideal dashboards where multiple insights from the NLP is combined with other business data. For instance, while promoting a product through a campaign, a marketing team may turn to a sentiment dashboard to see the trends in consumers' feelings towards the campaign, and decide on the pros and cons of the campaign from that perspective.

5. 2 Implementation Strategies

Failure to accomplish these tasks implies that effective solutions must be put in place based on NLP best practices and methodology for the actual deployment of these technologies.

Define Clear Objectives: Hence, first, they should set the appropriate goals and KPIs for NLP solutions that they plan to integrate. Know about these specific objectives of NLP application like what the client wants to achieve like enhancement of customer satisfaction, market trend analysis, writing content conclusion and many others, it assists the NLP designer and implementer of the entire procedure. Well-stated objectives guarantee the efforts of the solution align with the scope of the business problem and the final outcomes achieved.

Select the Right Tools and Technologies: To ensure appropriate implementation of expert systems/NLP, it is essential to select right tools and technologies. The selection of the NLP tools depends on the scale of the data, the level of processing needed, and the level of integration possible. it is now time to consider the various solutions such as open source libraries (for example spaCy, NLTK), Cloud-based services (Google Cloud Natural Language API, IBM Watson) and Big data (Hadoop, Spark). For instance, Google Cloud Natural Language API contains features for sophisticated sentiment analysis, and entity recognition; Apache Spark is designed for large-scale data set processing.

Data Quality and Preprocessing: NL processing needs quality data for it to be effective; thus, the need for reliable data. Make sure that the data which are employed for training and further analysis are free from defects and are typical for the target domain. To wash the data go through a process like- cleaning of text, tokenization, normalization of the text. Overcome shortcomings like the noisy and multi-lingual text and other data inconsistencies in order to establish a higher degree of dependability in the field of NLP models (Manning et al., 2008).

Model Training and Evaluation: NLP models should be trained with large datasets to enhance the efficiency and applicability of the models where ever used. In testing, the effectiveness of one or several models should be estimated with the help of proper coefficients that encompass accuracy, precision, recall, F1 score performance. Regularly update the models to reflect data on machines and the feedback received in the field in order to keep the models as updated as possible. For example, sentiment analysis model can be assessed with the help of evidently marked set of customer reviews to estimate the model's accuracy regarding sentiment classification (Joulin et al., 2017).

Integration with Existing Systems: NLP solutions should be made to work and interact with the rest of the systems and processes for it to run effectively and for the data to flow smoothly. When integrating the NLP application think about how it will fit into other technologies – CRM, data warehousing, and analytics. APIs can be used to provide a foundation or a standard way in which the systems will share data, data connectors can also be used to enable this. For example, applying NLP-based chatbots for CRMs will improve customers experience and support activities.

User Training and Adoption: Offer competent capacity building for the users to encourage its implementation of NLP solutions. Teach users how to better analyze and use NLP findings and provide materials for problem solving and contacting for help. Ask the users for feedback so that potential strengths and weaknesses could be revealed and the created NLP solution would correspond to their requirements. For instance, live training sessions regarding the utilization of NLP dashboards can clarify how to analyze the trends of sentiment and make proper decisions.

Ethical Considerations and Compliance: Include ethical concerns and regulate adherence to the existing legislation in relation to NLP solutions. Identify data privacy and transparency, and possible bias, and come up with ways of reducing risks on the same. Make sure that the implemented NLP applications respect the law, including, but not limited to, the GDPR in the EU or the CCPA in the United States.

6. CONCLUSION AND FUTURE SCOPE

NLP has helped businesses change refractory text into data they can use in their line of work. It enables one to interact with clients on auto-pilot through the use of chatbots and virtual assistants and offer correct information on inquiries. Consumer sentiments and trends are something which NLP can provide at a very profound level so that the businesses can adapt themselves according to the situation. In market research, NLP's technological features define the decision-making process and strategic planning. Still, NLP technologies' application has many difficulties such as data quality, preprocessing, integration with pre-existing systems, and ethical issues. The chosen processes have to be aligned with the industry standards and key principles like definitive goals and scope, proper tools and methods, and accurate data, in addition to constant end-users' education and support.

The future of NLP is bright because of the upgrades associated with technology and changes that are noticeable in business settings. The areas of the future NLP growth are connected with the enhancement of the existing NLP models that could maximize the models' efficiency and with the concordance of the NLP with the perspective technologies such as augmented reality and virtual reality. Technology used for real time will grow and provide more efficient ways of analyzing and processing text data in real time to businesses. Combination of NLP with the new technologies enables novel models of the user's interaction and experience, like NLP-controlled AVAs in AR and NLP-supported virtual reality templates. This is due to the fact that the ethics of using AI and their fair use will be a trend, with no bias, cluttered interface, or lack of freedom that users will be forced into without their knowledge. As for the future development of NLP it will further concern different fields including the most relevant healthcare, finance and legal industry, with regard to the certain field's problems and perspectives. Future developments will also therefore encompass refined frameworks and methods of ethical artificial intelligence practices.

REFERENCES

Blei, D. M., Ng, A. Y., & Jordan, M. I. (2003). Latent Dirichlet Allocation. *Journal of Machine Learning Research, 3*, 993–1022.

Chen, M., Mao, S., & Liu, Y. (2014). Big Data: A Survey. *Mobile Networks and Applications, 19*(2), 171–209. DOI: 10.1007/s11036-013-0489-0

Hirschberg, J., & Manning, C. D. (2015). Advances in Natural Language Processing. *Science, 349*(6245), 261–266. DOI: 10.1126/science.aaa8685 PMID: 26185244

Joulin, A., Mikolov, T., Grave, E., Bojanowski, P., Mikolov, T., & Grave, E. (2017). Bag of Tricks for Efficient Text Classification. *arXiv preprint arXiv:1607.01759.* DOI: 10.18653/v1/E17-2068

Kreps, J., Narkhede, N., & Rao, J. (2011). Kafka: A Distributed Messaging System for Log Processing. *Proceedings of the NetDB Conference.*

Manning, C. D., Raghavan, P., & Schütze, H. (2008). *Introduction to Information Retrieval.* Cambridge University Press. DOI: 10.1017/CBO9780511809071

Nenkova, A., & McKeown, K. R. (2011). Automatic Summarization. *Foundations and Trends® in Information Retrieval, 5*(2), 103-233.

Pang, B., & Lee, L. (2008). Opinion mining and sentiment analysis. Foundations and Trends® in information retrieval, 2(1–2), 1-135.

Roy, P., Podder, A., & Roy, S. (2023). A Voting classification approach for Sentiment Extraction from Bengali text. *International Journal of Emerging Trends in Engineering Research, 11*(5), 132–136. DOI: 10.30534/ijeter/2023/021152023

Chapter 2
Applications of Sentiment Analysis on Customer Service by Mediation of Market Research in the Horn of Africa

Shashi Kant
http://orcid.org/0000-0003-4722-5736
DMI-St.Eugene University, Zambia

Shashank Mittal
http://orcid.org/0009-0007-8643-4350
O.P. Jindal Global University, India

Pawan Kumar
http://orcid.org/0000-0001-7501-3066
Lovely Professional University, India

ABSTRACT

The main facets of digital transformation and their effects on the retail industry are covered in this chapter. Digital transformation and its significance in the current corporate environment are defined at the beginning of the chapter. It talks about how the retail industry is changing as a result of cutting-edge technology like artificial intelligence (AI), big data analytics, and the Internet of Things (IoT). The chapter looks at how merchants are using these tools to improve customer service, streamline processes, and obtain a competitive advantage. The significance of the customer experience in the digital era is one of the main topics discussed in this chapter. It

DOI: 10.4018/979-8-3693-8327-8.ch002

explores how merchants are personalizing their goods, enhancing customer interaction, and fostering greater brand loyalty with data-driven insights. The chapter also looks at the importance of cooperation and knowledge exchange in the retail sector. Upon finishing this chapter, readers will possess a thorough comprehension of the digital transformation tendencies influencing the retail sector.

INTRODUCTION

Sentiment measurement has become a necessity to companies and organizations worldwide as it provides informative information regarding consumer satisfaction, preferences, and opinions. The application of measurement of sentiments in the study of market and services of customers has significant implication in most parts of the world and particularly in the Eastern Africa and Ethiopia. Ethiopia has experienced remarkable financial sustainability and transformation in the last few years, which is ranked as the second-most populated African nation. The rapidly expanding knowledge economy in the country, which includes such industries as fintech, telecom, and retail, has increased the need of their smart services of customers tactics. Sentiment measurements can be very applicable in such a background in order to make businesses more attuned to consumer experiences and tailor their products (Jafari et al., 2021). The theory of measurement of sentiments was first introduced in the field of natural language processing. There, researchers have developed algorithms to automatically identify and extract the feeling expressed in the text data, such as social media posts, customer services, and customer reviews. Evidence based research on the application of measurement of sentiments in research in market and services of customers in Ethiopia and the Eastern Africa generally does not exist in any significant way. The lack of research specifically examining the aspect of sentiment measurement is present, but some studies have been conducted on the application of the concept in the context of other similar challenges as analysis of social media data or online reviews (Tseng et al., 2021).

Implementation of sentiments measurement in this context has various practical issues due to the diversity of languages in the region and quality of data, as well as the need to have background knowledge of social and cultural norms. Moreover, lack of technological experience and resources to apply and sustain measurement of sentiments systems successfully can occur. This chapter attempts to address all these gaps and resolve the challenges by providing an in-depth discussion of the applications of measurement of sentiments on customer services, mediated by study of market, within the context of the Eastern Africa, especially Ethiopia. The chapter will provide a comprehensive study of the pertinent literature, go over the process logical strategies and techniques used in measurement of sentiments, and look at case stories that highlight the useful demonstrate the practical implementation and impact of these techniques in the region (Balasubramanian et al., 2021). By doing this, this chapter emphasized the potential of measurement of sentiments to improve services of customers, drive research in market, and ultimately contribute to the monetary and social sustainability of the Eastern Africa. It will also provide insightful advice for future investigators, policymakers, and business leaders in the region.

BACKGROUND OF STUDY

Ethiopia, Eritrea, Djibouti, and Somalia make up the Eastern Africa, a strategically important region that has seen substantial monetary and social shift in recent years. Particularly Ethiopia has become a major regional monetary force, and the sustainability of the country as a whole is greatly aided by its knowledge sector. The necessity of excellent services of customers techniques has augmented in Ethiopia due to the fast expansion of businesses including retail, telecommunications, and fintech. Firms operating in these domains are rapidly realizing that, in order to be competitive and cultivate enduring customer loyalty, they must comprehend and respond to the changing tastes as well as attitudes of their clientele (Huang & Chiu, 2021). Within the larger subject of natural language processing, measurement of sentiments has become a useful process to meet this requirement. Measurement of sentiments makes it possible to systematically identify, extract, and quantify subjective information from a variety of data sources, including social media postings, customer care conversations, and reviews from customers, by utilizing sophisticated computer approaches. Businesses can gain a better manifesting of their customers' experiences, preferences, and pain points by utilizing measurement of sentiments in the background of research in market and services of customers. The aforementioned data may be utilized to improve decision-making, elevate the caliber of services, and formulate more efficacious marketing tactics (Huang & Rust, 2021).

Although measurement of sentiments has shown promise in the Eastern Africa, especially in Ethiopia, there is a dearth of evidence-based research on the topic. There is a need for more in-depth research that focuses on the intersection of measurement of sentiments, services of customers, as well as research in market within the Eastern Africa region, even though some studies have looked at the use of measurement of sentiments in related backgrounds, like the measurement of social media data or online reviews. In order to close this gap, this study offers a thorough examination of the uses of measurement of sentiments in services of customers, mediated by research in market, throughout the Eastern Africa, with an emphasis on Ethiopia (Jiang & Zhao, 2021). To shed light on the prospects, problems, and future research directions in this sector, the research will employ relevant theoretical models, factual data, and case studies. The results of this study should be of great use to firms, decision-makers, and scholars throughout the Eastern Africa. They will enable them to better understand how measurement of sentiments can be used to improve services of customers, inform research in market, and advance the general social and monetary advancement of the area.

STATEMENT OF PROBLEM

For firms operating in the Eastern Africa, especially Ethiopia, it would be ideal to have a comprehensive manifesting of the attitudes, inclinations, and experiences of their clientele. With this knowledge, they could then use it to provide outstanding services of customers, create focused marketing campaigns, as well as ultimately spur business expansion and success. But the actual situation on the ground paints a more ambiguous picture. There is a paucity of evidence based research on the use of measurement of sentiments in this setting, despite the quick expansion of Ethiopia's knowledge sector and the growing significance of services of customers. The literature that has already been written has a tendency to concentrate on more comprehensive, cross-national assessments or investigate measurement of sentiments in similar but unrelated fields (Miao et al., 2021).

Our theoretical as well as practical knowledge of how measurement of sentiments may be effectively implemented to improve services of customers and inform research in market in the Eastern Africa is still lacking due to the paucity of study in this field, which has produced inconclusive findings. For instance, little is known about the unique possibilities and difficulties that firms in the area have when putting measurement of sentiments systems into practice, as well as the backgroundual elements that might affect how effective these processes are. In addition, there exist notable deficiencies in manifesting concerning the accessibility and caliber of data sources, the linguistic as well as cultural subtleties that must be taken into account, and the operational and technical prerequisites for the effective implementation of measurement of sentiments solutions in the Eastern Africa (Molina-Castillo et al., 2021). Businesses, legislators, and academics looking to use measurement of sentiments's capacity to enhance services of customers and guide research in market tactics in the area face a great deal of difficulty because of these background-specific limitations. By offering a thorough investigation of the uses of measurement of sentiments on services of customers, mediated by research in market, in the background of the Eastern Africa, with an emphasis on Ethiopia, this study seeks to close these gaps. The study will investigate the theoretical foundations, evidence-based data, and real-world obstacles related to the application of measurement of sentiments in this field. In the conclusion, it will provide insights as well as suggestions to direct future investigations, regulatory actions, and corporate decision-making (Sohn & Ju, 2021).

The chapter contributed to a better manifesting of how measurement of sentiments may be used to improve services of customers, inform research in market, and advance the overall monetary and social sustainability of the Eastern Africa area by bridging these important knowledge gaps.

RELATED THEORIES

Using research in market as a middleman, this study examines how measurement of sentiments is used to services of customers in Ethiopia and other countries in the Eastern Africa. Furthermore, the research will be guided in identifying the gaps among customer expectations and experiences by the Customer Satisfaction Theory, which postulates that customer satisfaction is a function of the discrepancy among customers' expectations and their perceptions of the actual service performance (Srisawatsakul & Jermsittiparsert, 2021).

The research will also be conducted through the framework of the six-step Marketing Research Process that is grounded on the research in the marketplace and entails the following steps: issue description, research design, data collecting, data measurement, result interpretation, and reporting. Sentiment measurement can be applied at various stages of this process in order to gain a better understanding of the market. Also, the study will rely on the Segmentation, Targeting, and Positioning (STP) Framework, which emphasizes the importance of understanding customer segments, targeting the most promising segments, and positioning the product or the service to meet the needs of the target market (Sumitha et al., 2022).

Also, the research will utilize measurement of sentiments theory. It will use lexicon-based process(s) where a predefined lexicon or dictionary of words are used to classify text; machine learning based-processes where supervised or unsupervised algorithms are used to identify patterns in the data and classify sentiment; and hybrid-processes where the benefits of both processes are combined. The backgroundual factors, including the influence of language and cultural factors, the level of sociomonetary development, and the level of digital adoption, which can potentially affect the usage of the measurement of sentiments in the Eastern Africa will also be put into consideration by the study (Thakur and Srivastava, 2023).

EVIDENCE BASED LITERATURE REVIEW

Measurement of sentiments on services of customers

The investigators classified customer evaluations as good, negative, or neutral using a hybrid approach that included lexicon-based and machine learning techniques. The results imply that measurement of sentiments might offer insightful information about client satisfaction as well as assist hotel managers in pinpointing areas in need of sustainability. Nevertheless, the research was restricted to the hotel sector and did not investigate the wider consequences for services of customers (Tuan, 2021).

In order to gain a deeper manifesting of Ethiopian consumers' attitudes regarding telecommunications services, a different research applied measurement of sentiments on data from social media. The investigators analyzed Facebook posts and tweets from customers using a combination of rule-based and machine learning techniques. The findings showed that measurement of sentiments, especially in the quickly changing telecommunications sector, might be a helpful tool for tracking and reacting to consumer input (Turkyilmaz & Ozkan, 2021). Investigators examined the application of measurement of sentiments on user evaluations of e-commerce platforms across multiple African nations, including Ethiopia, in a cross-national research. In order to categorize customer evaluations and pinpoint the main causes of both consumer contentment as well as discontent, the investigators employed both lexicon-based and machine learning approaches. Though the study did not go into the particular difficulties and possibilities in the Eastern Africa, the results showed the potential for measurement of sentiments to guide services of customers strategies and product sustainability decisions (Van Eck et al., 2021).

More thorough, background-specific study is obviously needed on the uses of measurement of sentiments to services of customers in the Eastern Africa, especially in Ethiopia, even if these studies offer insightful information. The extant research predominantly concentrates on particular industries or conducts more comprehensive, cross-national evaluations, so resulting in deficiencies in our comprehension of the distinct obstacles and prospects that enterprises in the area encounter while using measurement of sentiments tools (Verhoef et al., 2021). Moreover, there is a dearth of studies on the incorporation of measurement of sentiments into research in market procedures, which may offer a more comprehensive comprehension of the ways in which these processes might be utilized to improve services of customers as well as guide strategic decision-making. This study's primary goal will be to fill these evidence based gaps, which will advance knowledge of measurement of sentiments's useful applications and implementation in the Eastern Africa.

Services of customers and research in market

Although still small, the evidence-based literature on the use of measurement of sentiments to research in market and services of customers, especially in the background of Ethiopia and the Eastern Africa, is expanding. Reviewing the existing literature, however, offers insightful information and emphasizes the need for more study in this area. Consumer evaluations of Ethiopian e-commerce sites were measured in one study by using measurement of sentiments. The researchers categorized customer reviews and also determined the primary causes of customer satisfaction and dissatisfaction through a hybrid approach that incorporated methods of lexicon and machine learning. The findings show that sentiment measurement can be used to help e-commerce companies improve the customer care and support by providing valuable information on the consumer experience. The study emphasized the significance of the inclusion of the measurement of sentiments into the general services of customers strategy (Widjaja et al., 2021). Another study investigated the application of measurement of sentiments to the data of social media to know more about the attitudes of Ethiopian consumers towards telecommunications services. The researchers examined the Facebook posts and tweets of the customer using a rule and machine learning method. The results indicate that emotion measurement, particularly of the fast-evolving telecommunications industry, could prove a useful instrument of monitoring and responding to consumer feedback. The study was also clarified about the significance of considering language and cultural background to assess the measurement of sentiments data and include it in the services of both customers and the research in the market procedures (Wu et al., 2022).

On the regional level, the analysis of sentiments among users of e-commerce platforms was conducted in several African countries, including Ethiopia. To classify customer ratings and identify the key factors contributing to consumer satisfaction and dissatisfaction, the researchers used not only lexicon based but also machine learning methods. Though the study did not specifically address how measurement of sentiments may be integrated with research in market procedures, the findings highlighted the potential for measurement of sentiments to guide services of customers strategies and product sustainability decisions (Zhang et al, 2024). More thorough, background-specific study is obviously needed on the use of measurement of sentiments to research in market as well as services of customers in the Eastern Africa, especially in Ethiopia, even if these studies offer insightful information. There are gaps in our knowledge of how firms in the area might use measurement of sentiments to improve their services of customers and research in market capacities because the literature that is currently available tends to concentrate on particular industries or more general, cross-country assessments (Zhu et al., 2024). Furthermore, not much study has been done on the practical difficulties and issues that need to be taken into account when putting measurement of sentiments systems into practice, such as data accessibility, language and cultural concerns, and technological infrastructure. This project will place a strong emphasis on filling in these evidence based gaps in order to further knowledge of the real-world uses of measurement of sentiments and its incorporation into research in market and services of customers procedures in the Eastern Africa.

Research in market and services of customers

The body of evidence-based research on the use of measurement of sentiments in research in market and services of customers, with a focus on Ethiopia and the Eastern Africa, is still small but expanding. Through the review of the available literature, nevertheless, it is possible to obtain valuable information and accentuate that the research in this direction should be continued. In one of the studies, consumer ratings of Ethiopian e-commerce websites were measured in the form of sentiments. A hybrid approach that integrated lexicon-based and machine learning methods helped the investigators characterize the evaluations of customers and define the primary determinants of customer happiness and discontent. The findings suggest that sentiment measurement can not only provide valuable information on the consumer experience but also help e-commerce companies to improve their customers and support services, therefore, having an effect on the research in market and customer care (Zhang et al, 2024).

The application of measurement of sentiments to data on social media was also considered in another study to understand the attitude of Ethiopian consumers towards telecommunications services better. The researchers examined Facebook posts and tweets of the customers in a form of rule-based plus machine learning. As the results indicate, the sentiment measurement, particularly in the rapidly evolving telecommunications industry, can be a useful instrument in monitoring and responding to consumer feedback. The research highlighted the importance of considering the language and cultural background in the process of measuring sentiments into services of customers and research in market procedures (Widjaja et al., 2021). In instances where sentiments were measured to analyze consumer reviews of e-commerce platforms in different African countries, such as Ethiopia, it was carried out on a regional basis. To cluster customer reviews and identify the primary factors that lead to consumer satisfaction and dissatisfaction, the researchers used lexicon-based and machine learning techniques. The findings revealed the way in which sentiments measurement can be applied in making product sustainability decisions and customer services strategy, hence creating a relationship between measurement of sentiments and market research.

More thorough, background-specific study is obviously needed on the use of measurement of sentiments to research in market and services of customers in the Eastern Africa, especially in Ethiopia, even if these studies offer insightful information. There are gaps in our knowledge of how firms in the area might use measurement of sentiments to improve their research in market and services of customers capabilities because the literature that is currently available tends to concentrate on particular industries or more general, cross-country assessments (Verhoef et al., 2021). Furthermore, not much study has been done on the practical difficulties and issues that need to be taken into account when putting measurement of sentiments systems into practice, such as data accessibility, language as well as cultural concerns, and technological infrastructure. This project will place a strong emphasis on filling in these evidence-based gaps in order to further knowledge of the real-world uses of measurement of sentiments and its incorporation into services of customers and research in market procedures in the Eastern Africa.

Measurement of sentiments, services of customers and research in market

The available body of literature highlights the ability of measurement of sentiments as a medium of connection between the research in market and services of the customers and providing a more complete process of understanding and responding to the needs of the clients. They would be able to better address their customer service offerings, and more effectively manage problems of consumers through the use of sentiment measurements to steer research in market (Widjaja et al., 2021). Consumer evaluations of Ethiopian e-commerce sites were determined using measurement of sentiments in one study. The researchers found that the sentiment measurement can provide e-commerce companies with valuable data concerning the consumer experience, which can help them determine which aspects of customer satisfaction and dissatisfaction are primary. The research findings may be used to create a feedback loop between the research in market and services of customers by using the findings to control the product sustainability, services improvement and services of customers tactics (Zhang et al, 2024).

Similarly, one study has questioned the way sentiments measurement can be used to social media data in determining the attitude of the Ethiopian consumers to telecom services. The role of considering the language and cultural background in interpreting measurement of sentiments results and integrating them into research in market and services of customers procedures were highlighted by the investigators. By understanding the peculiarities of consumer perceptions and emotions, businesses can develop more professional and specific services of customers solutions. Another study considered how measurement of sentiments were utilized in consumer reviews of online stores in various African countries, such as Ethiopia, at the local level. The findings underlined the correlation of research in market and services of customers by emphasizing the possibility of measuring sentiments to support the decisions related to sustainability of products and services of customers tactics (Verhoff et al., 2023). These researches emphasize the necessity to implement measurement of sentiments to establish a connection between services of customers and market research. The companies can develop more knowledgeable and responsive customers approaches and ultimately enhance the overall customer experience by exploiting measurement of sentiments to gain a more manifesting of consumer perceptions and preferences (Widjaja et al., 2021).

The existing literature, however, does as well underline the necessity of more background-specific research in the utilization of measurement of sentiments to services of customers and market research in the Eastern Africa, particularly, in Ethiopia. To allow the effective implementation of measurement of sentiments systems in business, additional studies are required. Such practical issues and concerns involve the availability of data, the variables related to culture and language and technological infrastructure (Zhang et al, 2024). In general, the researches in question indicate immense opportunities of applying the research on market-mediated measurement of sentiments to customer-service synthesis in Eastern Africa. By applying the knowledge provided by sentiment measurement, businesses can enhance customer satisfaction and customer loyalty by improving their services of customers offerings to match the needs and desires of the targeted market.

CONCEPTUAL FRAMEWORK

Figure 1. Conceptual Framework

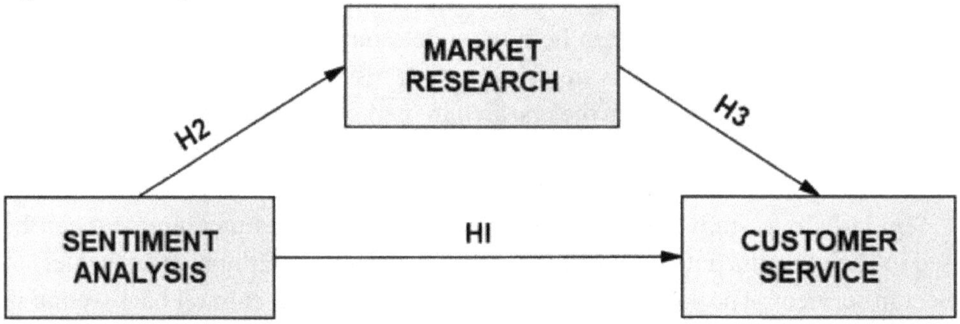

RESEARCH METHODOLOGY

A cross-sectional survey approach was employed in the research design to gather data from a sample of 390 enterprises that operate in different industries within the region. A power measurement and suggestions for a structural equation modeling (SEM) study were used to establish the sample size. The participants, who were corporate managers or executives in charge of services of customers, research in market, as well as measurement of sentiments implementation, were chosen using a purposive sample approach. Through research in market, the study created a new scale to assess how well measurement of sentiments is integrated into services of customers. To guarantee the validity and reliability of the instrument, the scale creation procedure included a comprehensive assessment of the literature, expert panel evaluation, and pilot testing. The scale included factors including the degree of measurement of sentiments adoption, the way measurement of sentiments is included into research in market procedures, the ways measurement of sentiments findings are used to services of customers tactics, and the perceived advantages of this integration. A 5-point Likert scale was used to measure the items on the scale.

A variety of statistical techniques were used to analyze the survey data. SEM was used to test the hypothesized associations among the integration of measurement of sentiments, research in market, and services of customers performanceCFA was used to validate the factor structure. In order to examine the mediating function of research in market in the link among measurement of sentiments integration and services of customers performance, the study also used mediation measurement. To guarantee the caliber of the measuring scales, reliability and validity evaluations, such as internal consistency, convergent validity, and discriminant validity, were carried out.

DATA MEASUREMENT

Table 1. KMO Test

Sampling Adequacy.		**.863**
Bartlett's Sphericity	Chi-Square	6322.130
	df	666
	Sig.	.000

Source: Authors

The results of table 1 show that factor measurement may be performed on the data. Kaiser's criteria classify Sampling Adequacy at 0.863, which is deemed "meritorious". This implies that there are enough significant partial associations among the variables to support component measurement. Sphericity has 666 degrees of freedom and an estimated chi-square value of 6322.130, making it highly significant ($p < .001$). The null hypothesis, according to which there are no associations among the variables and the association matrix is an identity matrix, is tested in this test. The noteworthy outcome demonstrates the association among the variables and the suitability of the data for factor measurement. Overall, the findings of the KMO and Bartlett's Test show that there is enough common variation in the data to carry out a useful factor measurement.

Table 2. Total Explained Variance

C	Initial Eigen			Extraction			Rotation		
	Total	% of Variance	Cumulative %	Total	% of Variance	Cumulative %	Total	% of Variance	Cumulative %
1	8.886	24.015	24.01	8.886	24.015	24.015	6.414	17.334	17.334
2	3.645	9.851	33.86	3.645	9.851	33.866	4.728	12.779	30.113
3	2.140	5.784	39.65	2.140	5.784	39.650	3.529	9.537	39.650

Source: Authors

The table 2 shows the total variance explained by the principal component measurement. The first component has an initial eigenvalue of 8.886, which explains 24.015% of the total variance. The second component has an eigenvalue of 3.645, explaining an additional 9.851% of the variance, for a cumulative total of 33.866%. The third component has an eigenvalue of 2.140, explaining a further 5.784% of the variance, resulting in a cumulative total of 39.650% of the variance explained by the first three components. After extraction, the first component still accounts for 24.015% of the variance. The second component explains an additional 9.851% of the variance, while the third component explains a further 5.784%. When the components are rotated, the first component explains 17.334% of the total variance, the second component explains 12.779%, and the third component explains 9.537%. Together, the rotated first three components account for 39.650% of the total variance in the data.

Table 3. Covariances

Covariance			Estimate	S.E.	C.R.	P	Hy.
Research in market	<-->	**Measurement of sentiments**	**.242**	**.021**	**8231**	***	**H2**
Research in market	<-->	Services of customers	.303	.032	7.692	***	**H3**
Measurement of sentiments	<-->	Services of customers	.254	.24	7.831	***	**H1**

Source: Authors

The covariances among the study's major constructs are shown in Table 3's results. Supporting H2 was the association among research in market and measurement of sentiments, which was.242 with a standard error of.021, a C.R. of 8.231, and a p-value less than.001. This implies that there is a strong association among the use of research in market and the incorporation of measurement of sentiments. H3 was supported by the covariance of.303 among research in market and services of customers, a standard error of.032, a C.R. of 7.692, and a p-value less than 0.001. This result suggests a substantial positive association among services of customers effectiveness and the application of research in market. Furthermore, the association among services of customers and measurement of sentiments was 0.254, confirming H1, with a standard error of 0.024, a C.R. of 7.831, and a p-value less than.001. This suggests that the performance of services of customers and the incorporation of measurement of sentiments is significantly positively correlated. As predicted by the suggested research process, the results show that the three major constructs measurement of sentiments integration, research in market, and services of customers performance are strongly positively correlated with one another.

Table 4. Validity Concern

	CR	AVE	MSV	MaxR(H)	SA	MR	CS
SA	0.732	0.643	0.219	0.852	**0.654**		
MR	0.758	0.657	0.132	0.763	0.171	**0.665**	
CS	0.793	0.603	0.274	0.797	0.383	0.193	**0.684**

Note: SA= Measurement of sentiments; MR= Research in market; CS= Services of customers
Source: Authors

The findings shown in Table 4 provide light on the measurement model's validity issues. Measurement of sentiments (SA), research in market (MR), and services of customers (CS) are the three constructs. The suggested limit of 0.50 is exceeded by the AVE values for SA (0.643), MR (0.657), and CS (0.603), indicating that the constructs account for more than 50% of the variation in their respective indicators.

The constructs have appropriate discriminant validity when the MSV values for each construct are less than the corresponding AVE values.

Figure 2. Structure Equation model

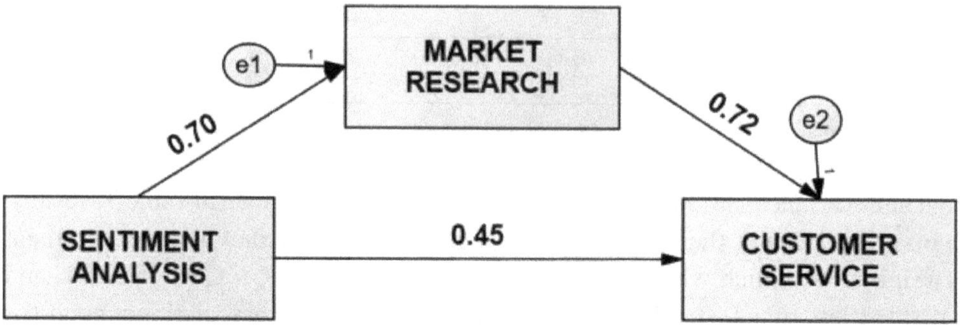

Source: Authors

Table 5. Fitness

Sig.	Chi-Sq	RMR	Goodness	Confirmatory	TLI	RMSEA
0.004	1.854	.039	0.927	0.923	0.907	.032

Source: Authors

An overview of the model fit indices is given in Table 5's results. The suggested criterion of 0.08 is not met by the RMR value of 0.039, indicating a satisfactory match among the estimated and observed covariance matrices. A excellent overall fit of the model is shown by the GFI and CFI, which are 0.927 and 0.923, respectively, both surpassing the suggested threshold of 0.90. A further indication of the model's strong fit is the TLI of 0.907, which is higher than the suggested cut-off of 0.90. Ultimately, a tight match among the model and the data is shown by the RMSEA of 0.032, which is below the suggested criterion of 0.08. The structural equation model employed in the study appears to have a good overall fit to the data, as indicated by the model fit indices shown in Table 5. This gives confidence in the validity and reliability of the hypothesized associations among measurement of sentiments integration, research in market, and services of customers performance.

Table 6. Regression

Relative			**Approx.**	**S.E.**	**C.R.**	**P**	**Ass.**
Research in market	**<---**	**Measurement of sentiments**	**.864**	**.143**	**7.583**	***	**H2**
Services of customers	<---	Research in market	.328	.131	2.853	***	H3
Services of customers	<---	Measurement of sentiments	.957	.192	7.958	***	H1

Source: Authors

The findings displayed in Table 6 shed light on the regression. The C.R. is 7.583, the p-value is less than 0.001, the standardized regression weight (relative) is 0.864, and the standard error is 0.143. This provides evidence in favor of H2, which states that there is a strong association among the use of research in market and the incorporation of measurement of sentiments. The regression route among services of customers performance and research in market is examined in the second row. The p-value is less than 0.001, the standardized regression weight is 0.328, the standard error is 0.131, and the proficient of determination is 2.853.

This result lends credence to H3, which holds that services of customers performance is positively impacted by research in market utilization. The regression route among measurement of sentiments and services of customers performance is the subject of the third row of the table. With a standard error of 0.192, a confidence interval of 7.958, and a p-value less than 0.001, the standardized regression weight is 0.957. This proves the first H1, which states that services of customers performance are favorably correlated with measurement of sentiments integration. All three of the study's H1, H2, and H3 have substantial evidence-based support, according to the regression assessment results shown in Table 6. The results indicate that the use of measurement of sentiments has a favorable impact on research in market and services of customers effectiveness, while research in market also has a positive impact on services of customers performance.

Table 7. Mediation

	worth
Measurement of sentiments → Services of customers	.45
Measurement of sentiments → Research in market → Services of customers	.70*.72=49
	.94

Source: Authors

Table 7 looks at the variables' mediating function. Measurement of sentiments has a 0.45 direct impact on services of customers. The calculation of measurement of sentiments's indirect impact on research in market, which in turn affects services of customers, is $0.70 * 0.72 = 0.49$. When the direct and indirect effects are combined, measurement of sentiment's "whole" impact on services of customers is 0.94. This suggests a partial mediation effect, in which the indirect channel through research in market explains a portion of the link among measurement of sentiments and services of customers. Stated differently, measurement of sentiments affects services of customers directly as well as indirectly through its connection to research in market. The total effect size is 0.94, suggesting a fairly strong overall effect of measurement of sentiments on services of customers, with both direct and indirect components.

DISCUSSION

Assuring the accuracy and suitability of the data utilized in the study, the findings shown in Table 4 show the measurement model's validity and dependability. While the low MSV values imply that the constructs are unique and assess various parts of the overall model, the high CR and AVE show that the constructs are well-defined and internally consistent. The study's structural equation model's validity is further supported by the model fit indices listed in Table 5. There is confidence in the model's ability to accurately represent the associations among the variables because the chi-square statistic, all meet or exceed the suggested thresholds. The findings of the regression measurement, which are shown in Table 6, offer substantial evidence based backing for the suggested theories. The results indicate that the inclusion of measurement of sentiments has a beneficial impact on research in market usage (H2) and services of customers performance (H1). Furthermore, it is discovered that the application of research in market improves services of customers outcomes (H3). These findings emphasize how crucial it is to use research in market and measurement of sentiments to improve services of customers results.

Moreover, the examination of research in market's mediating function, as indicated in Table 7, indicates that it mediates the link among measurement of sentiments integration and services of customers performance to some extent. This suggests that whereas measurement of sentiments improves services of customers directly, it also improves services of customers indirectly by enhancing research in market efforts.

CONCLUSION

The results indicate the positive relationship among these key business activities and between them, which gives informative data in both theoretical and practical research. It is seen that services of customers performance is directly benefited by incorporation of measurement of sentiments and indirectly through the intermediary position of research in the market. This reiterates the importance of applying measurement of sentiments to increase market endeavors research and gain a stronger displaying of consumer preferences and perceptions. Both of these objectives result in improved services of customers outcomes. The research is also effective in confirming the role of research in ensuring effectiveness of services offered by customers in the market. This highlights why it is so essential that companies are well researched on market capabilities so that they can understand their target markets, anticipate client desires and develop winning strategies of delivering high quality services of customers. The results and their applications are valid because the study was done in a strong way that incorporated elaborate structural equation modeling measurement, reliability and validity tests among other processes. These insights can be used to assist the managers and decision-makers to focus on strategic investments and activities, particularly regarding the strategic integration of research in the market and the measurement of sentiments, which can result in the long-term returns in the services of customers performance.

IMPLICATIONS

To begin with, the report points to the significance of investing in the measurement of sentiments skills. By measuring sentiments, organizations can get more insights into the perceptions, preferences, and pain areas of their clients by evaluating their sentiments, which allows them to understand their target markets better and develop more responsive services of customers strategies. To collect and study customer feedback in a systematic manner, through different sources, one of these being social media, customer reviews and even service of customers contacts, managers must prioritize most on installation of measurement of sentiments tools and processes. The paper shows the importance of using research in the market as an additional means to improve the manifesting received after measurement of sentiments. Although research in market may give a deeper understanding of broader industry trends, competitive activities and emerging customer needs, sentiment measurement can give real time, in depth insights into customer sentiments. By combining the two sources of data, managers can make superior decisions about product sustainability, strategic positioning and improvements in services of customers. Thirdly, the findings show the relationships between measurement of sentiments, market, and customer quality services are all interrelated. The supervisors need to possess an inclusive position that recognizes the mutually-profitable relationships between different aspects of operation. By aligning their plans and endeavours in such areas, organizations could form a positive feedback loop where research and market sentiments measurement informs such research which in turn improves services of customers.

To begin with, the report underscores the importance of ensuring that the firm develops powerful measurement of sentiments skills. To processively collect, analyze, and extract meanings of consumer feedback information on a multitude of channels, such as social media, customer reviews, and services of customers exchanges, this means investing in the latest text mining and natural language processing technology. By automating and scaling the sentiments measurement process, organizations can get real-time and detailed information on consumer perceptions and pain areas. This will aid them to adjust in a better manner according to the evolving needs of their customers. Second, the findings demonstrate the value of ensuring that businesses enhance their research in market department and that measurement of sentiments is well incorporated with it. To share knowledge and work towards continuous enhancement, this can involve creating cross functional groups or centers of excellence comprising data analysts, market enquisitors and services of customers experts. Another idea that organizations should consider implementing is the idea of installing integrated data management systems, which connect services of customers data, research in market, and measurement of sentiments data without difficulties to provide a clear vision of the customer experience. Thirdly, the report suggests that the businesses should prioritize most the development of dynamic feedback loops which would involve market, customer services and sentiments research. Organizations can change the processes of their services of customers, product offers, and marketing by continuously revising and enhancing their understanding of the consumer feelings as well as the market trends.

The paper also discloses the role of research in the market as an intervening variable in the relationship between the measurement of sentiments and services of customers effectiveness. This finding enhances our theoretical knowledge of the interdependent relationship of multiple data-driven capabilities and their effect on business activities that deal with customers. The study reveals that the incorporation of measuring of sentiments enhances the services of customers directly and indirectly. The reason is that it reinforces and educates research in market endeavors, which subsequently result in enhancement in the delivery of customer support. Thirdly, the study findings underline the importance of treating services of customers management as cross-functional and data-driven tactics. Using evidence based showing the interdependence between measurement of sentiments, market, and services of customers performance, the study challenges the traditionally isolated approach and points to the need of more integrated approach.

RECOMMENDATIONS

Development of effective measurement of sentiments skills should be given the top priority by the organizations. This would involve investing in the latest technology in the area of text mining and natural language processing, the establishment of accurate procedures and governance systems to collect, analyze, and integrate consumer feedback information across various sources. By leveraging the measurement of sentiments, organizations will have the ability to make smarter and more responsive services of customers decisions, getting real-time information on consumer perceptions, tastes, and pain points. Second, companies need to enhance the research process in the marketplace and ensure that the measurement of sentiments is well incorporated in the research. This can involve creation of cross-functional teams or centers of excellence that combine data analysts with market investigators and services of customers experts to collaborate in data-driven decision making. Another consideration that organizations ought to consider is the implementation of integrated data management systems that interconnect services of customers data, market research and sentiments measurement data in a seamless manner to create a holistic view of the customer experience. Thirdly, an organization should prioritize developing dynamic feedback between research on market, services of customers and measurement of sentiments. Organizations can respond to the ever-evolving consumer expectations by adapting their marketing messages, product proposals, and customer services tactics to suit the changing requirements by frequent changes and enhancement of their expression of market and customer trends and perceptions.

Organizations are also advised to align their procedures, incentives, and organizational culture to enable them integrate research in market as well as measuring sentiments in services of the customers operations. This could involve installing performance metrics and incentive schemes that motivate the effective deployment of these data-driven capacities, and provision of customer support departments tools and training they require to know and act on the insights generated. By implementing these recommendations, facilities will be able to harness the symbiotic relationships of measurement of sentiments, market research and customer service to generate long-lasting improvements in consumer satisfaction, loyalty, and ultimately, their corporate well-being.

REFERENCES

Balasubramanian, S., Raghavan, V. V., Selvaraj, R., & Geetha, M. (2021). Effect of big data analytics capability on firm performance: Mediating role of competitive strategy. *Journal of Business Research, 131*, 113–131. DOI: 10.1016/j.jbusres.2021.03.023

Huang, K. H., & Chiu, C. J. (2021). Integrating measurement of sentiments and social network measurement to explore customer-brand associations. *Industrial Management & Data Systems, 121*(2), 296–316. DOI: 10.1108/IMDS-05-2020-0258

Huang, M. H., & Rust, R. T. (2021). A strategic framework for artificial intelligence in marketing. *Journal of the Academy of Marketing Science*, *49*(1), 30–50. DOI: 10.1007/s11747-020-00749-9

Jafari, H., Sheikhi, A., & Fathi, M. R. (2021). The impact of digital transformation on customer experience and business performance. *Journal of Enterprise Information Management, 34*(3), 768–789. DOI: 10.1108/JEIM-09-2020-0377

Jiang, Y., & Zhao, Q. (2021). The impact of online brand community engagement on brand loyalty: The mediating role of brand trust and brand affect. *Journal of Product and Brand Management, 30*(4), 562–576. DOI: 10.1108/JPBM-03-2020-2822

Miao, C., Humphrey, R. H., & Qian, S. (2021). A meta-measurement of emotional intelligence and work attitudes. *Journal of Occupational and Organizational Psychology, 94*(1), 78–112. DOI: 10.1111/joop.12297

Molina-Castillo, F. J., Rodríguez-Escudero, A. I., Munuera-Aleman, J. L., & Marks, M. (2021). The role of internal dynamics and external mechanisms in the success of new product launches. *Industrial Marketing Management*, *92*, 128–140. DOI: 10.1016/j.indmarman.2020.11.013

Sohn, S. Y., & Ju, Y. H. (2021). Identifying potential causes of customer churn in the mobile communication industry using decision tree measurement. *Expert Systems with Applications, 163*, 113794. DOI: 10.1016/j.eswa.2020.113794

Srisawatsakul, C., & Jermsittiparsert, K. (2021). The impact of big data analytics capability on firm performance: Moderating role of organizational culture. The Journal of Asian Finance. *Monetarys and Business*, *8*(1), 475–487. DOI: 10.13106/jafeb.2021.vol8.no1.475

Sumitha, R., Dhanalakshmi, R., & Senthamaraikannan, K. (2022). Evaluating the impact of measurement of sentiments in services of customers interactions. *International Journal of Speech Technology*, *24*(1), 125–138. DOI: 10.1007/s10772-020-09747-x

Thakur, R., & Srivastava, M. (2023). Linking brand engagement to loyalty: Role of perceived risk and relative advantage. *International Journal of Retail & Distribution Management, 49*(2), 193–212. DOI: 10.1108/IJRDM-06-2020-0220

Tseng, F. C., Wu, H. H., & Wu, M. C. (2021). Manifesting the impact of artificial intelligence on individual employees. *Internet Research, 31*(1), 311–331. DOI: 10.1108/INTR-06-2019-0236

Tuan, L. T. (2021). Drivers of customer engagement and customer loyalty in retail fintech. *Journal of Retailing and Consumer Services, 59*, 102372. DOI: 10.1016/j.jretconser.2020.102372

Turkyilmaz, A., & Ozkan, C. (2021). The impact of employee engagement and knowledge sharing on service innovation performance. *Journal of Business Research, 125*, 679–689. DOI: 10.1016/j.jbusres.2020.01.012

Van Eck, P. S., Jager, W., Leeflang, P. S., & Wieringa, J. E. (2021). Chasing the tail: When do cumulative advantage processes drive Internet markets and when do they not? *Journal of Interactive Marketing, 53*, 100–116. DOI: 10.1016/j.intmar.2020.08.004

Verhoef, P. C., Broekhuizen, T., Bart, Y., Bhattacharya, A., Dong, J. Q., Fabian, N., & Haenlein, M. (2021). Digital transformation: A multidisciplinary reflection and research agenda. *Journal of Business Research, 122*, 889–901. DOI: 10.1016/j.jbusres.2019.09.022

Widjaja, A. E., Chen, C. H., & Hsu, J. S. C. (2021). Manifesting the role of text analytics in improving services of customers quality. *Information & Management, 58*(1), 103273. DOI: 10.1016/j.im.2020.103273

Wu, C. H., Kao, S. C., & Shih, Y. W. (2022). Linking transformational leadership and knowledge sharing: The mediating effects of perceived intrinsic and extrinsic rewards. *Leadership & Organization Sustainability Journal, 42*(2), 275–291. DOI: 10.1108/LODJ-05-2020-0184

Zhang, Z. L., Li, X. Y., Cao, X. H., Liu, Y., & Liu, J. (2024). Determinants of customer satisfaction and customer loyalty in social commerce. *Industrial Management & Data Systems, 121*(3), 678–703. DOI: 10.1108/IMDS-06-2020-0319

Zhu, Q., Wang, T., & Pourhejazy, P. (2024). The effect of data-driven innovation on firm performance: The mediating role of business model innovation. *Journal of Business Research, 126*, 110–120. DOI: 10.1016/j.jbusres.2020.12.058

KEY TERMS AND DEFINITIONS:

Artificial intelligence (AI): The simulation of human intelligence processes by machines, especially computer systems, to perform tasks such as learning, problem-solving, decision-making, and perception.

Big data analytics: The process of examining large and complex data sets to uncover hidden patterns, unknown associations, market trends, customer preferences, and other useful information to help organizations make more informed business decisions.

Brand loyalty: The commitment and positive attitude a customer has towards a particular brand, which leads to repeated purchases and a resistance to switching to competitor brands.

Customer experience: The overall experience a customer has with a firm or brand, including their perceptions, emotions, and interactions across different touchpoints and stages of the customer journey.

Digital transformation: The process of using digital technologies to create new or modify existing business processes, culture, and customer experiences to meet changing business and market requirements.

Knowledge sharing: The process of exchanging information, skills, and expertise among individuals, teams, or organizations to improve performance, innovation, and competitive advantage.

Chapter 3
Entertainment Revolution and Applications of Machine Learning Innovations

Soham Kapur
http://orcid.org/0009-0007-1620-9828
Vellore Institute of Technology, Chennai, India

A. Arivarasi
http://orcid.org/0000-0001-6774-0626
Vellore Institute of Technology, Chennai, India

ABSTRACT

The entertainment industry, comprising a vast array of technical and non-technical domains, sees a massive explosion with every new form of accessibility – beginning from street plays to printed books, then on to television and finally digital content. Considering the role of entertainment as a whole in civilized society, it can be seen to have an incredible impact on other scientific domains of research in psychology, economics and technology, including specialized fields like human-computer interaction and biological effects of handheld devices. For the industry, the Artificial Intelligence boom in the past decade has exponentiated the number of possible outputs that could be created in the name of entertainment, sparking several debates over the prospects of its monetary, technical, ethical and authentic outputs.

DOI: 10.4018/979-8-3693-8327-8.ch003

INTRODUCTION

Consumption of entertainment has been increasing year on year for the past few decades due to fast and easy access through the internet (Hong, 2207; S. J. Fowler and J. J. Fowler, 2011). The top contenders in the field are online streaming (movies, web series, etc.) and gaming. These domains rely greatly on the technological capacity of the media. Increase in online streaming through OTT demands high bandwidth for transmission of high-resolution videos, which contributed to encouraging research into faster wireless internet solutions like 4G and 5G networks (Somani et al, 2024). High-speed, high-engagement games like the various versions of Call of Duty require players to see the game elements in real-time which ignites the development of powerful Graphics Processors. These examples just scratch the surface on this perspective of the impact of the entertainment industry on technology.

The next industrial revolution being powered by Artificial Intelligence seeps well into this domain as well. The prime exhibit is Nvidia, one of the first few to roll out the new versions of their chips – GeForce RTX – that are optimized for Machine Learning and AI in 3D design, rapid game development and world-building. Meta, which initially spearheaded the Virtual Reality sector in large-scale production with Oculus as a consumer electronic, intended it primarily for content consumption; now Apple, a forerunner in the smartphone sector, has produced one of the leading and most popular VR products of the year – the Vision Pro – which has opened up countless new opportunities for passive as well as interactive content development (Hu, 2024). This gives a push to further study and work in spatial computing with computer vision, mixed with compact cyber physical systems that facilitate smooth connectivity.

Ideations and explorations by designers from both technical and non-technical backgrounds focusing on enhancing user experiences continue in the context of such gadgets. New products integrate existing concepts and find unprecedented applications for them, and in most cases a fine-tuned machine learning model built using consumer inputs can significantly improve the quality of these products and thus make them "smart". It allows productive usage of seemingly unproductive services, such as enhancing educational games as Jaferian et al (2024) describe.

This chapter discusses the areas in which developments in technology have improved digital recreational experiences, describes problems such as ethics as well as environmental and social impacts of those developments, and proposes a framework by which media can be categorized across various aspects of technology and user experience.

DOMAINS OF DEVELOPMENT

Modernizing entertainment, not just by content but also by media, requires multifaceted research and development into new technologies. Some may be general developments in technology that happen to be useful here, while some are primarily aimed at leisure activities only. Such products and concepts have been under work for quite a few years, but they have gained more attention since the period of Covid-19 lockdown.

Artificial Intelligence

Artificial Intelligence (AI) has been the talk of the town for a while now. It is a software solution which is meant to learn from given data and make predictions based on the same, or suggest an action to achieve a desired output, with minimal to no active participation of the user. It has multiple use cases, and Chawla et al (2024) discuss how it can be used to make gaming more inclusive.

Extensive studies have been done and are ongoing on Large Language Models (LLMs). They are optimized for Natural Language Processing, which means communicating using high level languages that humans can understand normally or "naturally". They are trained on vast amounts of data from the internet, which helps keep them updated with the latest socio-linguistic developments. These models are capable of answering complex logical questions based on given information, and understand and explain realistic scenarios. This would make it much easier for developers to design storylines for games, movies, shows etc. so they could simply be prompt ideas while the LLM does most of the work. In randomization scenarios such as gacha-gaming or lottery-based game scenarios (Kesuma and Princes, 2024), these models can give output based on the gameplay. Additionally, in interactive media, such models could be used to restructure the dialogues, story or gameplay based on inputs by the user, such as dialogue selections, plot selections and other activities. Such a dynamic form of entertainment helps cater the finer details to the specific consumers. Currently, Generative Pre-trained Transformer (GPT) 4.0 by OpenAI, Gemini by Google, Large Language Model Meta AI (LLaMA) by Meta are some of the mainstream LLMs. Their performance in terms of correctness and coherence has been showcased through usage by millions of consumers for both personal and commercial use. Abbas (2024) similarly discusses the use of Machine Learning techniques in making games more realistic, including interactions with non-player characters (NPCs).

Prompt:

You are a wise trinket trader in India in the year 1950 BC. You have a secret map to reach the location of a magical gem hidden in the midst of a mountain range. I am a swordsman who approaches you asking about the history of the gem and whether anybody around your locality would have come across it. What should I say to convince you to give me this secret map to help in my quest to find this gem?

□ *Response by Bing Copilot:*

Ah, noble swordsman, your quest for the gem is one of great valor and courage. The gem you seek is the Amara Mani, a jewel of legend said to grant immense power to its holder. It was lost to the ages, and many have sought it, but none have returned.

To gain my trust and the map, you must prove your pure intentions, for the gem has a history of attracting the hearts of men not with valor, but with greed. Share with me a tale of your past deeds that reflects your honor and the righteousness of your quest. Swear by the sword you wield that your purpose is noble and that the power of the Amara Mani will be used for the good of all.

If your heart is true, I shall entrust you with the map, for it is not just a path to the gem, but a journey that tests the spirit. May your sword stay sharp, and your will unbroken.

□ *Response by Google Gemini:*

(Squinting at you over my spectacles, I, the wizened trinket trader, stroke my long beard thoughtfully.)

Ah, warrior, the whispers of forgotten legends always pique the curious mind. The gem you seek, some say, is the "Eye of the Mountains," a sapphire imbued with the power to grant wishes whispered on the wind.

As for its whereabouts... obtaining such knowledge doesn't come freely. Many have sought this gem, some for good, some for nefarious purposes. Tell me, brave one, why does this gem call to you? What purpose drives you to brave the treacherous mountain paths?

Here's how you can convince me to consider parting with the map:

- *Appeal to My Curiosity: Tell me a genuine story about a vision or prophecy that led you to the Eye of the Mountains. A wise trader appreciates a good tale.*
- *Offer a Trade: Do you have any rare artifacts or forgotten lore you could exchange for the map? Knowledge is a valuable currency. Perhaps an ancient weapon your family has passed down?*

- *Demonstrate Worthiness: Show me your skills! A demonstration of swordsmanship or a display of strength could convince me you're capable of handling the dangers that lie ahead.*
- *A Promise of Respect: Vow to use the gem's power for good and to bring prosperity to this land. A worthy cause can sway a cautious heart.*

Remember, a good swordsman isn't just strong, they're also strategic. Choose your approach carefully, for a map in the wrong hands can bring chaos.

(A sly twinkle enters my eye.) Who knows, if you impress me enough, I might even point you towards someone who can help you decipher the map's ancient script.

The choice is yours, warrior. Will you convince me you're worthy of the Eye of the Mountains, or will this legend remain a mere whisper on the wind?

The above original prompt is a hypothetical excerpt from a fantasy game in which the player is looking for a fictional relic. The responses of the LLMs show that they are capable of expanding the stories even with minimal information and adding details of their own to suit the theme, making it even more interesting. Using such tools, games could be made more dynamic. Tang et al (2020) analyze such potential of AI in gaming.

Similar to LLMs, which focus on text and language, generative AI (GenAI) has the capability to produce visual outputs as well, such as images and videos. Enhancing computer vision in game engines further improves the capabilities of companies for faster and more complex worldbuilding in free-world and immersive games. Dall-E is an image generation tool, which can create animated pictures based on given prompts and is even able to interpret complicated fictional structures which may not exist in the real world. Gemini is a multipurpose AI tool which is similarly capable of generating images. Sora, recently launched by OpenAI, produces short realistic video clips from text prompts. Integrating such a feature in interactive gaming media could allow user-specific customization to an unprecedented level. Even without interactive features, a tool like this can expedite the process of creating animations for commercial artists, making it much more economic and most certainly disrupting the animation industry in aspects of worldbuilding, character design and more – be it movies, shows or advertisements. However, these tools still need some development to maintain logical connections between multiple sequential prompts, which affects the continuity and consistency of a visual product.

Both the models generated multiple images for the same prompt, shown in Figures 1 and 2. It shows that, although they can fulfill the requirements mentioned by the user, it is tricky to stay coherent on the same image for multiple prompts in a continual manner.

Prompt:

Image of a creature with the head of a dog, snout of a crocodile, humanoid body with the hide of a tiger, limbs of a gorilla and the tail of a long fish.

Figure 1. Images generated by Bing Copilot – Designer (Dall-E) as response to given prompt.

Figure 2. Images generated by Google Gemini as response to given prompt.

Extended Reality

Extended Reality (XR) is the general term for any experience that blends the physical world with the digital world. It includes Augmented Reality (AR), Virtual Reality (VR) and Mixed Reality (MR). These technologies require additional hardware and software to take effect, but come with highly immersive content consumption. Kalaiarasan et al (2024) comment on the usage of this technology in the gaming industry, while Creed et al (2024) suggests on making it more inclusive.

Augmented Reality consists of content digitally overlaid on a natural environment in real time without actually making any changes to the image of the natural world. It allows the user to interact with digital entities through a screen. A fitting example of entertainment through AR is the game 'Pokémon Go'. It caused stirs across social media for its public safety hazards, but remains popular to this day. The game requires users to collect Pokémon, which are a variety of fictitious creatures with supernatural abilities found in the animated franchise of the same name. The app displays various Pokémon moving and interacting with the real world as seen by the phone camera. It essentially allows the player to see the game happening in real life as they can find any Pokémon at any time and place they may be. This makes the user deeply engaged in the experience.

Virtual Reality takes it a notch higher. It comprises an entire virtual world around the user and allows interaction with the digital elements present in it. This does not typically involve any objects from the real environment of the user. Meta has shifted its focus in the past decade from superficial digital experiences to highly immersive experiences by creating the 'Metaverse'. The Metaverse is intended to be the next form of social connectivity, and appears to be blooming economically as well. It allows creators to create custom environments within the virtual world, in which virtual space is sold commercially. These environments could potentially allow entire physical experiences, such as amusement parks, cinema screenings, and more to be felt digitally. It might also facilitate immersive content consumption similar in theory to reverse-augmented reality, wherein the user can find themselves virtually present in the fictional world of a movie and see the events of the movie happen around them while not engaging with them directly. The Metaverse could therefore add a whole new element to Gaming as well as Over-The-Top (OTT) platforms. Bian (2023) discusses in depth the characteristics and applicability of VR in games. Cheiran et al. (2025) present detailed user feedback of VR devices.

Mixed Reality is essentially a gray area between Augmented and Virtual realities, wherein the real world is taken as reference and its elements are digitally altered in real time according to the features of the application. Facial filters on social media are a day-to-day example, where a person's actual face is seen digitally edited for recreational purposes. This is a prime example of the advancements of computer vision technology applied here, which needs to be fast and versatile to adapt to the natural environment of the user. Another theoretical aspect of this technology is Spatial Computing. Through the lenses of VR goggles and other supplementary gadgets, the user must experience digital entities such as virtual screens, 3-dimensional objects and content displayed in a real 3-dimensional space. This requires the VR-enabling devices to have the ability to correctly compute positions of everything around them and the size and intensity of the generated objects as per how the user shall perceive it. Apple Vision Pro is the trending product on extended reality, which allows users to engage with applications and their surroundings at a digitally deeper level. It is evident that this technology is quite expensive for consumer electronics.

Display and Sound Technology

Display technology has come a long way since the Cathode ray Tube (CRT) all the way to Organic Light Emitting Diode (OLED) screens. Majorly only two techniques are used for display – either light emitting screens (Liquid Crystal Display - LCD, Light Emitting Diode – LED) and projectors (Micromirror projectors, LCD projectors, Film Print projectors). Woo et al (2024) propose a method for combining these two technologies for enhanced viewer experience in a new era of entertainment.

Sound technology is being intensely researched upon. Active Noise Cancellation (ANC) is currently a premium feature for sound gear sought after for comfortable audio experiences. Samsung has made great leaps using ML in background noise reduction during live communication such as phone calls. Some products are rather unconventional in the norm of earphones and headphones. Open earphones by Bose are attached to the ears but do not insert fully into the ear, which gives better health, safety and comfort. Bone conduction earphones are exclusively worn out of the ears, and rather transmit soundwaves through the skull bone to the ears. This is a subtle move towards versatile wearables and covers some basics for implantable consumer gadgets.

VR Goggles are the primary tool for users to have a deeper virtual reality experience. They are a compact device consisting of display and sound of such quality that blends the digital world into reality. Having the form factor of comfortable headsets, these 'goggles' enable portability and enhanced immersion into the content they interact with. However, they are expensive to develop and thus to purchase. Further work is required to make them more affordable and accessible.

Processors and Computer Chips

When multiple technologies are combined to create immersive experiences that Partarakis and Zabulis (2024) study, the need for processing capability increases. The domains discussed above require immense computing power in order to provide a satisfactory user experience at a commercial scale. Intel and Nvidia are some of the industry leaders in making new, specialized processors optimized for AI, Machine Learning, Graphics processing and more.

Intel advertises their Core series as suitable for gaming, and Core Ultra series as enhancing the gaming experience with AI. The Atom series is particularly designed for small form-factor IoT designs that require edge implementation of AI – suitable for devices such as VR goggles.

Nvidia originally introduced Graphics Processor Units (GPU) to consumer hardware with the GeForce 256 (NV10). Their graphics cards are renowned for high performance and are used by computer gamers across the globe. Recently the company has shifted their focus majorly towards AI computing, such as the GeForce RTX series which supports high FPS (Frames Per Second), low latency AI-powered graphics – another boon for virtual reality applications. These graphics drivers support plug and play compatibility with various VR headsets.

Apple Vision Pro uses the Apple M2 system on chip (SoC) with the R1 co-processor to read sensor inputs, and has memory of options of several gigabytes. This is a small testament of how much computing power a VR headset really requires, considering that the M2 is the same chip used in their laptops, desktops and tablets.

Controllers and Haptics

Controllers for televisions need to be inherently straightforward. Since they are meant for simple, fast and non-continuous usage, they should have direct buttons to access various features of the television system. This is particularly important for smart televisions which have more features. Gaming controllers, on the other hand, are a canvas for innovation – as seen in the variety of handsets made by PlayStation, Nintendo and Xbox over the years. As adult gamers typically enjoy complex high-stimulation experiences, gaming handsets can be made elaborate and advanced, but if the target audience is adolescents and children, they need to be made simple and less stimulating too.

However, the idea of 'controllers' is no longer limited to buttons. PlayStation Move and Wii Remote are classic examples of motion-based controllers, which allow the in-game character to simulate the real movements of the user to some extent. One Kinect by Xbox was a revolutionary device in itself, by allowing gesture control using a camera, implementing a unique use case of computer vision at the time it was launched. Gesture control still has a slight drawback – it inhibits user experience by disrupting usage as the user has to stop their game and make specific gestures to execute commands. The next evolution to this – merging the two concepts of contact-based and gesture-based controls into a unified haptic and wearable control. Xi et al (2024) highlight the use of wearable devices in gaming.

Haptic gloves, like most other technologies mentioned above, have been under development for decades now; but their execution in the form of updated digital functionalities has only been done recently. They are also known as VR gloves as they allow the user to interact with the virtual world. They can simulate some sensations like touch, pressure, various textures for the user to feel, and the other way round by sensing hand movements and projecting similar actions in the digital world in three dimensions. This requires proper utilization of sensors to detect the signals from the hand and a mix of chemistry, biology and psychology to produce sensory outputs for the consumer. By virtue of AI-enhanced edge computing, this technology can greatly reduce the latency of interactions between the glove and the console by using deep learning to predict user movements in advance, and thus make the experience seamless.

Interaction with the User

All the technologies mentioned above act as an intricate system to make the user interact with the media. This system works at various stages to efficiently deliver new forms of content. The adjoining Figure 3 depicts these stages and how closely the work with the user.

PROBLEMS AND CRITICISM

The entertainment industry has succeeded in capturing a wider, more diverse audience. While that is a positive result from a financial point of view, it is a risky attribute given the advancement of the artificial intelligence industry and its obsession with data. It provides several threats from an ethical perspective.

Data Privacy

Highly customizable content or media which requires high amount of user interaction is likely to generate significant amount of data with respect to the user's personal choices and preferences. For an organization to have such data and use it for commercial purposes is a violation of privacy of the users. Ugwu et al. (2022) discuss through a case study how major AI tools target personal data, from the healthcare industry in this case. If the entertainment data provides similar insights in the context of consumer psychology, access to user trends beyond a typically available level of depth, it will be susceptible to similar attacks. The work by Menard and Bott (2025) highlights this concern against the misuse of AI.

Producing Sensitive Data

In contrast to AI extracting sensitive data, we also have the issue of AI producing sensitive data. Despite several safeguards in place, prompt injection and jailbreaking can successfully trick an LLM into producing sensitive or harmful content. Wang et al. (2025) and Dong et al. (2025) present some examples of such techniques. This fragile restriction, paired with recommendation systems, may cause a self-modifying media to repetitively generate harmful content beyond the control of the creators, or even the users. This poses a serious threat to youth and children being exposed to sensitive content, unwittingly and in an unregulated manner.

Social Impact and Addiction

High-stimulation media is often considered harmful for youth, as it desensitizes them to basic social experiences. The problem of isolated entertainment raised by these media is also discussed by Ergin (2024). Incomplete entertainment leading to social deformity and addiction is a serious risk. The study by Singh et al. (2025) emphasizes this problem, noting that a majority of their sample proved to be addicted to OTT platforms.

Physical Usage and Disability

A variety of gadgets require a variety of physical interaction with media that did not previously exist. VR sickness is a known issue, causing physical discomfort to the users after prolonged usage of the device, which poses a higher risk for those with high sensitivity to temperature and physical contact. Rupp (2024) highlights the negative user experiences faced due to thermal discomfort and VR sickness. Furthermore, the requirement of increased motion to effectively utilize the media experience limits its usage by people with motor impediments and disabilities causing restricted motion. It poses a paradoxical challenge to inclusive design, where the visual nature of a media can be replaced by haptic design for users with vision impairments, but the implementation of increased motion-based gadgets reduces its usability for audience with physical disabilities.

Resource Hungry AI

Since recent developments in high-performance LLMs, major organizations have been spending increasing amounts of money and energy for the training and further development of their AI models. Energy in this case also refers to literal energy, which is the electricity supply. Multiple data centers in the USA are known to be consuming as much energy alone as entire towns, as well as significant amounts of water supply for cooling – causing water shortages for use by humans. The major environmental risk put forth by the supposedly improving technology is a matter of serious debate worldwide and needs swift and strict regulations to maintain the ecological balance of humans and technology with the biosphere. Additionally, the powerful chips needed to train these models are being produced and traded in massive quantities, indicating a new genre and wave of electronic waste. This waste would be particularly novel in nature as it is produced with newer and more advanced technology nodes, with smaller transistor sizes and higher count. While there is a broader shift towards green electronics, it has not been implemented and adopted at the scale at which the demand for chips is growing.

Governance

High-performing AI models, which are in high demand, are known to consume high amounts of data from various digital sources – some licensed, and some allegedly unlicensed. Gumusel (2025) studies the threat to privacy from as basic a tool as a chatbot. Protecting user rights is essential and ethical use of AI needs to be legislated thoroughly. Batool et al. (2025) review various frameworks that have been implemented to regulate AI and provide insights into this necessity.

Training on personal data allows AI to mimic an individual's digital persona, as has been witnessed in various reported cases of people being defrauded by AI-generated personas. It puts people's identity at risk of being misidentified as a criminal in a crime they did not commit, and also endangers the victims who are being made to believe that they are interacting with someone else. Since facing such criminal cases, various governments are working towards appropriate action and safeguards against AI being let loose online.

METHODOLOGY

Previous methodologies to assess user experience with respect to performance of the products are intended for user feedback, and dependent on subjective assessments. They are also limited to specific media or products and, though helpful in evaluating the product after or during development, do not provide a metric for categorizing and demarcating the properties of the product. Faruk et al. (2025) present a framework for assessing user experience but specifically for AI conversational models, while Vergari (2025) proposes an evaluation methodology for extended reality products. These examples show the general concentration of existing frameworks.

The field of entertainment now comprises more supplementary features than ever before. It is imperative that creators focus not only on the content but also on the medium of endorsement for maximum impact. The following framework is proposed with the intention to help the designers involved in making products and services in the entertainment industry systematically design a prototype rapidly to meet their requirements. It is intended to apply for business, research and regulatory purposes.

Figure 3. Sample of Experience Design Framework as a horizontal bar graph.

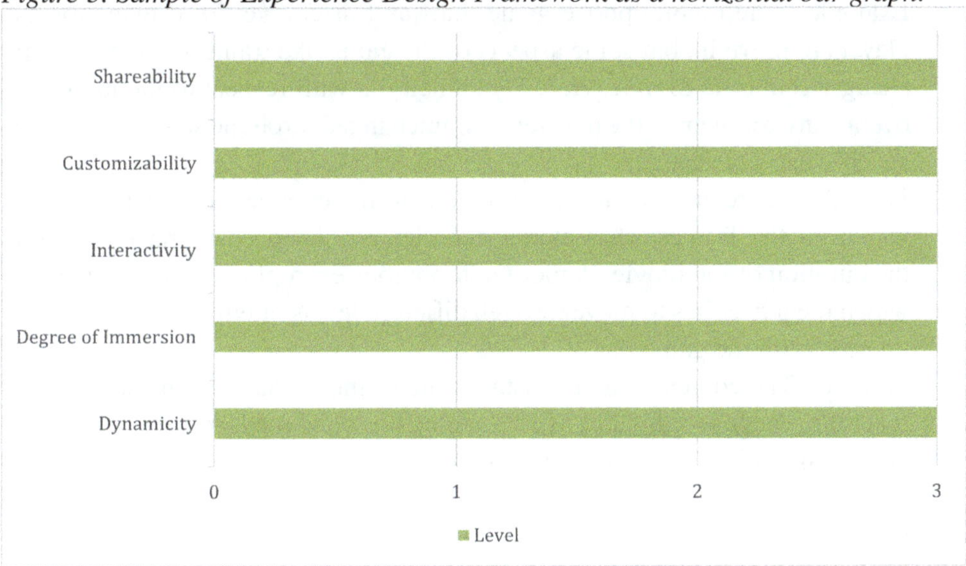

We can dub this the "Experience Design Framework" or EDF. The name indicates that this framework is used to design the experience of the user. This framework takes into consideration how the user perceives the features of a product by their experience and defines the elements that the maker should use through a rubric. It aims to bring under a common umbrella any product, service, content, or idea generated in the entertainment industry.

Figure 3 shows the 'level' of each parameter, which essentially means the extent to which the parameter is implemented in the product. Nevertheless, the levels do not indicate whether a product is better or worse than another. Naturally, Level 1 is the least implementation and Level 3 is the highest. However, there can be a Level 0 for a parameter as well which indicates that the respective feature does not exist at all in the product. Each level has certain properties depending on the parameter. The parameters and their levels are as defined below.

Dynamicity

This refers to the variability of the content. A simple explanation for this is the comparison of an image and a video. An image stays the same whenever seen – which is less dynamic – but a video is continuously changing – which is more dynamic. Essentially, it is a measure of the changes in media without any modifications made by the user.

Level 1 – There are partial changes in the content with increase in usage. Example – the mobile phone game Subway Surfers has fixed maps for the players to move in, but some aspects of the game like trains and hurdles will change from time to time. Here Dynamicity is with respect to the map. The overall environment of the map remains unchanged throughout the game while specific aspects change.

Level 2 – There are continuous variations to the content, such as a movie in which all the frames, characters, sceneries etc. keep changing throughout the duration of the movie. A more non-obvious example would be a game in which the player has to move through different levels or environments as they proceed with the gameplay.

Level 3 – The content is in a constant state of motion and can be accessed in real time, which is similar to live streaming on social media or other channels. Online multiplayer games can also be included in this.

Degree of Immersion

The term 'Degree of Immersion' can be used to describe to what depth the user can experience the digital content. It is a very straightforward measure of how many dimensions of usage the creator needs to add to their product.

Level 1 – The first level of immersion is standard viewing on screens, such as television, computers and mobile phones.

Level 2 – The second level contains Mixed reality, having digital media overlaid on the real-world environment.

Level 3 – The third and last level has complete immersion into the media, which is Virtual Reality. This would involve highly experiential content such as virtual worlds like the Metaverse.

Interactivity

This feature involves how much the user can interact with the media in order to change or affect the content. In this context it takes into consideration only the extent, not the method in which the user shall interact. Interaction may include anything from motion controls (games) to search history (OTT).

Level 1 – Only the designated interactions in the media are allowed. Similar to games like Temple Run and Mortal Kombat, the player can only perform a fixed number of actions. Generally, movies and shows do not have any form of interaction, but recently Netflix has introduced non-gaming interactive content as well.
Level 2 – The user can interact with non-designated elements in the media, which includes free-world games where the player can roam around in the digital world and interact with aspects of the game that are not mandatory for the promised experience.
Level 3 – Every element in the content is accessible to some extent. Games like Minecraft and Fortnite which allow the players to interact with and build their own environments fall into this category.

Customizability

There are some products that stay as they are until the end of their lifecycle, and there are some which cannot be identified after usage – plenty of users want at least some variations in the product from what was originally made to be. Customizability shows how much of that is possible.

Level 1 – Nothing more than basic features can be changed from pre-defined options, such as changing settings like color themes, character outfits in games, language preferences etc.
Level 2 – Inputs given by the user can indirectly affect the content, such as a dialogue choice from the player leading to a different output in the game including significant changes in the storyline. Recommender systems from search histories may also be included here as they change based on indirect input.
Level 3 – The game or media can analyze the usage patterns of the consumer and restructure the content completely with or without conscious choices from the user. This can also be seen akin to advanced algorithms implemented by social media applications that are intended to engage the user by showing content that is predicted to be liked by them.

Shareability

This parameter conveys to what extent multiple users can use the same product or content from the same or a connected network of devices. This includes physical as well as online connectivity in consoles. The extent of this affects whether the consumer can enjoy the service alone or with company, both known and unknown.

Level 1 – The first level has products that can be used alone, but also with a deterministic number of companions – either by physical or wireless connection. This includes gaming consoles and games such as EA Sports Fifa, which can be played by a group of people by connecting multiple controllers to the same console. It also includes OTT platforms which allow password sharing with a small finite number of companions, making them accessible by multiple people online.

Level 2 – This level describes server-based limited multiplayer environments in which for one iteration of a game, the user is matched with a finite number of other players who are all placed in a single server to interact with each other through the internet. Games like Fortnite and Among Us showcase this aptly, as they group a small number of online players randomly, but also allow the multiple users who want to stay together to join the same group together.

Level 3 – The final level of Shareability essentially means one can intentionally interact with any other user connected on the network of devices. There are a few games which allow the users to find anybody playing that game and perform some activities with them. Technically, social media also falls under this category.

ILLUSTRATION OF FRAMEWORK

This proposed framework is applicable in many ways to entertainment designers in classifying and developing both new and old products. The feature ratings make it clearer to all parties involved in the creation of the product which specific features and components need to be included based on the content. It also streamlines the study of these products and enables better structuring of data to train and implement deep learning models, whether to classify existing products or to generate ideas for new products by testing various combinations.

Demonstration

The framework is meant to simplify the description of a product from the perspective of design and features by reducing it to 5 features. It makes it easier to compare different products and predict other aspects like components and cost of development in order to meet user requirements.

The following are some demonstrations of representing existing products to explain how this framework is intended to be used. These sample products are arbitrarily chosen to include various combinations of features. It shows that content, hardware, platforms, products and more can be represented through this framework.

OTT Platforms

Figure 4. OTT Platforms represented through Experience Design Framework.

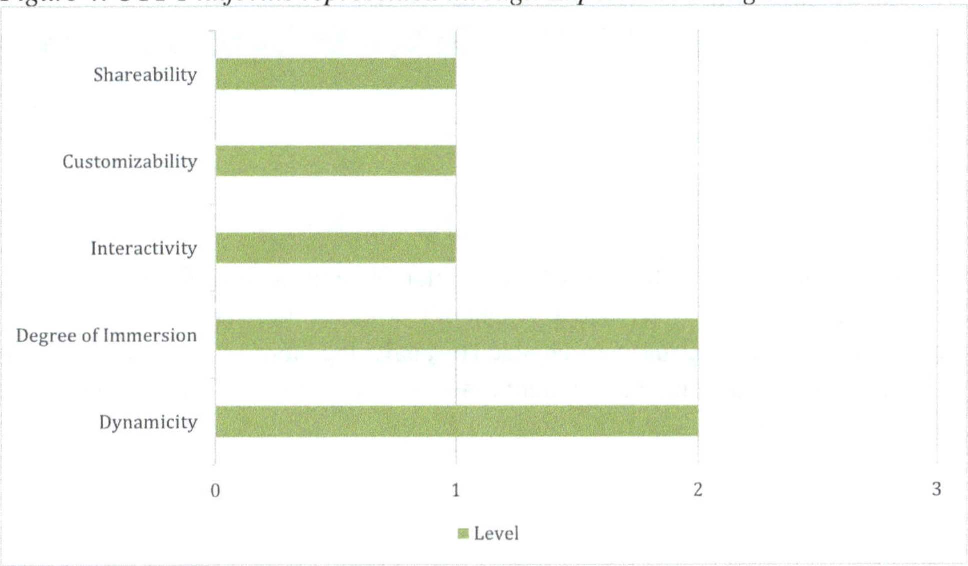

OTT platforms, which provide the most basic form of entertainment through movies and shows, emerged as a successful business model in the past couple of decades. Simple wireframes and easy accessibility make them popular. Figure 4 describes these platforms.

Social Media Application

Figure 5. Social Media Applications represented through Experience Design Framework.

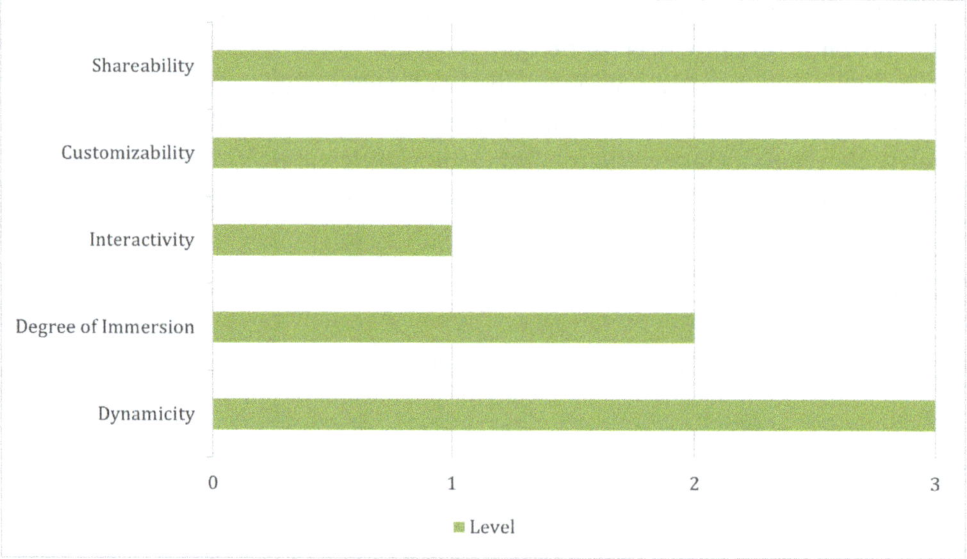

Most social media applications have similar features with different names or interfaces; hence Figure 5 is made as a generalization for these applications. These apps are designed to keep the users engaged by analyzing their consumption through likes and shares, and displaying content that is expected to keep them engaged for longer periods of time.

Fortnite

Figure 6. Fortnite represented through Experience Design Framework.

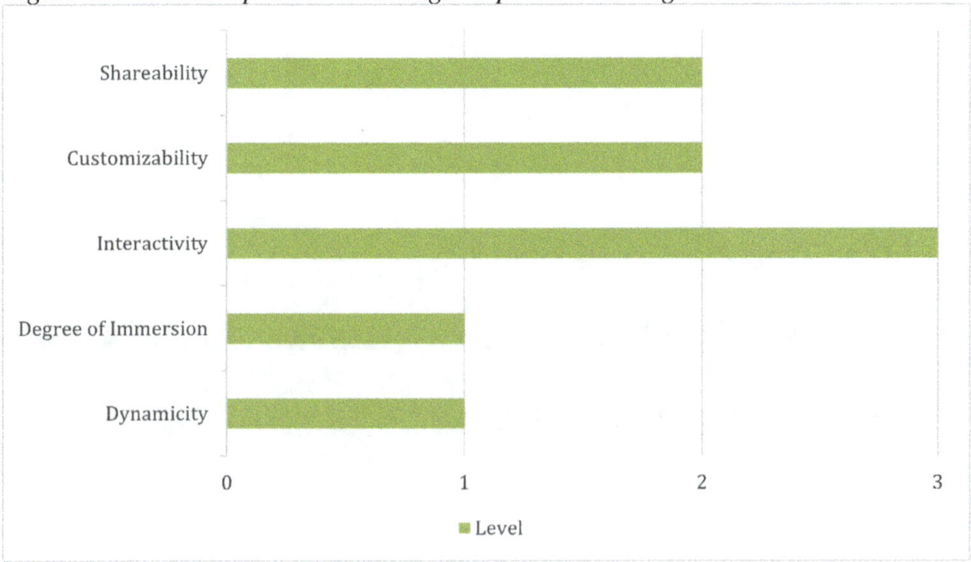

Figure 6 elaborates on Fortnite, one of the most popular battle-royale games. It allows the players to compete with each other to fight for the position of last surviving player or team in a map, giving the chance to acquire various gaming items as they go and defeat others. It is free-to-play and developed by Epic Games. It also has a feature through which the players can build their own maps with the landscape features supported by their gaming engine, such as mountains, water bodies etc. and play in it.

Decentraland

Figure 7. Decentraland represented through Experience Design Framework.

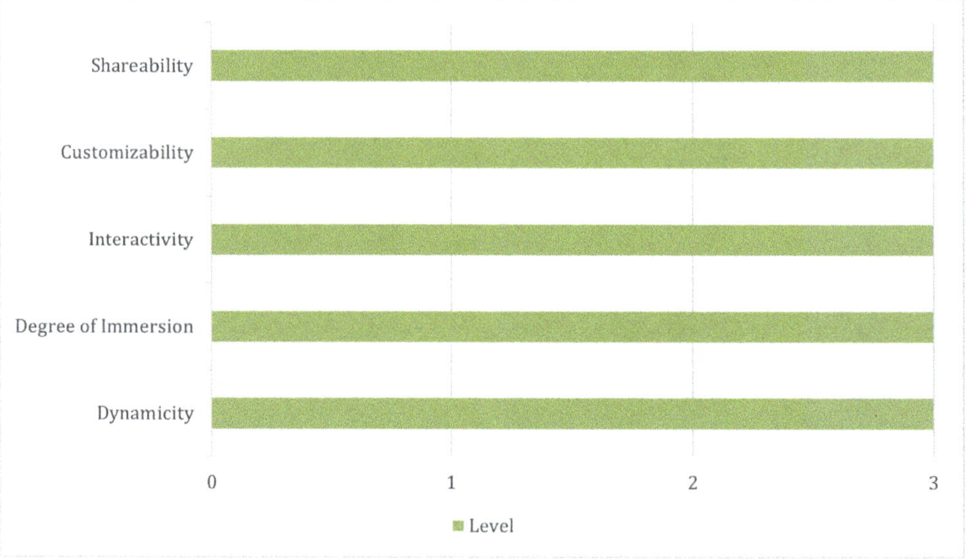

Since the VR industry is still under development, there are not many games that are commonly known or available which support VR equipment. Decentraland is a game and platform in which users are allowed to access a custom-made virtual universe, interact with its components, design and publish new elements, and do all of this either with or without VR devices. It is made as an open world where anybody can express their creativity. Figure 7 showcases the attributes of this platform.

PlayStation 5

Figure 8. PlayStation 5 represented through Experience Design Framework.

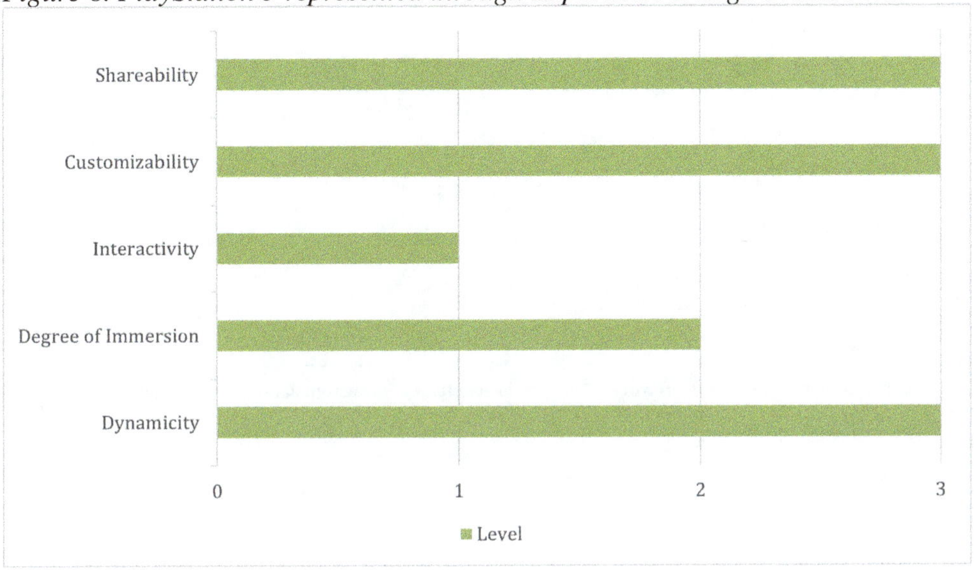

The latest gaming console by Sony Interactive Entertainment in its PlayStation franchise took the internet and its customers by storm. It comes with a wireless controller named 'Dual Sense' which has enhanced haptic feedback, built-in microphone and adaptive control triggers. The console itself contains custom processors and memory drives which enable high speed applications for game creators. It also supports high quality displays, higher refresh rate and enhanced realistic graphics. Figure 8 is a representation of this console through the Experience Design Framework.

Alternative Illustrations

The framework is conceptual in its essence and therefore it can be illustrated in various types of statistical visualizations as needed or desired by the user. Since this is a broad framework, it should be able to accommodate any form of communication. Some alternate illustrations of EDF continuing the example of PlayStation 5 are as demonstrated in Figures 9 to 12.

Figure 9. Experience Design Framework represented as a Line Graph.

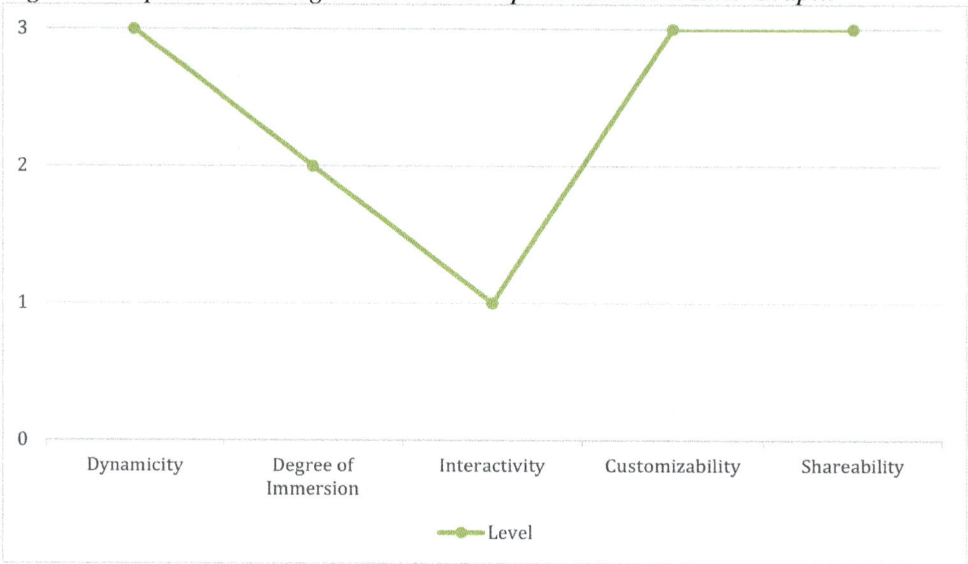

Figure 10. Experience Design Framework represented as a Scate Plot.

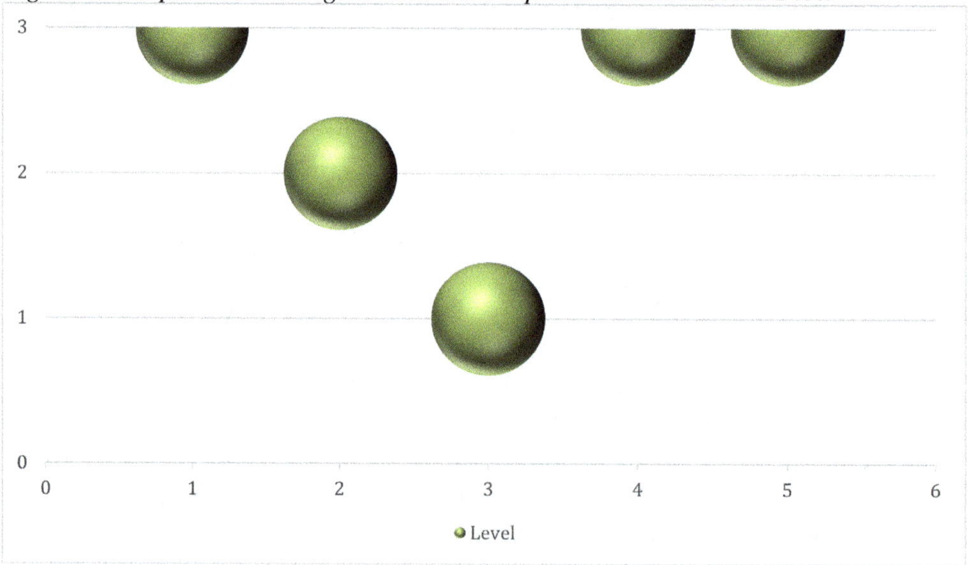

Figure 11. Experience Design Framework represented as a Radar.

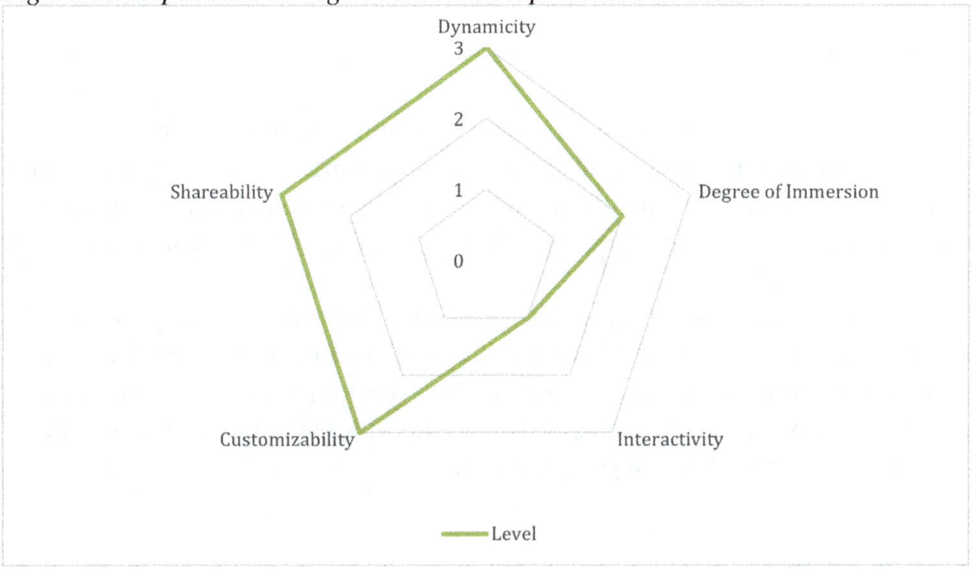

Figure 12. Experience Design Framework represented as a Vertical Bar Graph.

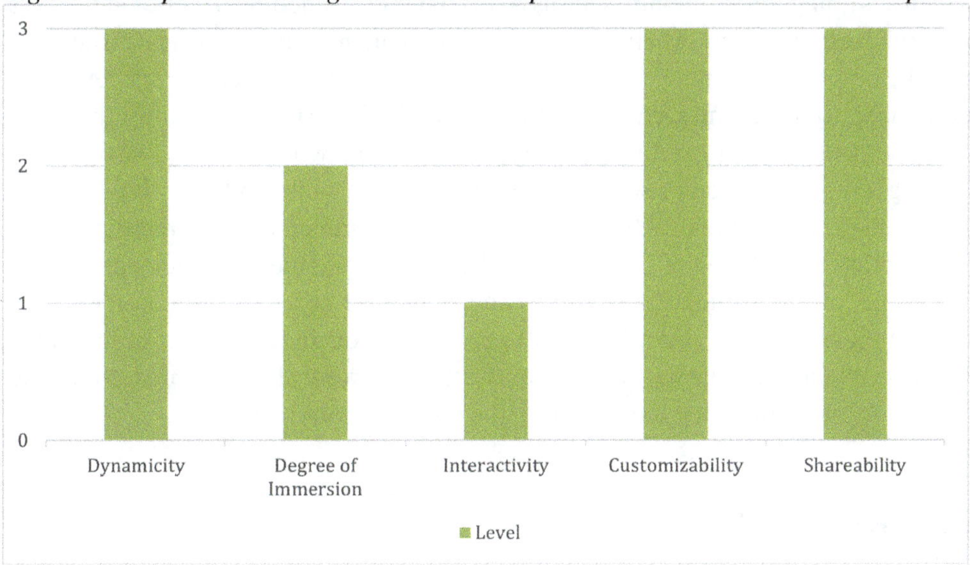

Advantages

This framework enables the user to deconstruct their product or service into various categories so that they can adopt a modular approach to their design. It clarifies the specific aspects that need to be implemented at different stages in its working cycle, such as tools used for the features – machine learning for greater customizability, additional hardware for more degree of immersion and so on. The framework also allows a designer to define end goals for their product to aid in a top-down approach.

Moreover, it provides specific data parameters for understanding user trends, and consequent legislations. Understanding which categories of products cause addiction, exposure to harmful content, or data sensitivity issues becomes clearer with this categorization. Thus, it is easier for authorities to regulate specific aspects of media in the interest of the general public.

CONCLUSION

This chapter covers the various domains involved in the materialization of the entertainment industry. It highlights recent developments and the future direction in which it is going. Each domain, such as Artificial Intelligence and Haptic Controllers are explained separately. Their importance and pertinence are shown using examples of existing products launched commercially in the past few years. A framework is introduced to represent each product through which attributes it allows the users to implement to what extent. The usage of this framework was demonstrated by making a representation of some existing products from the industry. It takes note of five main parameters – Dynamicity, Degree of Immersion, Interactivity, Customizability and Shareability. These are the general parameters which apply to all electronic leisure products, keeping it independent of cost and content in order to make it more modular, lest it become an analysis of business or arts. Additionally, alternate methods of illustrating the same framework were also presented to indicate that the framework is not dependent on the mode of communication.

FUTURE WORK

It is possible to use the Experience Design Framework to classify products, old and new, into various categories to study attributes like their psychological and physiological impacts on humans, consumption rates, production costs, feature-specific elements such as hardware components, software solutions and media requirements among other things. They could also be studied for their impact on sustainability. This will result in relevant data that can be used to train deep learning models to predict realistic future market trends, and also generative models to design new feasible products optimized for both business and client. The framework can be adapted to include more classes like stimulation, processing power, bandwidth requirements in order to suit the needs of a specific product or business model being designed.

REFERENCES

Abbas, B. (2024). Elevating Realism: Cutting-Edge AI NPCs and Environments Transform Gaming in'VirtualEra.'.

Batool, A., Zowghi, D., & Bano, M. (2025). AI governance: A systematic literature review. *AI and Ethics*, •••, 1–15.

Bian, S. (2023). Research on the Application of VR in Games. *Highlights in Science, Engineering and Technology*, *39*, 389–394. DOI: 10.54097/hset.v39i.6558

Chawla, M., Panda, S. N., Khullar, V., Garg, K. D., & Angurala, M. (2024). Deep learning based next word prediction aided assistive gaming technology for people with limited vocabulary. *Entertainment Computing*, *50*, 100661. DOI: 10.1016/j.entcom.2024.100661

Cheiran, J. F. P., Bandeira, D. R., & Pimenta, M. S. (2025). Measuring the key components of the user experience in immersive virtual reality environments. *Frontiers in Virtual Reality*, *6*, 1585614. DOI: 10.3389/frvir.2025.1585614

Creed, C., Al-Kalbani, M., Theil, A., Sarcar, S., & Williams, I. (2024). Inclusive AR/VR: Accessibility barriers for immersive technologies. *Universal Access in the Information Society*, *23*(1), 59–73. DOI: 10.1007/s10209-023-00969-0

Dong, X., Hu, W., Xu, W., & He, T. (2025, July). Sata: A paradigm for llm jailbreak via simple assistive task linkage. In Findings of the Association for Computational Linguistics: ACL 2025 (pp. 1952-1987).

Ergin, P. (2024). Are video streaming services offering incomplete entertainment? *Media Culture & Society*, *46*(2), 414–424. DOI: 10.1177/01634437231216443

Faruk, L. I. D., Pal, D., Funilkul, S., Perumal, T., & Mongkolnam, P. (2025). Introducing CASUX: A standardized scale for measuring the user experience of artificial intelligence based conversational agents. *International Journal of Human-Computer Interaction*, *41*(9), 5274–5298. DOI: 10.1080/10447318.2024.2359206

Fowler, S. J., & Fowler, J. J. (2011). A quantitative analysis of entertainment consumption: 1984-2009. *MEIEA Journal*, *11*(1), 39–61. DOI: 10.25101/11.2

Gumusel, E. (2025). A literature review of user privacy concerns in conversational chatbots: A social informatics approach: An Annual Review of Information Science and Technology (ARIST) paper. *Journal of the Association for Information Science and Technology*, *76*(1), 121–154. DOI: 10.1002/asi.24898

Hong, S. H. (2007). The recent growth of the internet and changes in household-level demand for entertainment. *Information Economics and Policy*, *19*(3-4), 304–318.

Hu, X. (2024). Analysing the new marketing model for entertainment companies: A case study of SM. entertainment. In SHS Web of Conferences (Vol. 181, p. 01007). EDP Sciences.

Jaferian, G., Ramezani, D., Polyak, E., & Wagner, M. (2024). Exploring blockchain's horizons in educational gaming. Inted2024 Proceedings, 5050-5058.

Kalaiarasan, S. M.. (2024). Can we engage players with extended reality in gaming applications? A Stimulus-Organism-Response framework. *Entertainment Computing*, *50*, 100651. DOI: 10.1016/j.entcom.2024.100651

Kesuma, A. E., & Princes, E. (2024). Antecedents of Gacha gaming intention: Extending UTAUT2 with structural video game characteristics. *Computers in Human Behavior Reports*, *14*, 100405. DOI: 10.1016/j.chbr.2024.100405

Menard, P., & Bott, G. J. (2025). Artificial intelligence misuse and concern for information privacy: New construct validation and future directions. *Information Systems Journal*, *35*(1), 322–367. DOI: 10.1111/isj.12544

Partarakis, N., & Zabulis, X. (2024). A review of immersive technologies, knowledge representation, and AI for human-centered digital experiences. *Electronics (Basel)*, *13*(2), 269.

Rupp, M. A. (2024). Is it getting hot in here? The effects of VR headset microclimate temperature on perceived thermal discomfort, VR sickness, and skin temperature. *Applied Ergonomics*, *114*, 104128. DOI: 10.1016/j.apergo.2023.104128 PMID: 37708655

Singh, S., Debata, I., Behera, A. A., Panda, P. S., Samantaray, A., & Behera, B. K. (2025). Over-the-top (OTT) entertainment viewership addiction among the undergraduates of a medical college in Bhubaneswar, Odisha. *Journal of Family Medicine and Primary Care*, *14*(3), 1110–1115.

Somani, P. P.. (2024). *"The Rise of OTT: A Dynamic Shift Towards Binge Watching, an Increase for On-Demand Entertainment." The Rise of Over-the-Top (OTT) Media and Implications for Media Consumption and Production*. IGI Global. DOI: 10.4018/979-8-3693-0116-6.ch012

Tang, C., Wang, Z., Sima, X., & Zhang, L. (2020, October). Research on artificial intelligence algorithm and its application in games. In 2020 2nd International Conference on Artificial Intelligence and Advanced Manufacture (AIAM) (pp. 386-389). IEEE.

Ugwu, A. O., Gao, X., Ugwu, J. O., & Chang, V. (2022, September). Ethical implications of AI in healthcare data: a case study using healthcare data breaches from the US department of health and human services breach portal between 2009-2021. In *2022 International Conference on Industrial IoT, Big Data and Supply Chain (IIoTBDSC)* (pp. 343-349). IEEE.

Vergari, M. (2025). User experience for public usage of extended reality (Doctoral dissertation, Technische Universität Berlin).

Wang, H., Li, H., Zhu, J., Wang, X., Pan, C., Huang, M., & Sha, L. (2025, November). Diffusionattacker: Diffusion-driven prompt manipulation for llm jailbreak. In *Proceedings of the 2025 Conference on Empirical Methods in Natural Language Processing* (pp. 22193-22205).

Woo, J., Kim, D., Lee, J., & Jang, S. (2024, January). Enhancing Viewer Experience: Combining TV and Projector Technologies for a New Era of Entertainment. In *2024 IEEE International Conference on Consumer Electronics (ICCE)* (pp. 1-3). IEEE.

Xi, N., Buruk, O. O., Chen, J., Jabari, S., & Hamari, J. (2024). Wearable gaming technology: A study on the relationships between wearable features and gameful experiences. *International Journal of Human-Computer Studies, 181*, 103157. DOI: 10.1016/j.ijhcs.2023.103157

Chapter 4
Predictive Modelling of Drivers' Positions in Formula 1 Racing Using Ensemble Machine Learning

Shilpa Mahajan
http://orcid.org/0000-0001-8975-8114
The NorthCap University, India

Ragni Sharma
http://orcid.org/0009-0009-3666-7476
The NorthCap University, India

ABSTRACT

Formula 1 racing is a data-driven sport, where applying data science techniques can provide competitive edge. This chapter explores machine learning models to predict driver positions on a given racetrack. Utilizing machine learning models like Random Forest, Gradient Boosting, Support Vector Classifier, K-Nearest Neighbors, Gaussian Naive Bayes, Decision Trees, and Multi-layer Perceptron, we have explored their efficacy in forecasting race outcomes. The analysis is based on historical data encompassing of driver skills, team performance, weather conditions, and track characteristics. The goal is to provide insights that can help teams to optimize their race strategies, identify areas for improvement, and gain an advantage over competitors. The analysis revealed that Gradient Boosting and Decision Trees

DOI: 10.4018/979-8-3693-8327-8.ch004

emerged as the top-performing models, showcasing their ability to capture complex patterns within the data. Additionally, The methodologies defined can potentially be applied to other motorsports as well.

INTRODUCTION

In the split-second world of Formula 1, any advantage can be the difference between winning and losing. That's where data science comes in. This research dives into using machine learning to predict where drivers will place on a given racetrack circuit. Predicting driver positions means analyzing a huge range of factors - driver skills, team performance, weather, track layouts, and more. By mining historical F1 datasets and building predictive models, we aim to accurately forecast each driver's finishing position on any circuit.

The study tests out multiple machine learning algorithms like neural networks, boosting, decision trees, naive Bayes, k-NN, SVMs, and random forests. The top performers are gradient boosting and decision trees, which proven adept at capturing the complex patterns in F1 data. Careful data preprocessing and engineering extract the most relevant features from the raw data - driver experience, team histories, weather data, track maps, and any other variables that could impact position.

Introducing machine learning prediction to F1 could transform how teams approach strategy and decisions. Accurate position forecasts let teams optimize pit stops, adjust tactics mid-race, and make smarter calls that boost performance. The techniques explored here could also extend to other racing disciplines beyond F1. Successful gradient boosting and decision tree models pave the way for further developing these algorithms specifically for motorsport predictions and analysis.

LITERATURE REVIEW

Predictive modeling and performance analysis have become integral components of Formula 1 racing, leveraging advanced computational techniques to gain competitive advantages. Various studies have explored different methodologies to enhance the accuracy and efficiency of these predictive models. Casella and Vidoni (2017) utilized Generalized Additive Models (GAMs) to model lap times, providing a flexible approach to understanding the multifaceted factors that impact race performance (Casella & Vidoni, 2017). Sobrie (2020) demonstrated the application of tree-based models, which excel in sifting through the noise inherent in Formula One data, thereby enhancing predictive performance (Sobrie, 2020).

Generalized Additive Models (GAMs) have been employed to model lap times, offering flexibility in understanding the complex factors that influence race performance. Casella and Vidoni (2017) utilized GAMs to capture the nuances of lap time data, demonstrating the potential of this approach in providing detailed insights into race dynamics (Casella & Vidoni, 2017).

Neural networks have also been extensively explored for their potential in race prediction. Franssen (2021) conducted a comparative study of various neural network architectures, highlighting their relative strengths and limitations in predicting race outcomes (Franssen, 2021). Stoppels (2017) similarly applied artificial neural networks to predict race results, showing significant promise in this domain (Stoppels, 2017). Additionally, Liu and Fotouhi (2020) combined neural networks with Monte Carlo tree search techniques to develop sophisticated race strategies, further advancing the predictive capabilities in the field (Liu & Fotouhi, 2020).

Bayesian analysis has also been employed to disentangle complex variables in racing performance. Van Kesteren and Bergkamp (2023) utilized Bayesian methods to separate the influence of driver skill from constructor advantage, providing deeper insights into performance determinants (Van Kesteren & Bergkamp, 2023). Machine learning frameworks, as discussed by Sicoie (2020), have been developed to predict race winners and championship standings, showcasing the versatility and robustness of these models (Sicoie, 2020).

Tree-based models have been extensively explored for their ability to sift through the noise in Formula 1 data. Sobrie (2020) highlighted the effectiveness of these models in predicting race outcomes by reducing the impact of irrelevant features and focusing on the most significant variables (Sobrie, 2020). The use of tree-based models has shown promise in handling the high dimensionality and variability inherent in race data.

Machine learning frameworks designed specifically for predicting race winners and championship standings have also been developed. Sicoie (2020) presented a comprehensive framework that integrates various machine learning techniques to enhance the predictive power of race outcome models (Sicoie, 2020). This framework underscores the importance of combining multiple approaches to capture the full complexity of Formula 1 races.

The integration of weather data into predictive models is essential for understanding the impact of environmental conditions on race outcomes. Salazar, Balerna, and Elbert (2017) highlighted the significance of real-time control algorithms that incorporate weather variables, demonstrating their influence on race performance (Salazar et al., 2017). This integration allows for more accurate and robust predictions under varying conditions.

Optimal control and strategy development play crucial roles in maximizing performance under dynamic race conditions. Kehrle et al. (2011) explored the optimal control of Formula 1 race cars within a virtual environment, demonstrating how simulations can inform real-world strategies (Kehrle et al., 2011). Heilmeier et al. (2018) provided a race simulation framework for making strategic decisions, such as tire changes and energy allocation, underlining the practical applications of these models in race scenarios (Heilmeier, Graf, & Lienkamp, 2018). Duhr et al. (2023) focused on minimum-race-time energy allocation strategies for hybrid-electric power units, further emphasizing the importance of efficient resource management (Duhr, Buccheri, & Balerna, 2023).

Pit stop strategies are another area of interest, as highlighted by Estes (2023) in his Poisson analysis of pit stops. This study provided insights into the timing and frequency of pit stops, which are critical for optimizing race strategies and improving overall performance (Estes, 2023).

DATASET

The datasets utilized in this study encompass a wide range of historical and recent data related to Formula 1. The primary dataset, "Formula 1 World Championship 1950-2020," sourced from Kaggle and FastF1 API, includes comprehensive historical data covering multiple aspects of the championship from 1950 to 2020. This dataset consists of several CSV files that provide detailed information on races, drivers, constructors, race results, lap times, pit stops, qualifying sessions, constructors' results, constructors' standings, drivers' standings, circuits, and seasons. For instance, it contains race information such as race ID, year, circuit ID, and race name, as well as driver details including driver ID, name, and nationality. It also features extensive race result data, detailing each driver's performance metrics like grid position, race position, points, laps, and fastest lap times.

Complementing this, the "F1 Weather Dataset 2018-2023" offers weather-specific data for Formula 1 races held between 2018 and 2023. This dataset includes parameters such as race ID, year, circuit ID, temperature, humidity, wind speed, and descriptive weather conditions. This data is crucial for understanding the impact of weather on race outcomes and driver performance.

METHODOLOGY

The methodology for this study involves a comprehensive process that includes data collection, preprocessing, feature engineering, model development, evaluation, and deployment. Each step is critical to ensure the robustness and accuracy of the predictive models.

1. Data Collection and Preprocessing

Datasets: Multiple datasets containing detailed information about Formula 1 races were utilized. These datasets included information on circuits, constructors, drivers, lap times, pit stops, qualifying results, race results, and weather conditions from 2018 to 2023. The datasets were imported into pandas Data Frames for manipulation and analysis. The inclusion of diverse datasets allowed for a comprehensive analysis of factors influencing race outcomes (Casella & Vidoni, 2017) (Sobrie, 2020).

Web Scraping: To enhance the dataset, additional features such as the length and number of turns for each circuit were extracted from Wikipedia. This was achieved using web scraping techniques with the BeautifulSoup library. By parsing the HTML content of Wikipedia pages, we were able to extract specific information and merge it into the main dataset. This additional data was crucial for understanding circuit characteristics and their impact on race performance (Casella & Vidoni, 2017).

Figure 1. Data Preprocessing Outliers (Lap times)

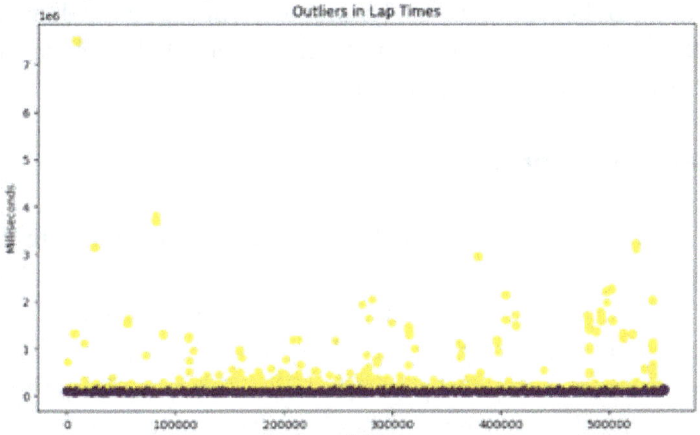

Figure 2. Data Preprocessing Outliers (Pit Stop Times)

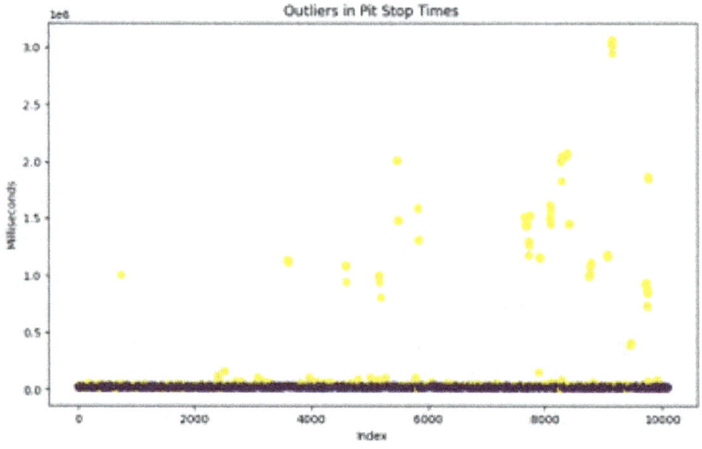

Data Cleaning and Imputation: The initial datasets contained missing values and outliers, which were addressed to ensure data quality. Missing values were replaced with the mean values of their respective columns. Outliers were identified using the Interquartile Range (IQR) method (as shown in Fig. 1 and 2) and were managed appropriately to avoid skewing the analysis. Data cleaning ensured that the datasets were consistent and complete, which is essential for reliable model training and evaluation (Casella & Vidoni, 2017) (Sobrie, 2020).

2. Feature Engineering

Experience Metrics: We calculated experience metrics for both constructors and drivers based on the number of races they participated in (as shown in Fig.3). Constructor experience was determined by the cumulative count of races each constructor had participated in. Similarly, the driver's experience was calculated by counting the races each driver had participated in. These metrics provided insights into the experience and consistency of teams and drivers over time (Franssen, 2021).

Figure 3. Constructor Experience

Performance Metrics: Historical performance metrics such as driver age, wins, and constructor wins were included as features. Driver age was calculated based on the date of birth and the date of each race. The number of wins for each driver and constructor was determined (in Fig. 4) by counting their first-place finishes. These performance metrics were critical for capturing the historical success and reliability of drivers and constructors (Sicoie, 2020).

Figure 4. Performance

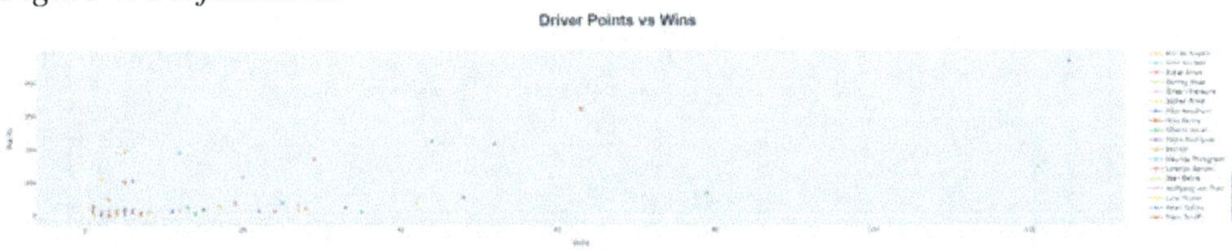

Track Characteristics: The characteristics of each circuit, including location (Fig. 5), length and the number of turns, were integrated into the dataset. This information was obtained from the web scraping process and provided insights into how different circuit features might influence race outcomes (Fig. 6). Circuit length and the number of turns is significant factors that can affect race strategies and performance (Van Kesteren & Bergkamp, 2023).

Figure 5 Folium map indicating locations of the Circuits

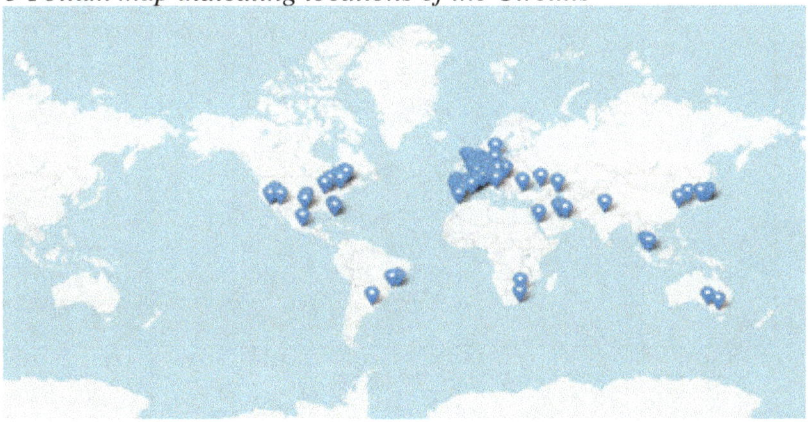

Weather Impact: Weather conditions, particularly rainfall, were included in the analysis to assess their impact on race outcomes (Fig. 7). The weather data was merged with race data to correlate weather conditions with race results. This analysis was essential for understanding how different weather conditions, such as rain, could affect race dynamics and driver performance (Tulabandhula & Rudin, 2014).

Figure 6. Effect of grid position on winning stats

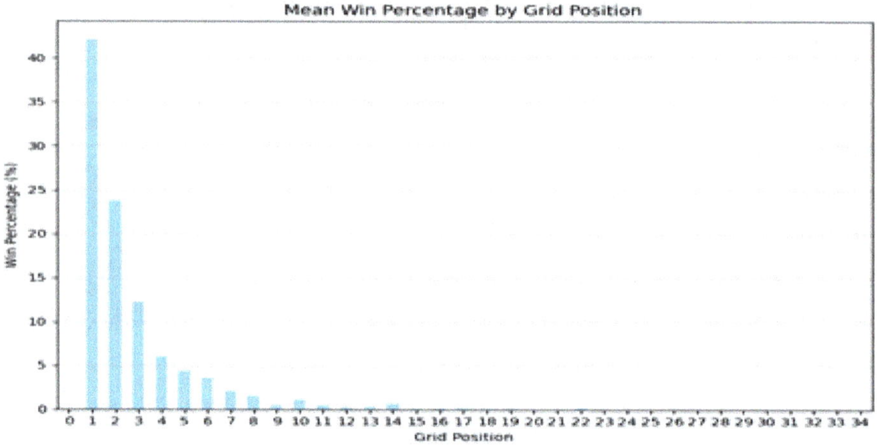

Figure 7 Effect of weather (rain) conditions on winning stats

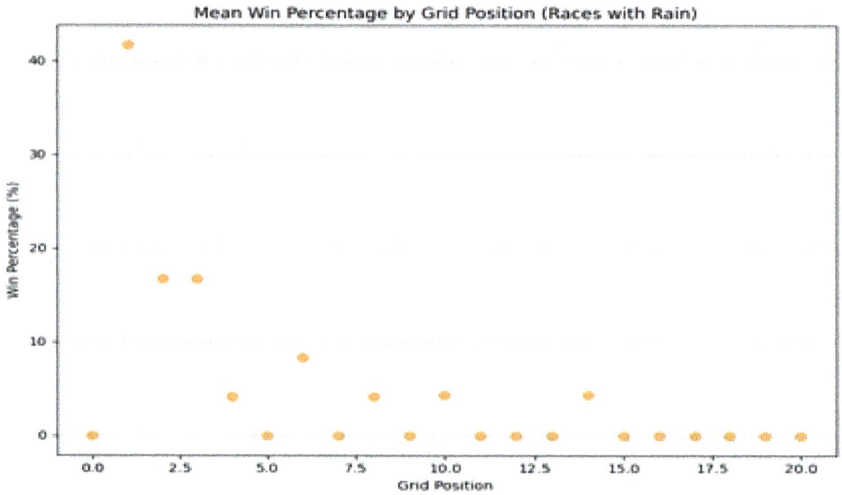

3. Model Development

We employed various machine learning models to predict race outcomes. Each model was evaluated using cross-validation techniques to ensure robustness.

Random Forest Classifier: The Random Forest classifier is an ensemble method that combines multiple decision trees to improve classification accuracy. Each tree is trained on a random subset of the data, and the final prediction is made by averaging the predictions of all trees. This method reduces overfitting and improves generalization. Random Forests are particularly effective in handling large datasets with complex interactions among features (Mahajan, 2023; Stoppels, 2017).

Figure 8. Random Forest Classifier

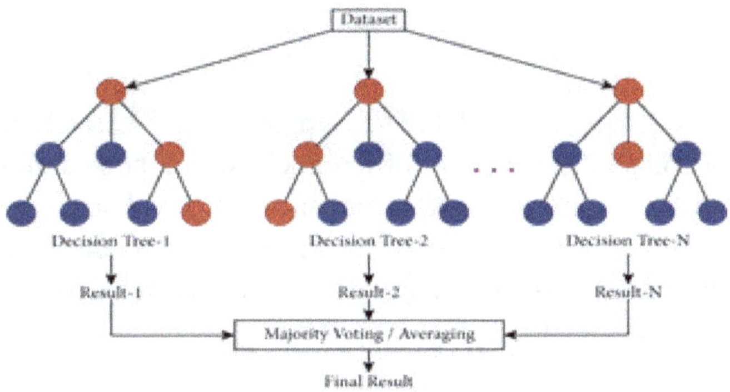

Gradient Boosting Classifier: Gradient Boosting is another ensemble technique that builds trees sequentially. Each tree is trained to correct the errors of its predecessor, and the final model is a weighted sum of all trees. This method aims to minimize a specified loss function, typically through gradient descent. Gradient Boosting is known for its high predictive accuracy and ability to handle various types of data, making it suitable for our race prediction task (Sicoie, 2020) (Stoppels, 2017).

Figure 9. Gradient Boosting Classifier

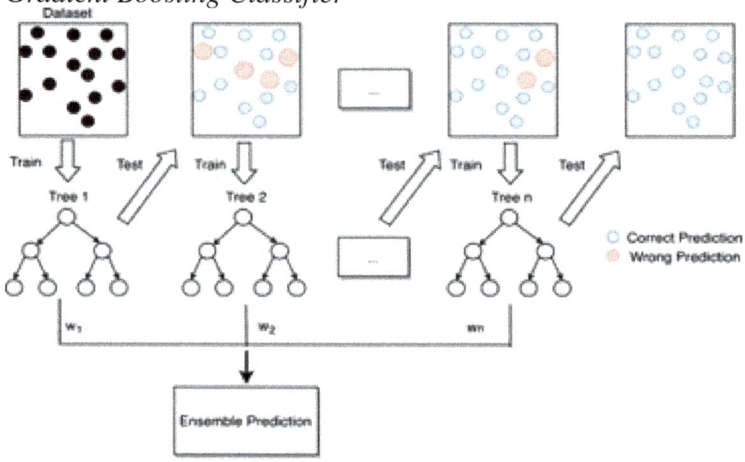

Support Vector Classifier (SVC): The Support Vector Classifier aims to find the optimal hyperplane that separates different classes in the feature space. It uses a kernel trick to transform data into a higher-dimensional space where a linear separator can be found. SVC is effective in cases where the decision boundary is complex and non-linear. It is particularly useful for classification tasks with high-dimensional data (Sobrie, 2020).

Figure 10. Support Vector Classifier

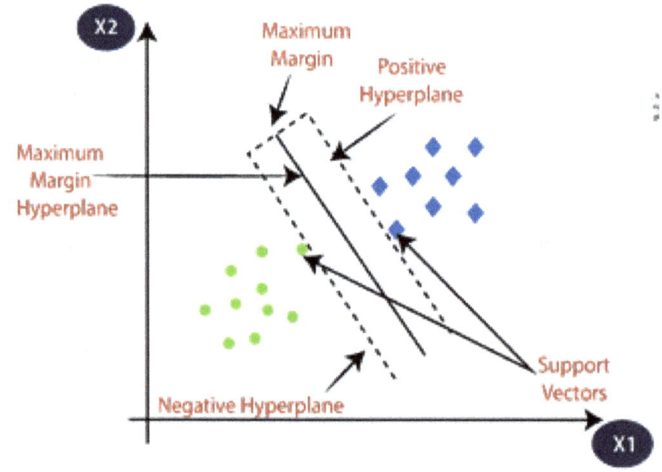

K-Nearest Neighbors (KNN): KNN is a simple yet powerful algorithm that classifies a data point based on the majority class of its k-nearest neighbors. It is a non-parametric method that is effective when the decision boundary is irregular. KNN can adapt to the local structure of the data, making it useful for predicting race outcomes based on the characteristics of similar past races (Franssen, 2021).

Figure 11. K-Nearest Neighbors

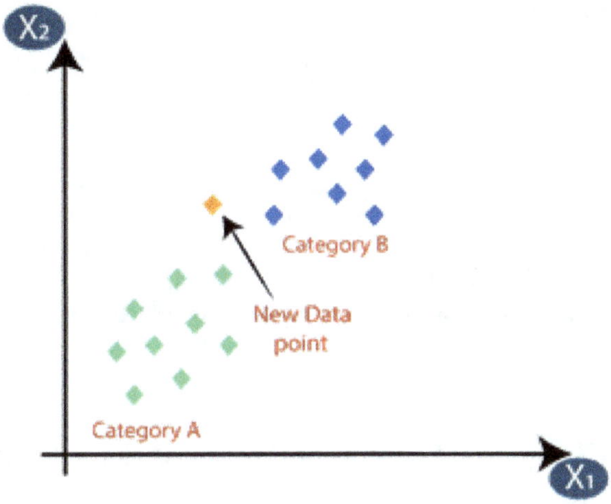

Gaussian Naive Bayes: Gaussian Naive Bayes assumes that the features follow a normal distribution and uses Bayes' theorem for classification. Despite its simplicity, it performs well in many real-world applications, especially when the assumption of feature independence holds true. It is computationally efficient and provides probabilistic predictions, which can be useful for understanding the confidence of the model's predictions (Peng et al., 2021).

Figure 12. Gaussian Naive Bayes

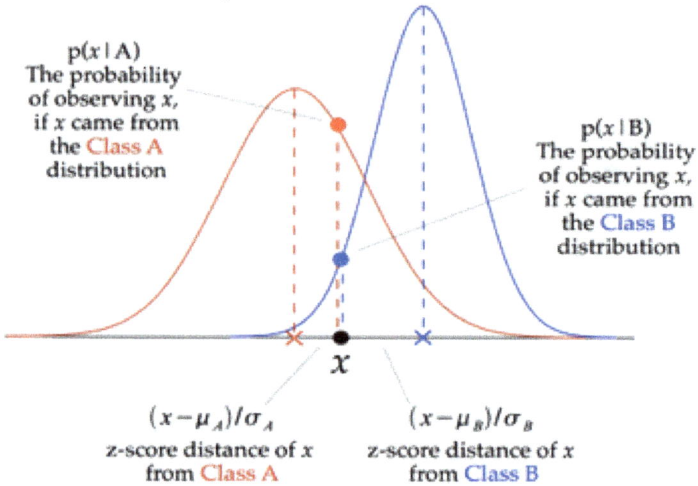

Decision Tree Classifier: The Decision Tree classifier splits the data into subsets based on feature values, creating a tree-like structure. Each node represents a feature, each branch represents a decision rule, and each leaf represents an outcome. Decision Trees are easy to interpret and visualize, making them useful for understanding the decision-making process of the model. However, they are prone to overfitting, which can be mitigated by pruning or using ensemble methods like Random Forests (Sicoie, 2020).

Figure 13. Decision Tree

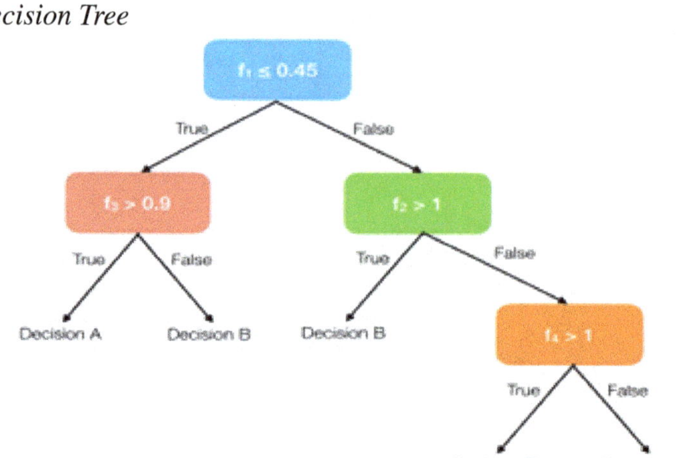

Multi-layer Perceptron (MLP): MLP is a type of neural network that consists of multiple layers of nodes (neurons), with each layer fully connected to the next one. It uses backpropagation to learn the weights that minimize the prediction error. MLPs are capable of learning complex non-linear relationships in the data, making them suitable for tasks where feature interactions are intricate. They require careful tuning of hyperparameters and a large amount of data for training (Franssen, 2021).

Figure 14. Multi-Layer Perceptron

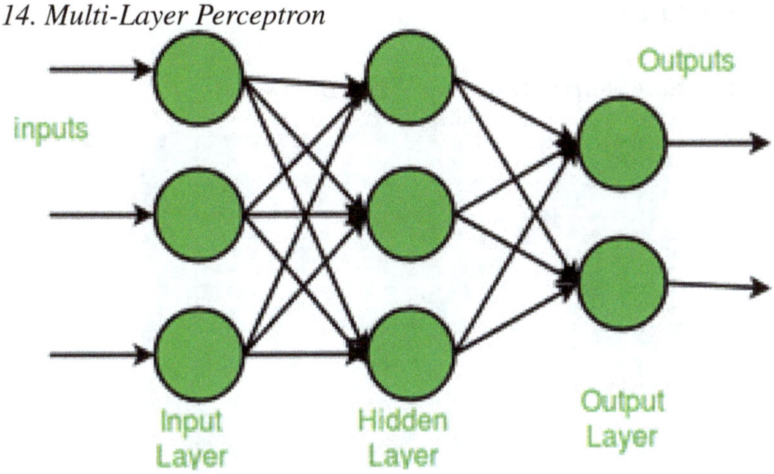

4. Model Evaluation and Comparison

The models were evaluated using stratified K-fold cross-validation to ensure robustness and avoid overfitting. Accuracy and F1 score were the primary metrics used for model evaluation. Cross-validation ensures that the model's performance is consistent across different subsets of the data, providing a reliable estimate of its generalization ability (Sobrie, 2020) (Stoppels, 2017).

After training and evaluation, the models' performances were compared. The model with the highest accuracy and F1 score was selected as the best-performing model. This model was then saved using joblib for future use and deployment. The deployment included a prediction function that could predict race outcomes based on input features such as driver name, grid position, and circuit location (Sicoie, 2020).

Confusion Matrix

To evaluate the performance of the developed models, a confusion matrix was employed. The confusion matrix provides insights into the accuracy, precision, recall, and F1-score of the predictive models, helping to fine-tune and improve their performance for better race outcome predictions. It also highlights the correct and incorrect predictions made by the model, allowing for a detailed analysis of its performance across different classes (Ikram & Mahajan, 2016). This is essential for understanding the model's strengths and weaknesses and making necessary adjustments to enhance its predictive capabilities.

Gaussian Naïve Bayes

Figure 15. Confusion Matrix: Gaussian Naive Bayes

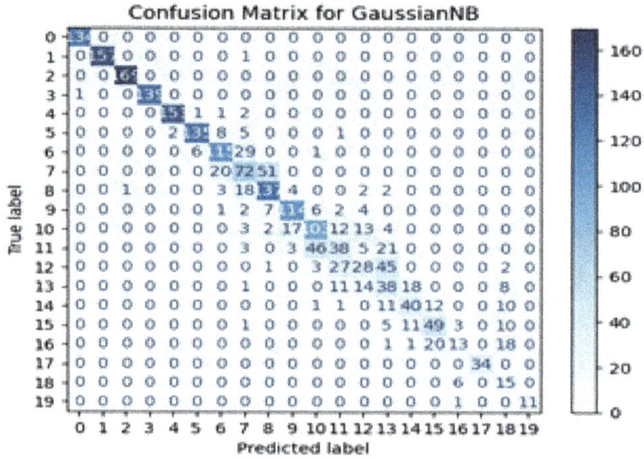

The confusion matrix for the Gaussian Naive Bayes (Fig. 15), indicates good performance for classes 0, 1, 2, 3, and 5, with high true positive counts along the diagonal, but significant misclassifications for classes 4 and 11, indicating confusion with other classes.

Decision Tree

Figure 16. Confusion Matrix: Decision Tree

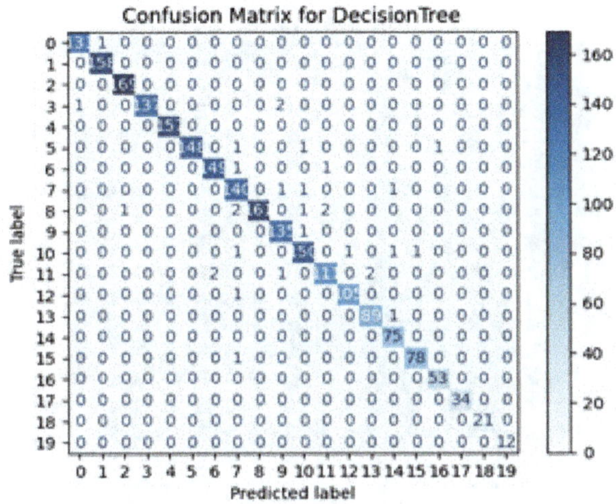

The Decision Tree classifier's confusion matrix (Fig 16) reveals high accuracy for classes 0, 1, 2, 3, 5, and 9, with fewer misclassifications compared to Gaussian Naïve Bayes, although some errors are present in classes 8 and 13.

Support Vector Classifier

Figure 17. Confusion Matrix: SVC

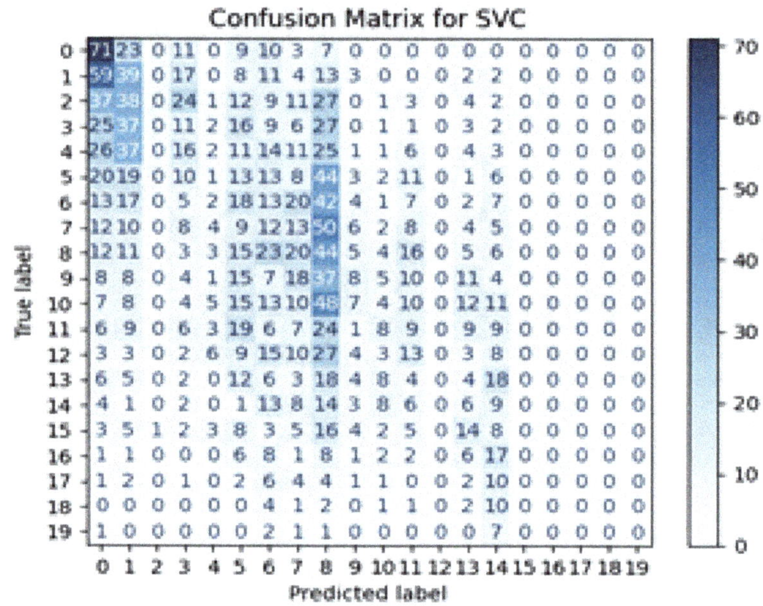

The SVC (Support Vector Classifier) confusion matrix (Fig. 17), generally performs well but shows notable misclassifications across several classes, particularly for classes 1 and 2, which exhibit considerable confusion with other classes.

K Nearest Neighbors

Figure 18. Confusion Matrix: KNN

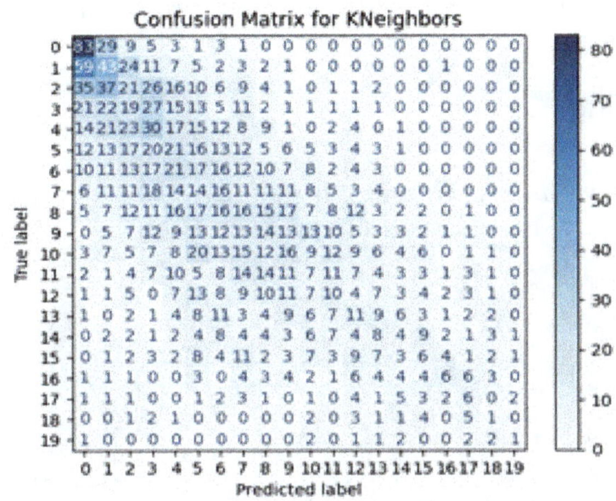

The K-Nearest Neighbors classifier's confusion matrix (Fig.18), indicates high levels of misclassification across many classes, struggling particularly with classes 3, 4, 7, and 10, demonstrating a difficulty in distinguishing between different classes.

Random Forest

Figure 19. Confusion Matrix: Random Forest

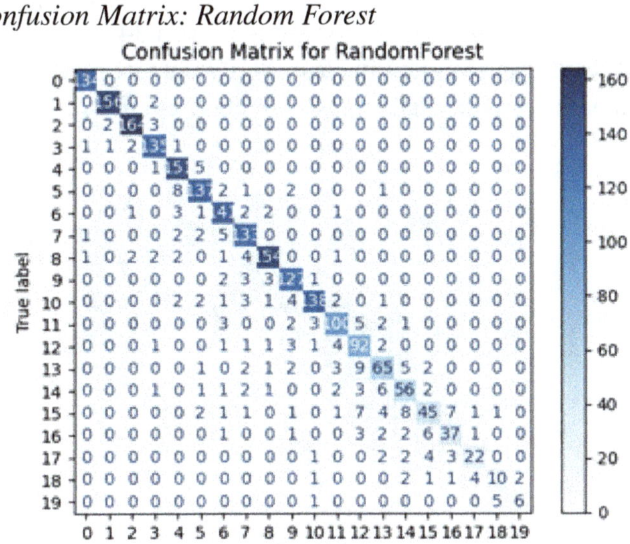

The confusion matrix for the Random Forest classifier (Fig. 19) shows strong performance with correct predictions for class 0 (34 times) and some confusion for class 1 with class 3, and a notable struggle with class 15, which was misclassified as class 16 57 times, yet performs relatively well across most classes.

Gradient Boosting

Figure 20. Confusion Matrix: Gradient Boosting

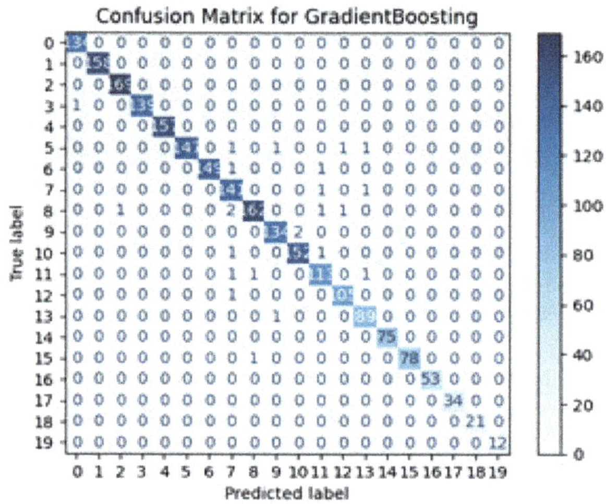

The confusion matrix for the Gradient Boosting classifier (Fig. 20) shows improved performance compared to Random Forest, with 34 correct predictions for class 0 and significant improvement in class 3 (137 correct predictions and only 5 misclassifications), but similar challenges with class 15, misclassifying it as class 16 53 times.

MLP

Figure 21. Confusion Matrix: MLP

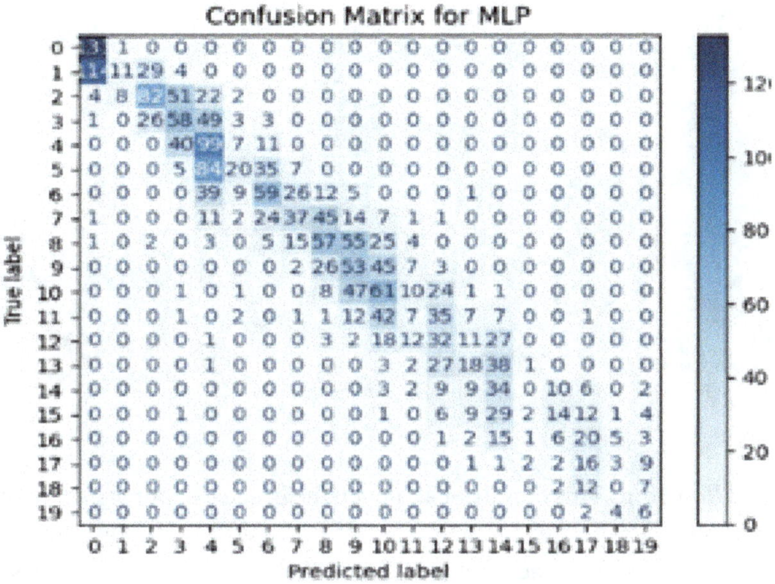

The confusion matrix for the Multi-Layer Perceptron (MLP) model (Fig. 21) demonstrates high accuracy for classes 0, 1, 4, and 6, but difficulty in distinguishing certain classes like 7 and 12, suggesting areas for model improvements through refining architecture, increasing training data diversity, and advanced feature engineering.

Model Comparison

To compare the performance of different classifiers, we analyzed their accuracy scores, as depicted in Figure 22. The bar graph illustrates the accuracy of each model, providing a clear visual comparison.

Figure 22. Model Performance Comparison

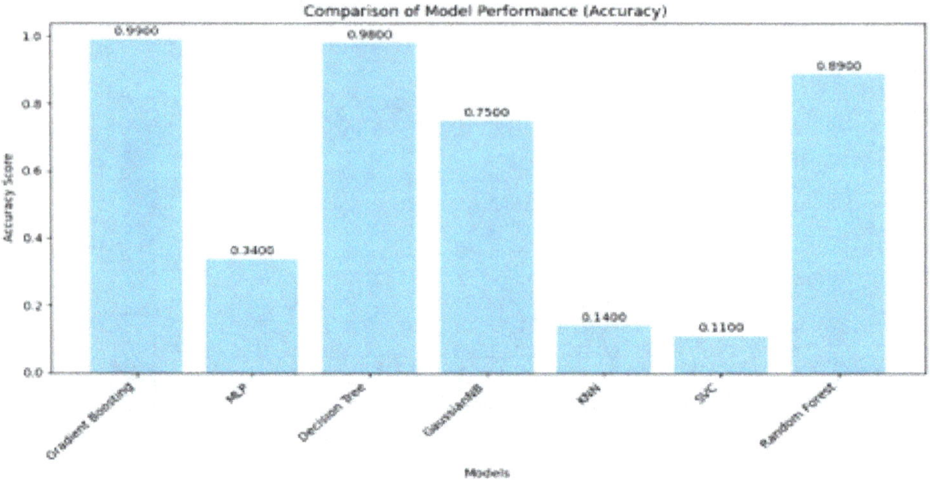

Gradient Boosting: This classifier achieved the highest accuracy score of 0.9900, indicating its superior performance in correctly classifying the instances.

Decision Tree: With an accuracy of 0.9800, the Decision Tree classifier also performed exceptionally well, closely following Gradient Boosting.

Random Forest: This model demonstrated robust performance with an accuracy of 0.8900, showing its effectiveness in classification tasks.

Gaussian Naïve Bayes: The Gaussian Naive Bayes classifier achieved a moderate accuracy of 0.7500, suggesting decent but not outstanding performance.

MLP (Multi-Layer Perceptron): The MLP classifier showed a significantly lower accuracy of 0.3400, indicating substantial room for improvement.

K-Nearest Neighbors (KNN): This classifier had a low accuracy score of 0.1400, reflecting its difficulty in distinguishing between different classes (Mahajan & Ikram, 2019).

SVC (Support Vector Classifier): The SVC model performed the least effectively with an accuracy of 0.1100, demonstrating its struggle in the classification task.

In summary, Gradient Boosting and Decision Tree classifiers outperformed the other models, showing the highest accuracy scores, while MLP, KNN, and SVC exhibited lower performance levels. This comparative analysis highlights the strengths and weaknesses of each model, guiding the selection of the most suitable classifier for specific tasks.

Use Case

Given the highly competitive nature of Formula 1, data accessibility is restricted, making it imperative to outline specific use cases for the project. The following use cases illustrate the practical applications of predictive models in enhancing various aspects of Formula 1 operations.

Use Case 1: Predictive Modeling for Race Outcomes

In this use case, the data scientist preprocesses raw data, which includes historical race results, weather conditions, and car performance metrics. This data is transformed into a structured format suitable for analysis. Machine learning models are then developed to predict race outcomes based on this preprocessed data. The performance of these models is evaluated using various metrics such as accuracy, precision, and recall. Once validated, the models are deployed in a live environment, providing real-time predictions that the F1 team uses to inform their race strategies and decision-making processes. The iterative cycle of model development, evaluation, and deployment ensures that the predictions remain accurate and relevant, helping teams maintain a competitive edge.

Figure 23. Predictive Modeling for Race Outcomes

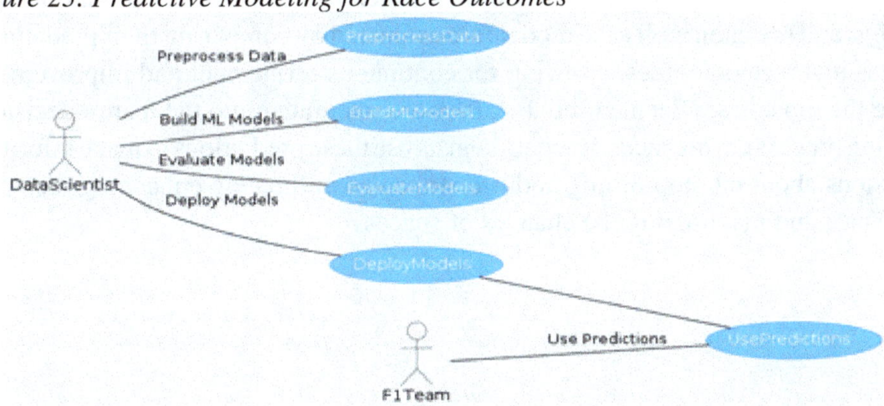

Use Case 2: Race Strategy Optimization

Figure 24. Race Strategy Optimization

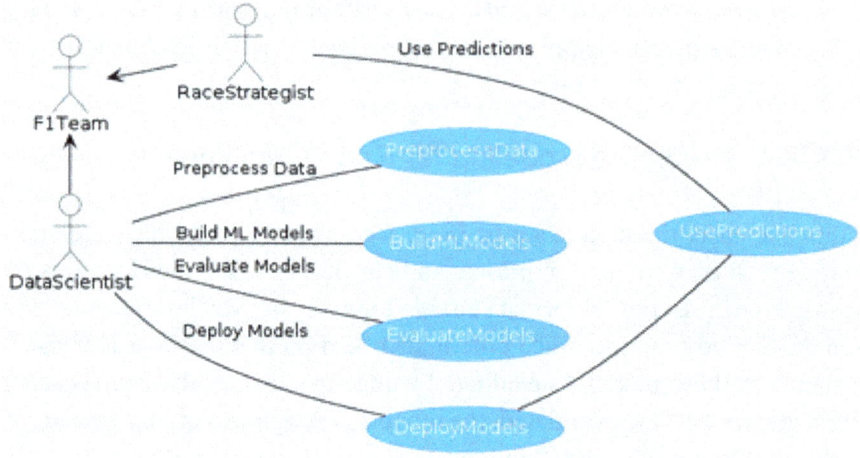

Race strategy optimization is crucial for achieving optimal results in highly competitive environments. In this use case, the data scientist aggregates historical race data, weather conditions, and tire performance data to preprocess into a usable format. Machine learning models are then developed to forecast optimal pit stop timings and tire choices. These models are evaluated by comparing their predictions with actual race outcomes, allowing for continuous refinement and improvement. Once the models are deemed reliable, they are integrated into the team's decision-making process during races. Race strategists use these predictions to make informed decisions about pit stop timing and tire strategies, ultimately enhancing race performance and maximizing the chances of success.

Use Case 3: Driver Performance Analysis

Figure 25. Driver Performance Analysis

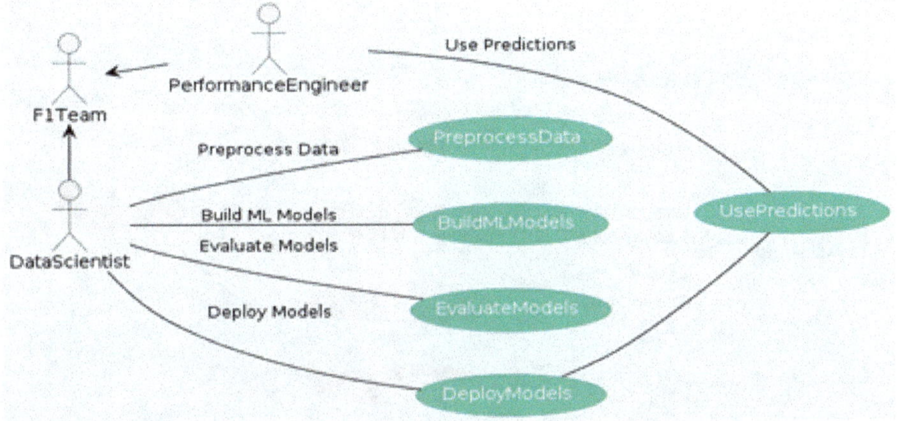

Analyzing driver performance is essential for optimizing training and race outcomes. In this use case, the data scientist collects extensive data on driver telemetry, lap times, and physical condition. This data is preprocessed and used to develop machine learning models that assess driver performance and predict fatigue levels. The models' accuracy is validated against actual performance metrics, ensuring their reliability. Once validated, these models are implemented in training sessions and race simulations. Performance engineers use the insights from these models to provide tailored feedback and optimize driver training programs. This approach not only helps in improving individual driver performance but also contributes to the overall success of the team.

Use Case 4: Predictive Maintenance

Figure 26. Predictive Maintenance

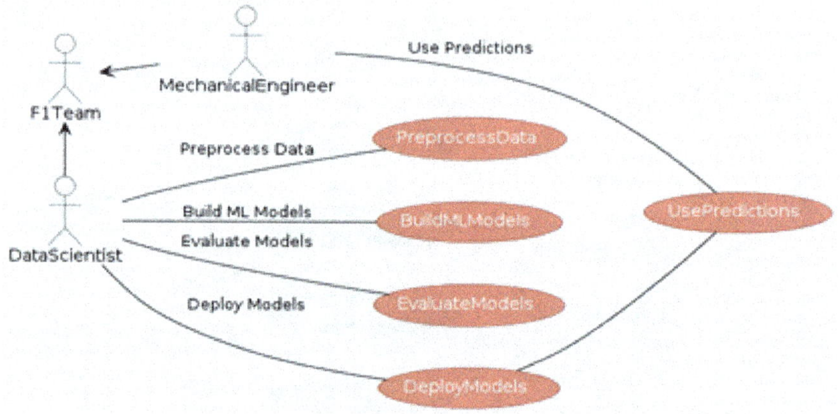

Predictive maintenance is vital for ensuring the reliability and performance of Formula 1 cars. In this use case, the data scientist gathers sensor data from various car components along with historical maintenance records. This data is preprocessed to develop models that predict component failures and maintenance needs. The models' predictions are tested against actual maintenance events to validate their accuracy. Once validated, these models are applied to the team's maintenance schedule planning. Mechanical engineers use predictive insights to proactively address potential issues, minimizing the risk of in-race failures and ensuring optimal car performance throughout the season.

Use Case 5: Aerodynamic Performance Improvement

Figure 27. Aerodynamic Performance Improvement

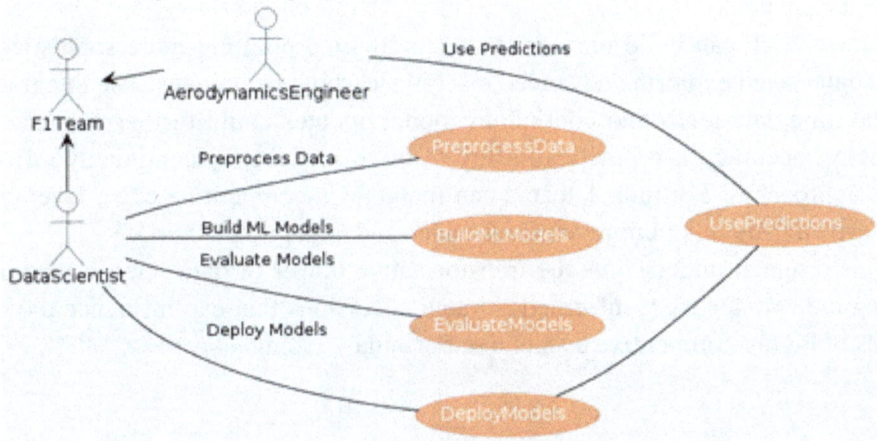

Aerodynamic efficiency plays a critical role in the performance of Formula 1 cars. In this use case, the data scientist compiles data from wind tunnel tests, computational fluid dynamics (CFD) simulations, and on-track performance measurements. This data is preprocessed and used to develop models that predict aerodynamic efficiency under various conditions. The models are validated against actual aerodynamic performance data to ensure their reliability. Once validated, these models are integrated into the aerodynamic development process. Aerodynamics engineers use predictive insights to design more efficient aerodynamic components, ultimately enhancing the car's performance on the track. This use case demonstrates the application of machine learning in optimizing technical aspects of car design, contributing to competitive advantage in Formula 1 racing.

CONCLUSION

By leveraging a variety of machine learning models, including Random Forest, Gradient Boosting, Support Vector Classifier, K-Nearest Neighbors, Gaussian Naive Bayes, Decision Trees, and Multi-layer Perceptron, we have explored their efficacy in forecasting race outcomes based on historical data encompassing driver skills, team performance, weather conditions, and track characteristics.

The analysis revealed that Gradient Boosting and Decision Trees emerged as the top-performing models, showcasing their ability to capture complex patterns within the data. The deployment of these predictive models offers significant potential for transforming race strategies, optimizing pit stops, and enhancing decision-making processes in real-time. Additionally, the methodologies outlined in this study can be extended to other motorsports, providing a framework for further advancements in sports analytics.

Future work can build on these findings by incorporating more sophisticated data sources and exploring advanced machine learning techniques. The integration of real-time data feeds and continuous model updates could further enhance the predictive accuracy and practical utility of these models. By continually refining these approaches, Formula 1 teams can maintain a competitive edge, leveraging data-driven insights to improve performance and strategic planning.

This research underscores the transformative power of data science in sports, paving the way for more informed, strategic decisions that can influence the outcomes of highly competitive events like Formula 1 racing.

REFERENCES

. Casella, C., & Vidoni, P. (2017). Formula 1 lap time modeling using generalized additive models. Proceedings of MathSport International.

Duhr, P., Buccheri, D., Balerna, C., Cerofolini, A., & Onder, C. H. (2023). Minimum-race-time energy allocation strategies for the hybrid-electric formula 1 power unit. *IEEE Transactions on Vehicular Technology, 72*(6), 7035–7050. DOI: 10.1109/TVT.2023.3237388

. Estes, A. (2023). A Poisson Analysis of Pit Stops in Formula 1

. Franssen, K. (2021). Comparison of neural network architectures in race prediction.

Heilmeier, A., Graf, M., & Lienkamp, M. (2018). A race simulation for strategy decisions in circuit motorsports. 2018 21st International Conference on Intelligent Transportation Systems (ITSC), 2351-2356.

Ikram, N., & Mahajan, S. (2016, March). Road accidents: Overview of its causes, avoidance scheme and a new proposed technique for avoidance. In 2016 3rd International Conference on Computing for Sustainable Global Development (INDIACom) (pp. 497-499). IEEE.

Kehrle, F., Frasch, J. V., Kirches, C., & Sager, S. (2011). Optimal control of formula 1 race cars in a VDrift based virtual environment. IFAC Proceedings Volumes, 44(1), 10062-10067. DOI: 10.3182/20110828-6-IT-1002.02954

Liu, X., & Fotouhi, A. (2020). Formula-E race strategy development using artificial neural networks and Monte Carlo tree search. *Neural Computing & Applications, 32*(18), 14525–14539. DOI: 10.1007/s00521-020-04871-1

Mahajan, S. (2023). Phishing uniform resource locator detection using machine learning: A step towards secure system. *Security and Privacy, 6*(6), e311. DOI: 10.1002/spy2.311

Mahajan, S., & Ikram, N. (2019). An android-based hardware system for accident avoidance and detection on sharp turns. *International Journal of Computer Aided Engineering and Technology, 11*(4-5), 543–560. DOI: 10.1504/IJCAET.2019.100450

Peng, B., Li, J., Akkas, S., & Araki, T. (2021). Rank position forecasting in car racing. *2021 IEEE International Conference on Data Mining (ICDM)*, 919-924.

Salazar, M., Balerna, C., & Elbert, P. (2017). Real-time control algorithms for a hybrid electric race car using a two-level model predictive control scheme. *IEEE Transactions on Intelligent Transportation Systems, 18*(12), 3308–3319.

Sicoie, H. (2022). Machine Learning framework for Formula 1 race winner and championship standings predictor. Bachelor's thesis, Tilburg University, School of Humanities and Digital Sciences.

Sicoie, H. (2022). Machine Learning framework for Formula 1 race winner and championship standings predictor. Bachelor's thesis, Tilburg University, School of Humanities and Digital Sciences.

Stoppels, E. (2017). Predicting race results using artificial neural networks. Master's thesis, University of Twente.

Tulabandhula, T., & Rudin, C. (2014). Tire changes, fresh air, and yellow flags: Challenges in predictive analytics for professional racing. *Big Data*, *2*(2), 97–112. DOI: 10.1089/big.2014.0018 PMID: 27442303

Van Kesteren, E. J., & Bergkamp, T. (2023). Bayesian analysis of Formula One race results: Disentangling driver skill and constructor advantage. *Journal of Quantitative Analysis in Sports*, *19*(4), 273–293. DOI: 10.1515/jqas-2022-0021 PMID: 38020583

Wischnewski, A., Euler, M., Gümüs, S., & Lohmann, B. (2022). Tube model predictive control for an autonomous race car. *Vehicle System Dynamics*, *60*(1), 26–44. DOI: 10.1080/00423114.2021.1943461

Chapter 5
Smart Logistics:
Designing and Implementing AI-Driven Decision Support Systems

Roop Kamal
http://orcid.org/0009-0001-8334-0101
Chandigarh University, Mohali, India

ABSTRACT

This chapter explores the transformative impact of these systems on logistics, highlighting their role in optimizing operations, enhancing decision-making, and improving overall efficiency. The chapter also examines implementation strategies, including the integration of machine learning models, real-time data processing, and predictive analytics, to facilitate informed decision-making across various logistics functions such as inventory management, route optimization, and demand forecasting. Case studies of leading logistics companies are presented to illustrate successful applications and the tangible benefits achieved. Additionally, the chapter addresses challenges related to data security, scalability, and the need for continuous system updates to adapt to changing market conditions. By providing a comprehensive overview of the design and implementation processes, this chapter aims to guide logistics professionals and researchers in leveraging AI-driven DSS to create smarter, more responsive logistics networks..

INTRODUCTION

Logistics is the science of managing indoor and outdoor transportation and associated storage economies; it being the planning of every detail to acquiring resources, procuring, selling, distributing and disposing of consumer goods, capital products, service products, and information. They have a central function of determining the

DOI: 10.4018/979-8-3693-8327-8.ch005

delivery of products that meet the business and consumer needs in terms of cost and efficiency (Yaiprasert & Hidayanto, 2024).

At its core, logistics involves several key components: Logistics involves transportation, storing of goods, managing inventory, picking and order fulfillment, and supply chain arrangement. Logistics is exercised mainly through the movement of products through vehicles by either road, rail, air or the seas (Gammelgaard, 2023). The efficient transportation systems help to reduce the time and cost of making deliveries so as to satisfy the customers. Warehousing also means the action of the keeping of goods in a particular place for some time before they are required. To enhance the flow of products and leverage the delivery cycle, the various strategies of warehousing are applied to ensure that products are easily accessible and with shortened lead times hence enhancing the service levels (Al-Talib, Al-Saad, Alzoubi, & Anosike, 2024).

EAC is also the strategic management of inventories concerning issues of stocks that are either too many or too few. This calls for a program that is accurate in its prognosis and mechanisms that gives the status of the inventory real-time (Louis & Hubert, 2024). Order fulfilment can be defined as all the activities that are associated with the receipt, handling and shipment of orders to customers. That is why it can be said that an effective organization of the order fulfillment process plays a crucial role in satisfying the needs of customers and in maintaining the competitive advantage (Ha, Akbari, & Au, 2023).

Co-ordination of supply chain is the broad factor that forms the basis of all these aspects. It incorporates the coordination of activities that cover supplier, manufacturers and retailers in the supply chain. Supply chain coordination means the smooth functioning of the total logistics; in other words, it eliminates gaps and improves performance (Cheah, Kersten, Ringle, & Wallenburg, 2023).

The result of globalization is the fact that the management of logistics in today's world has become more of a scientific challenge, which also entails the use of scientific and high technologies (Kamal & Sofat, 2024). Technologies such as GPS tracking, automated warehousing systems, and data analytics are redefining the facility logistics, by enhancing the capabilities of the organizations to adapt to the system changes. Given that business enterprises are gradually extending their span across countries and nations, there can be no denying that this is one area of commerce that cannot do with optimal methods of handling logistics, which is why it is one of the necessities of the present business world (Oriekhoe et al., 2024a).

AI IN LOGISTICS- SMART LOGISTICS

AI plays a significant role among business sectors as it optimizes time, increases precision, and improves logistical operations. There are discussions on using AI for demand statistics, which help companies to forecast the likely demand so that they are able to adjust their inventory levels and save costs. Furthermore, AI is used for route planning, where logistics companies find the best network for deliveries cutting on fuel and delivery time. Another major area is the robotic warehousing with the help of which tasks such as sorting, packing, and inventory are carried out through robots which increases the velocity of accurate and timely delivery of orders (Herbe et al, 2024). Additionally, this boosts supply chain visibility and enables real-time tracking and monitoring of supply to mitigate disruptions if they occur. In conclusion, the use of AI in logistics is in the process of recreating the supply chain as centrally connected, far less expensive, and highly reliable.

AI is slowly becoming the hottest tool in supply chain because of issues of efficiency, precision, and productivity in the operations. Of the many uses of AI in logistics, one of the most important is demand forecasting. Since AI can analyze large sets of data, it can determine future demand with much precision hence the ability to manage inventories prudently minimizing the costs of having too much of a product or none at all. This predictive capability is important in order to avoid disruptions of the supply chain, which is crucial for industries in which demand is variable.

Another important use is the optimization of routes; that is, how to navigate from one location to another (Kamal & Malhan, 2024). There is ability to determine in real-time with the help of AI the most suited routes for delivery vehicles to take depending on traffic congestion, adverse weather conditions and others. This does not only curb the use of energy and the time that is taken in making deliveries but also has the effect of making the logistics firms to have decreased impact on the physical world. Also, AI is applicable in automation of warehousing through use of autonomous robots and systems such as self-sorting, packing and shipment of goods. They cut down on costs, reduce human interference and that sharply enhances efficiency and faster delivery of orders (Yaiprasert & Hidayanto, 2024).

Another area where AI is quite useful is in the case of predictive maintenance. Some of the major benefits of incorporating the use of artificial intelligence include; the ability of the AI systems to predict when the condition of the vehicles or any of the equipment is likely to cause a breakdown thus reducing on any form of disruption on the activities that would have been instigated by the same (Oriekhoe et al., 2024). In addition, AI also helped map out a better tracking information and initiated better and personalized communication with the customers making the clients' experience exceptional.

However, there are some disadvantages of using AI in the industry of logistics: for instance, using AI involves capital-intensive investment in technology together with the need for human resources experts who can handle AI tools. Nonetheless, due to the heels of improvement in the AI technology it will become easier for logistics to adopt the technology thus making the industry more efficient and sustainable (Ha, Akbari, & Au, 2023).

In the case of logistics, AI is enhancing multiple activities including demand forecasting, route optimization, and warehouse management as well as others. Thus, if we consider the further development of this technology, its contribution to the logistics industry is also in a continuous increase, which will eventually lead to the creation of the necessary conditions for sustainable development (Louis & Hubert, 2024).

ROLE OF AI IN LOGISTICS OPTIMIZATION

Machine learning specifically has become the new avatar to transform the look and feel of logistics optimization in every way imaginable, from better, smoother and cheaper to achieve. Several sectors, with logistics being one of the most prominent, were made to improve by utilizing AI for its' analysis and prediction, as well as for its capability to manage decisions (Al-Talib, Al-Saad, Alzoubi, & Anosike, 2024). Through machine learning, evaluation and analysis of value as well as other artificial intelligence technologies, the physical movement, handling and delivery of products is being revolutionized leading to evolution of supply chains.

There are several facets in which AI augments logistics optimisation, and one of the most crucial is predictive analysis. AI algorithms can analyze big quantities of historical data and provide patterns that a human may not find. This capability is useful in demand forecasting, inventory control, and vehicle routing and scheduling. For example, AI can forecast about changes in demand based on factors like historical sales, market condition, weather among others and even social media presence. These enable firms to determine appropriate stocks levels in reasonable stock out or stock in scenarios and storage expense (Cheah et al, 2023). Additionally, the advanced demand forecasts created with the help of AI can be used in the synchronizing of production and logistics and planning to have inventory in the right places at the right time.

Another area where AI penetration is deep is route optimization. Earlier, route planning was based on historical data and calculations done on paper and were thus likely to be less efficient besides leading to unnecessary consumption of fuel. AI, however, can learn from real-time data flow from traffic updates, weather conditions, telematics etc and adjust the route. This also saves on delivery times and fuel expenses at the same time helping customers to be happier with more accurate expectations of when to expect delivery. Besides, the use of AI in route optimization will help in controlling the carbon dioxide emission by logistics setup, which can be beneficial while executing the sustainability strategy (Xu et al., 2024).

AI is also seeping its way into warehouse management. In the contemporary depots, robotics and automated techniques controlled by the principles of artificial intelligence control operations such as picking, packing, and sorting. Such systems can work round the clock with no variance in their accuracy thus minimizing on human error and labour (Louis & Hubert, 2024). There are opportunities to use machine learning to control the location of stock in a warehouse, to put hot items closer to the doors for example in order to increase the speed of order realization. Furthermore, AI is also used to gather information on usage and maintenance requirements of the equipment; about their tendencies to fail; then plan the maintenance time to avoid it occurring at peak hours (Basingab et al., 2024).

Logistics and AI means more than choices for the optimization of methods but also about decisions and choices. Cutting through the complexity of such a network can be extremely challenging, more so when the supply chain involves flow based models with a complex array of inputs and outputs; this is where AI can be quite beneficial since it is able to model various scenarios and judge the probability and likely impacts of such a shift on the supply chain both in terms of resource allocation and selection of suppliers and in the management of risks (Al-Talib, Al-Saad, Alzoubi, & Anosike, 2024). For instance, in a large-scale emergency, for example, COVID-19, AI could identify potential risks of disruptions in supply chains and provide information on other options for sourcing of supplies or delivery, depending on changes in the circumstances (Gammelgaard, 2023).

Technology has been one major driver of change in the logistics space, with AI coming at a time when logistics has arguably never needed it more than it does now as it comes with countless advantages ranging from the demand function, haulage planning, warehouse management and even strategic functioning of the whole system. It is therefore expected that as new improvements in AI emerge the incorporation of AI in logistics will further intensify, enhancing the degree of optimization and inventions. Todays' buyer is a very demanding one mostly because of the advances in technology and one can predict that firms which incorporate AI in their supply chain management will be able to deliver their products faster, cheaper, and more sustainably than other firms (Shahzad et al, 2024).

Figure 1. Utilization of AI in Logistics

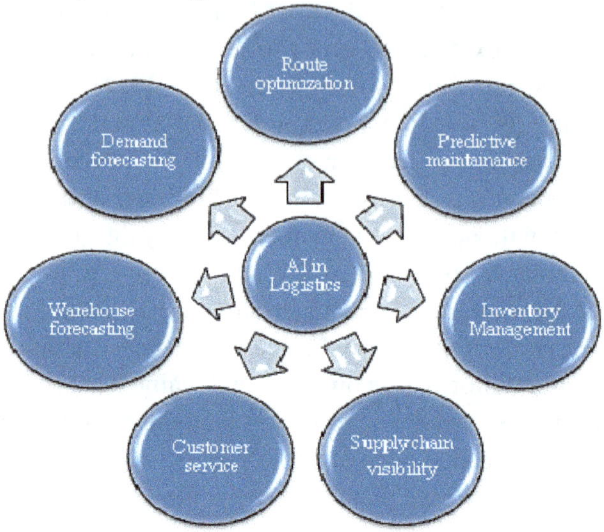

AI has a key part to be allocated when it comes to logistics optimization primarily in the efficiency, in the cost and in the satisfaction of the customers. Here are some key ways AI is utilized in logistics: Here are some key ways AI is utilized in logistics:

1. Route Optimization: A department of AI identifies the flow of traffic, weather and other relevant past information that helps to select the best routes for delivery and in this way helps to save fuel and achieve efficient delivery time.
2. Predictive Maintenance: By means of the predictive analytics, AI determines the time by which vehicles and equipment are likely to require repair and maintenance thus avoiding downtimes.
3. Inventory Management: AI in helping to monitor inventory on a real-time basis so that it effectively tracks optimal stock position without overstocking or obtaining stock out reports (Gammelgaard, 2023).
4. Demand Forecasting: Based on the past experiences, external factors such as trends and averages, as well as other factors, information is fed into machine learning models to get a probable demand in the future to makeup for a better plan in the future.
5. Warehouse Automation: Introduction of robotic and automated systems like those based on Artificial Intelligence enhance operational efficiency in warehousing involving sorting and packing as well as inventory management and others.

6. Customer Service: The use of artificial intelligence customer support and product and shipment update through chat and virtual assistants makes customers happy.
7. Supply Chain Visibility: With AI, one can better track the suppliers' performance and logistics and find out the strengths and weaknesses faster than traditional approaches.

Such applications of AI do not only enhance logistics functionality but also create a resilient and environment-friendly supply chain (Cheah, Kersten, Ringle, & Wallenburg, 2023).

AI IN LOGISTICS EFFICIENCY

Logistics has also benefited from AI integration and improved the delivery of services by most firms and organizations by cutting costs and increasing efficiency. As such, it will come as no surprise that with the subject area focusing on networks, big data, and timely delivery of products, the use of AI within logistics is not possible to overstate (Kamal & Malhan, 2024).

Among the ways that efficiency of the sphere can be improved with the help of AI is data analysis. Real-time processing of data from different sources i.e., transport networks, inventories, and customer orders is possible with AI systems. With this approach, companies are able to find out areas they need to improve on, the likelihood of disruptions and then make decisions that enable them to improve on their supply chain logistics. For example, AI can look into the records that consist of data of previous shipments, weather, traffic conditions in various regions and it can determine the most optimal paths for delivery trucks so that the transit or delivery time is minimized cutting on fuel consumption (Yaiprasert & Hidayanto, 2024). This alone reduces the operation expenses and at the same time increases reliability of delivery and customer satisfaction.

AI also expends productivity through automation. In logistics, a number of functions that in the past were done manually, are today performed by AI systems. This is reflected by cases such as; in warehouses the use of robots and the automated guided vehicles (AGVs) in tasks such as picking, packing and sorting of the goods (Kamal et al., 2024). They are effective than human staff since they minimize on mistakes hence enhancing the order processing. In addition, the AI-powered automation helps to open a new level of productivity since it does not get tired and needs no days off. This applies to clerical work too due to the ability of such systems to handle such things as invoice processing, shipping schedules and checking of stock levels while people are shifted to higher value-added tasks (Soori et al., 2024).

There are many more logistics efficiency areas in which AI contributes to the subject; one of these areas is predictive maintenance. The raw material handling in logistics involves the use various machinery like trucks, conveyors and forklifts that needs frequent service times due to frequent use. Another important usage is constant observation of the performance of such equipment, using sensors and machine learning algorithms to identify early sings of an equipment degradation. This way it is possible to have a prediction of when particular equipment is likely to develop faults thus helping the firm schedule maintenance on the equipment before a breakdown, hence be able to avoid immense losses from equipment breakdown. Not only does this approach keep operations going on but also preserve the life of equipments; a factor that leads to elimination of more costs (Dwivedi, 2024).

AI is also helpful in the effective running of the logistics system, and inventory management is part of the logistics system. The conventional methods of managing inventory have two major drawbacks: overstocking causes a lot of money to be tied down in idle stocks while stockouts can be very costly. Using such information as sales records, market characteristics and even macro factors like the state of the economy, it is possible to predict demand patterns with a considerably high level of accuracy. This makes it possible for 'way' companies to be in a position to order the right stock that they can sale to their customers without having to stock a lot of products that may cost a lot of money while waiting for customers to come. In addition, AI is capable of arranging inventory in a manner that enhances warehousing pick and ship rate and consequently, a boost in logistics (Gammelgaard, 2023).

Beyond the efficiency improvements, AI also supports a more sound decision-making process in decision-making tasks in the scope of logistics by extending the knowledge beyond operational level and allowing for analysis of 'what-if' situations. For instance, it can model different logistics situations including the variations in costs of the suppliers or in the time taken to transport the products and the effects that will result from the same (Torres et al., 2023). This in turn assists the companies to make better decisions in matters concerning resource allocation, management of risks and other contingencies thus enhancing efficiency.

AI can significantly enhance the various parts of operations in the logistics industry and hence is a powerful tool in operations. From improving the routing and automating logistics to improving stock control and making maintenance predictable, AI enables the flow of logistics to be better for any given company. Thus, AI technologies' effect on increasing the efficiency of logistics is expected to increase in the future holding more potential for company's competitive advantage improvement (Al-Talib, Al-Saad, Alzoubi, & Anosike, 2024).

AI –DECISION SUPPORT SYSTEM TO LOGISTICS

Figure 2. AI- Decision support system

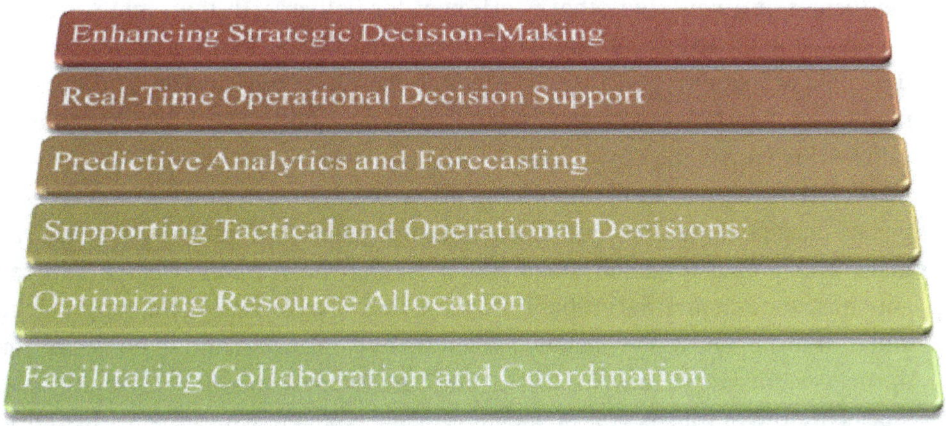

AI DSS systems are important in today's logistics since they offer efficiency in decision-making and the whole supply chain. These systems utilize data analysis, machine learning, and predictive modeling functions of AI to enable the logistics managers to easily and accurately make effective decisions hence enhancing efficiency, cutting down costs and achieving better operations.

1. Enhancing Strategic Decision-Making: A key purpose of applying the AI-based Decision Support Systems in logistics processes is to support the strategic levels of decision making. As is often the case with the work of logistics managers, the decisions they must make are multi criterion and depend on the assessment of significant amounts of data. AI DSS can analyze loosely coupled data input from different data sources such as supply chain, market data, weather data and status of the transportation networks etc. For instance, AI DSS can present a situation that may entail change in demand, a shift in supply, or fluctuation in transport costs and enable the managers to assess the effects of any of the situation on the supply chain. This allows them to be able to make good strategic decisions such as choosing the right supplier, how much stock to order or how to choose the most effective transport network among others (Xu et al., 2024).
2. Real-Time Operational Decision Support: Indeed, real-time decision making is a key element in logistics, when for instance, one has to cope with congested

traffic, adverse weather conditions or an increase in the demand for goods. Depending on the type of data incorporated in the AI DSS, real-time data can be tracked and valuable suggestions made to the logistics managers. For example, when a delivery route is are inaccessible because of an unfortunate event such as an accident, then it will alert the available AI DSS where the latter notifies the former of a new route that is efficient for delivery. In the same way, in a warehousing environment, the AI DSS can analyze the foot traffic or the real-time data of inventory and recommend the most efficient picking and packing model to service orders within the shortest time possible thus improving customer satisfaction (Basingab et al., 2024).

3. Predictive Analytics and Forecasting: AI or Decision Support Systems for logistics managers are optimally designed for prediction models so that you can make decisions beforehand. Basically, through historical analysis AI DSS can anticipate the demand and probably notice some issues regarding the supply chain and or transport cost. For instance when there is high demand in consumption during certain festive seasons, the AI DSS can forecast and make changes to the stocks in store or transportation means (Cheah, Kersten, Ringle, & Wallenburg, 2023). However, by using the forecast capability of the AI DSS, a firm can be aware of possible risks such as supplier disruptions or political instabilities, which assist in developing contingency plans with a view of minimizing their effects on the bit logistics.
4. Optimizing Resource Allocation: Of equal importance compared to procurement and distribution is the allocation of resources namely vehicles, labour, storage space all of which if allocated inefficiently can cost a lot and reduce efficiency. Resource allocation can be improved through AI DSS if real time information on current asset usage, demand for the resources and the operational constraints are available. For instance, an AI DSS can assist in identifying the suitable locations for delivery vans that are deemed appropriate in terms of relevance of deliveries, volume of cargo and fuel consumption. This in turn helps in avoiding wastage of resources, minimizes operational expenses while offering better services to the users (Kamal & Malhan, 2024).
5. Supporting Tactical and Operational Decisions: Other than strategic decisions, AI Decision Support Systems perfectly serve tactical and operational decisions within the logistics operations of an organization. First of all, using traffic data, fuel prices, and delivery timetables, AI DSS can help in the selection of routes that will be both the most inexpensive and shortest. It can also support decisions concerning stock replenishment by evaluate the sales records and lead times to indicate when and how much stock should be ordered. These tactical and operational decisions are quite pivotal for the efficient supply chain and ensuring customers with better service delivery (Ha, Akbari, & Au, 2023).

6. Facilitating Collaboration and Coordination: AI DSS can also improve the cooperation between the various players in the supply logistics chain including the suppliers, the transporters and the warehousing companies. As a central decision support system, AI DSS allows all the stakeholders to be on one page, hence they are all operating on the same knowledge base and level. This cuts the chances of misconceptions, time wastage, and general disruptions in most operations in the supply chain, thereby increasing synchronization of operations (Dwivedi, 2024).

Logistics Analytics and Decision Support System are the current trends that are revolutionizing the logistics industry by supplying advanced technology tools to improve the decision-making process on multiple levels it Logan. AI's certain skills in data processing, predictive analysis, and design of logical optimal solutions make such systems advantageous to the logistics managers by providing proactive insights to the problems, optimizing solutions to the problems and improve efficiency hence reducing costs for better performances. With the advancement of deep learning, their usage is seen in the decision making process of logistic chains and the benefits will only increase in the near future (Altay et al., 2024).

STRATEGIES OF AI-DECISION SUPPORT SYSTEM

Figure 3. AI-Decision support system Strategies

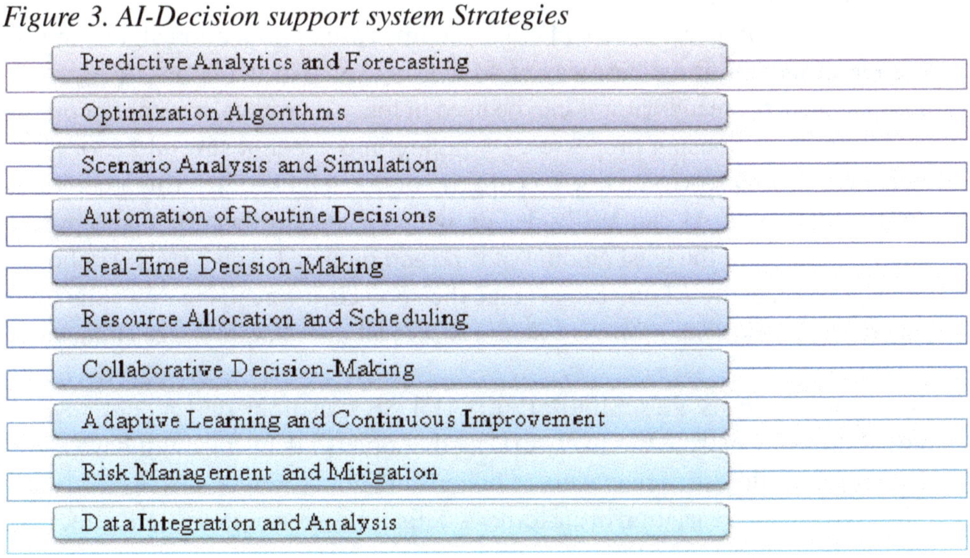

The primary intention of AI-DSS in increasing the effectiveness of the decision making practices are given below: These strategies take advantage of the strengths accorded by AI in the aspects of data analysis, prediction, automation, and optimization to deliver prescriptive solutions. Here are some key strategies employed by AI DSS in logistics. Here are some key strategies employed by AI DSS in logistics:

1. **Data Integration and Analysis:** AI DSS systems use inputs from various applications including inventory management systems, transportation networks, customers' orders and the conditions such as weather and markets. In this way, it will be possible to integrate this data and analyze it at once, which could help to discover connections, relations, and tendencies that might remain beyond notice if data were grouped (Torres et al., 2023). The concept encompasses ways through which the large amount of information produced can be systematically managed analyzed, and acted upon by leveraging on technologies like analytics, machine learning, and big data technologies.
2. **Predictive Analytics and Forecasting:** Another strategic approach of AI DSS is the use of analytics to help in predicting and predicting future trends, demand as well as any incidences that may disrupt the business. This is achieved through an analysis of previous trends of demand, supply, logistics, or other such factors that could affect the balance in the near future including high demands, supply chain constraints or transportation constraints. These predictions let the managers of logistics plan for the future decisions, including order quantities, route optimization of deliveries, or assigning of extra resources for the expected demand (Dwivedi, 2024).
3. **Optimization Algorithms:** AI DSS sometimes use optimization algorithms in the identification of the best way of addressing some of the issues in logistics. For instance, these algorithms can be used in logistics routes, inventory control and in the warehousing processes. By taking into account several factors like delivery time, fuel price, carrying capacity of the vehicle delivering goods and traffic conditions AI can easily decide which route can best be taken by the delivery trucks in the least amount of time and money. Likewise, in warehouse management, using AI one can arrange the goods in a way to cut down the time taken when picking to minimize on the cost of labour (Yaiprasert & Hidayanto, 2024).
4. **Scenario Analysis and Simulation:** AI DSS can help one model several possibilities to analyse the likely effects that diverse decisions will have. This strategy helps logistics managers to understand how changes such as new supplier agreements, variation in customer's demand or new routes would affect the real system. Lastly, by using the analysis of scenarios, one is able to determine the risks involved and have adequate precaution to make the best contingency plans for the occurrence of such event in the operation of the logistics system (Cheah, Kersten, Ringle, & Wallenburg, 2023).

5. **Real-Time Decision-Making**: Real-time decision-making support can be considered as one the most powerful strategies of AI DSS. By capturing real-time data from sensors and GPS and other related sources, the AI DSS can come up with real-time advice to the logistics managers on the best mode of transport to use. For instance, if the delivery route is blocked the system can recommend a new route available in the shortest time. It is this real-time responsiveness that ensures that the operations are effective and customers' expectations met whenever there is quick changes in the logistics industry (Xu et al., 2024).
6. **Automation of Routine Decisions**: AI DSS can control repetitive decisions so that routine decisions can be made by the AI DSS and human managers can take time to strategize. For instance; AI can automatically re-order merchandise when they run out of stock or adjust the vehicle delivery schedules depending on traffic congestion (Surabhi & Buvvaji, 2024). They help to avoid human error, and at the same time, the use of AI DSS shortens the time required to make decisions.
7. **Resource Allocation and Scheduling**: AI DSS enhances proper utilization of resources especially the transport vehicles, labour and storage facilities. As the current operation is studied and with future demands identified, the system can make suggestions on the most appropriate way to employ resources. For instance, in the case of delivery, a technique like a vehicle matrix that will indicate when a given vehicle is available or the shift in drivers can be employed by AI (Richards & Grinsted, 2024).
8. **Adaptive Learning and Continuous Improvement**: AI DSS systems are capable of learning from experience and therefore adapting to new conditions. Adaptive learning will make the system to continually improve its algorithms resulting from new data and performance appraisal of previous decisions made. Such a strategy makes the system better in its suggestions leading to a marked improvement in the exercise of logistics (Xu et al., 2024).
9. **Risk Management and Mitigation**: Another important aspect of the AI DSS it the assistance in the identification of the risks involved in the logistics supply chain and their management. AI can scout for potentially disruptive events by using data about suppliers' reliability, transportation issues, and geopolitical threats, after which indicate ways of handling the identified challenges. For example, if the system thinks that its key supplier will take longer time to deliver, it may advise the use of other suppliers or increase the inventory to avoid shortage of stock (Oriekhoe et al., 2024).
10. **Collaborative Decision-Making**: AI DSS enables group decision making whereby the user involving the various stakeholders like supplier, carriers, and logistics managers can make decisions based on one common data pool (Surabhi & Buvvaji, 2024). This is important because it enables all the stakeholders

involved in logistics to make decisions that would be complementary of those made by other stakeholders hence enhancing efficiency in the movement of supplies.

Decision Support Systems with the support of Artificial Intelligence's used several tactics to improve decisions in the scope of logistics: forecast, optimization, real-time decision making and risk management. Through the effective implementation of such strategies, the managers in the logistics sector can make better decisions in a timely manner hence improving operation performance, cutting on cost, and most importantly improving customer satisfaction. With the advancement of the AI technologies, these strategies will be more developed, which will change the logistics sector even more (Gammelgaard, 2023).

CASE STUDY OF LEADING COMPANY USING AI-DSS FOR LOGISTICS

One of the firms that have experienced the benefits of implementation of AI-DSS in logistics is DHL among other companies. DHL, an international express delivery and logistics company, is among the pioneers of companies using artificial intelligence innovations for the optimization of their activities. It has changed how they have adopted AI-DSS in various ways in their logistics operations where efficiencies and cost have been optimised, and customer satisfaction increased (Al-Talib, Al-Saad, Alzoubi, & Anosike, 2024).

DHL as a business is a division of the Deutsche Post DHL Group that is involved in the transportation of assorted products across the globe and has operations in more than 220 countries/territories. The complexity has a great impact on DHL because being one of the largest logistic organizations in the world it has numerous challenges in managing its logistic network within the scope of transportation, storage, and delivery (Yaiprasert & Hidayanto, 2024). Because of the enormity of these operations, sophisticated decision tools are applied in the determination of the best processes in terms of managing risks and satisfying customer needs.

IMPLEMENTATION OF AI-DSS

DHL has introduced AI-DSS into various aspects of its supply chain which includes, but not limited to, route improvement, and predicted forecast, as well as, storage and picking processes. Thus, ''Resilience 360'' and ''MySupplyChain'' of the company exemplify how the AI-DSS is applied to improve logistics decisions (Dwivedi, 2024).

1. Predictive Analytics with Resilience360

Resilience 360 is an Artificial intelligence based software which was designed by DHL to estimate and prevent supply chain vulnerabilities. The platform relies on artificial intelligence and machine learning techniques for processing big data and real-time information on the weather conditions, political and other threats (Basingab et al., 2024). The system then offers guidance as well as solutions that would be useful to logistics managers to enable them reduce on risks.

For instance, following the COVID-19 outbreak, Resilience360 helped to discover possible disruptions of the supply chain as a result of lockdowns and other restrictions in one country or another. In this case, the AI-DSS supported by multiple data sources helped the DHL recognize specific supply chain disruptions and inform the customers in due time, allocate the resources for the change of the shipment's route, and adjust inventory and other shipping conditions.

2. Optimization of routes and real time scheduling

DHL has also used AI-DSS to optimize routes and schedule the dynamic vital scheduling. The company's artificial intelligence based system examines real time data regarding traffic conditions delivery slots and the capacities of vehicles for delivery to make the delivery routes most efficient (Suganda, Buchory, & Aripin, 2024). It also helps in cutting down of fuel usage and operation expenses while at the same time also ensuring faster and efficient delivery to the customers.

For example, DHL applies artificial intelligence in its vehicles, dispatching delivery trucks in relation to real time traffic information. As an avenue is closed arising from an accident or other occasions of traffic jam, the AI-DSS will in a short span of time provide other feasible routes that can help the vehicle avoid unnecessary time wastage. This capability is special important for express delivery service, which is the main service of DHL, the timeliness of delivery is crucial.

3. Warehouse Automation with Robotics

The retail point is IA enabled through the mobile application; At the warehouses, Robotics & Automation assist DHL. These systems are interfaced with the AI-DSS in the manner that improves the picking, packing and sorting (Altay et al., 2024). The AI-DSS can use order patterns data, inventory data of the warehouse, and items' locations to guide robots to the most efficient pick paths for order fulfillment, thus lowering the time taken to complete the orders.

With the help of AI-DSS the potential of DHL in warehouse management has increased as it can now process a higher number of orders at a faster and more efficient manner. Also, the system is able to indicate when certain products will be required most to ensure that at DHL they are placed where they can easily be accessed by clients (Xu et al., 2024).

4. Improving the Customer Experience through MySupplyChain

MySupplyChain is the platform used by DHL to adopt AI-DSS as can be seen above. This platform offers its customers full visibility of their shipments and inventories in the entirety of supply chain. Built on AI technology, MySupplyChain has the capabilities of providing analytical proposals on possible delay, alternative mode of transportation and the most suitable supply chain models (Yaiprasert & Hidayanto, 2024).

The consumers of MySupplyChain can be provided with a status on their order, the delivery time and any hindrances to their consignment. The analytical AI-DSS behind the platform constantly updates data from different sources to give the best information to enhance the level of customer satisfaction and confidence in DHL'S services (Cheah, Kersten, Ringle, & Wallenburg, 2023).

RESULTS AND IMPACT

The implementation of AI-DSS at DHL has led to several notable improvements in logistics operations:The implementation of AI-DSS at DHL has led to several notable improvements in logistics operations:

- Efficiency Gains: Self-organizing routes as well as the implementation of Smart Warehouse concepts have caused lower costs and much faster order processing.
- Risk Management: The Resilience360 platform has improved the capability of DHL in risk mitigation and dealing with the disruptions in the supply chain to minimize the effects of such incidences on the company carries out (Altay et al., 2024).
- Customer Satisfaction: DHL'S efforts in attaining greater customer satisfaction through MySupplyChain has enabled real-time visibility and predictability of events leading to customer loyalty (Kamal et al., 2024).

- Sustainability: Real-time capacity matching and the implementation of dynamic scheduling has also helped DHL to minimize its carbon impact, and improve on the sustainability targets.

Decision Support Systems in DHL is one of the best-use cases of AI in logistics looking at the prowess at which the Company has adapted AI to serve its global operations. The application of AI-DSS in DHL various dimensions of supply chain can be evidenced as useful in improving on decision making, efficiency and risk management. Therefore, this paper finds that AI-DSS can bring about innovation and competitive advantage in the provision of logistics services as illustrated by the case of DHL (Dwivedi, 2024).

CHALLENGES RELATED TO AI-DSS

The study recognises that AI-DSS have numerous advantages especially in the field of logistics; however, there are drawbacks to the implementation and usage of the technology (Gammelgaard, 2023). These could be technical as well as operational in form or may be as ethically or regulation-wise severe. Here's a look at some of the key challenges associated with AI-DSS:Here's a look at some of the key challenges associated with AI-DSS:

1. Data Quality and Availability

Currently AI-DSS is dependent on large volumes of high quality data to work as required. However, challenges related to data quality, availability, and integration can impede the performance of these systems. However, challenges related to data quality, availability, and integration can impede the performance of these systems:

- Data Inconsistency: The information that is received tends to vary in format, accuracy and may not be complete hence causing inconvenience to AI-DSS in processing and analyzing it.
- Data Silos: In most organizations, data resides in different separate functional areas or information systems so that it becomes quite difficult to analyze and use for decision making.
- Data Privacy and Security: The need to maintain privacy and security of the data will always be important especially when dealing with people's data. There are disadvantages in using AI-DSS such as Legal requirements including GDPR compliance complicates data management.

2. The introduced measures of model uncertainty and its generalization ability describe the procedures for constructing an AI model that is both intricate and easily explain, including the benefits of interpretability over complexity (Basingab et al., 2024).

AI models, particularly those based on deep learning, can be complex and difficult to interpret, leading to challenges in understanding and trusting the decisions made by AI-DSS:AI models, particularly those based on deep learning, can be complex and difficult to interpret, leading to challenges in understanding and trusting the decisions made by AI-DSS:

- Black Box Nature: Most of the AI models particularly those under the machine learning category are black boxes whereby the decision making process cannot be explained. It can be especially challenging for those, who are to assign rational for a particular choice or an outcome of a venture.
- Lack of Transparency: Inability to see inside AI algorithms may render some decision making processes to be mostly secretive or arbitrarily made and this can be a let off for users or stakeholders who do not want to engage in systems they cannot easily decipher (Kamal et al., 2024).

3. Integration with Existing Systems

Integrating AI-DSS with existing IT infrastructure and legacy systems can be a significant challenge. Integrating AI-DSS with existing IT infrastructure and legacy systems can be a significant challenge:

- Compatibility Issues: They may also use equipment which is incompatible with many of today's AI-DSS, necessitating either costly upgrade or replacement.
- Scalability: Another challenge that organizations experience as they expand is that of accommodating the expansion in terms of data volume and complexities in decision making can be a challenge with AI-DSS.
- Customization: AI-DSS can easily be configured to operational business environments or personal requirements frequently calling for considerable adjustments that consumes both human resource and time (Cheah, Kersten, Ringle, & Wallenburg, 2023)..

4. Cost of Implementation

Implementing AI-DSS can be expensive, particularly for small and medium-sized enterprises (SMEs):Implementing AI-DSS can be expensive, particularly for small and medium-sized enterprises (SMEs):

- Initial Investment: The initial outlay for procuring and deploying AI technologies may be expensive, or the integration of those technologies with the existing systems may be expensive or highly time consuming, and the cost of personnel training could also be astronomical (Ha, Akbari, & Au, 2023).
- Ongoing Maintenance: A constant process of updating, monitoring and enhancement of operation is required to keep the AI-DSS at optimum value which can incurs additional operating expenses.
- Return on Investment (ROI): AI-DSS development can take time and measuring a definite return on investment is not easy doing so, in many cases it will be of indirect nature and spanning a long period of time (Basingab et al., 2024).

5. Imbalance between skills demand and supply and adjustment strategies.

The successful deployment of AI-DSS requires skilled personnel who can develop, manage, and use these systems effectively: The successful deployment of AI-DSS requires skilled personnel who can develop, manage, and use these systems effectively:

- Lack of Expertise: Several organizations complain of talent shortages in professionals with experience in AI, data science, and advanced analytics that affect the proper application of AI-DSS (Basingab et al., 2024).
- Training and Upskilling: AI-DSS depends on human capital in that employees require to be trained on how to operate in the system, and this can be a costly affair in terms of time and expenses.
- Resistance to Change: It may be difficult to introduce AI due to some employees may be concerned that their jobs will be eliminated with the upgrade and also those that are apprehensive about the use of technology, there are implementation challenges that are bound to come up (Cheah, Kersten, Ringle, & Wallenburg, 2023).

6. Ethical and Bias Concerns

AI-DSS, like any AI system, is susceptible to ethical issues, particularly related to bias and fairness. AI-DSS, like any AI system, is susceptible to ethical issues, particularly related to bias and fairness:

- Algorithmic Bias: There is always a risk that having been trained on a particular kind of data and therefore making decisions based on that data AI models will make unfair or discriminatorily prejudiced decisions (Altay et al., 2024).
- Ethical Dilemmas: When decisions are being made regarding deliverables, ethical issues may be created due to AI-DSS participation; For instance, giving priority to one delivery over the other strictly based on prejudice leads to ethical issues (Juliet, 2025).
- Accountability: It might be difficult to know who needs to take the primary responsibility for the actions performed by the AI-DSS, especially if the way that the AI-DSS makes decisions is not comprehensible to the human operators (Al-Talib, Al-Saad, Alzoubi, & Anosike, 2024).

7. Regulatory and Compliance Issues

The use of AI-DSS in logistics and other sectors is subject to regulatory scrutiny, particularly concerning data privacy, security, and decision-making transparency. The use of AI-DSS in logistics and other sectors is subject to regulatory scrutiny, particularly concerning data privacy, security, and decision-making transparency:

- Compliance with Regulations: Adhering to different legal requirements essential for AI-DSS at the local and national and even international level could be a concern if the company is operating in different regions (for example GDPR or CCPA).
- Liability and Legal Risks: Legal risks may ensue if through AI-DSS an organization comes up with a decision that causes or violates the law hence appropriate handling of the legal risks incurred (Dwivedi, 2024).

8. Dependence on AI-DSS

Over-reliance on AI-DSS can create risks, particularly if the systems fail or make incorrect decisions (Ukato et al, 2024). Over-reliance on AI-DSS can create risks, particularly if the systems fail or make incorrect decisions:

- System Failures: AI-DSS like any other technological invention is not without its dark-side that can manifest itself in form of technical problems, data problems, or even cyber incidents that might cause the system to shut down otherwise (Ha, Akbari, & Au, 2023).
- Decision-Making Autonomy: Deviation of reliance on the AI-DSS might lower the human intervention and deep thinking hence coming up with poor decision making that is mechanistic or does not consider the real-world situations (Nicoletti, 2025).

Hence, there are numerous advantages of applying AI for Decision Support Systems particularly for logistics operations and decisions; however, the following are the challenges that need to be well addressed (Cheah, Kersten, Ringle, & Wallenburg, 2023).. Solving these issues necessarily involves more technical knowledge and planning and less ad hoc decision-making concerning AI-DSS leveraging and creating efficient and ethical AI-DSS systems that fit an organization's goals. However, these challenges will have to be readdressed and faced time and again as the advancement of AI technology progresses in terms of adoption to provide a fulsome application of AI-DSS in logistics and in other areas of business (Ukato et al, 2024).

CONCLUSION

Integrating AI in Supply Chain managerial decision-making model to develop managerial information system that can be used to create smart logistics is an innovative process of making decisions which positively impacts efficiency and cost in the smart supply chain. AI-DSS uses high-level analysis, machine learning, and real-time data processing to help logistics managers improve routes, demand forecasting, risk, and recurring tasks. Such systems are promising to transform logistics managers and afford a competitive advantage in the increasingly cutthroat, high-speed global environment (Shahzad et al., 2024).

However, realized AI-DSS comes with a number of challenges which need to be solved such as data integration, system convertibility, ethical issues, and workforce flexibility. This paper has highlighted the need to achieve quality data, and embrace clear and understandable layout, as well as constant learning as key factors toward achieving the potential of AI-DSS. Moreover, there is a need for organizations not to leave all systems fully automated as this may lead to compromising too much on the employments of human input in some organizations.

Therefore it can be concluded that current advances in smart logistics allow AI-DDSS to become a critical enabler, emerging with huge benefits but also complexity. Those organizations which will carefully plan and execute these systems and manage the risks related to them will be able to take the lead in determining and shaping the future of logistics and achieve sustainable success.

REFERENCES

. Al-Talib, M., Al-Saad, W., Alzoubi, A., & Anosike, A. I. (2024). A systematic review of the literature on the use of information technologies in supply chain management. *International Journal of Industrial Engineering and Operations Management.*

Altay, N., Heaslip, G., Kovács, G., Spens, K., Tatham, P., & Vaillancourt, A. (2024). Innovation in humanitarian logistics and supply chain management: A systematic review. *Annals of Operations Research, 335*(3), 965–987. DOI: 10.1007/s10479-023-05208-6 PMID: 36777409

Basingab, M. S., Bukhari, H., Serbaya, S. H., Fotis, G., Vita, V., Pappas, S., & Rizwan, A. (2024). AI-Based Decision Support System Optimizing Wireless Sensor Networks for Consumer Electronics in E-Commerce. *Applied Sciences (Basel, Switzerland), 14*(12), 4960. DOI: 10.3390/app14124960

Cheah, J. H., Kersten, W., Ringle, C. M., & Wallenburg, C. (2023). Guest editorial: Predictive modeling in logistics and supply chain management research using partial least squares structural equation modeling. *International Journal of Physical Distribution & Logistics Management, 53*(7/8), 709–717. DOI: 10.1108/IJPDLM-08-2023-552

Dwivedi, D. N. (2024). The use of artificial intelligence in supply chain management and logistics. In *Leveraging AI and Emotional Intelligence in Contemporary Business Organizations* (pp. 306–313). IGI Global.

Gammelgaard, B. (2023). Systems approaches are still providing new avenues for research as the foundation of logistics and supply chain management. *International Journal of Logistics Management, 34*(1), 1–4. DOI: 10.1108/IJLM-01-2023-601

Ha, N. T., Akbari, M., & Au, B. (2023). Last mile delivery in logistics and supply chain management: A bibliometric analysis and future directions. *Benchmarking, 30*(4), 1137–1170. DOI: 10.1108/BIJ-07-2021-0409

Herbe, A., Estermann, Z., Holzwarth, V., & vom Brocke, J. (2024). How to effectively use distributed ledger technology in supply chain management? *International Journal of Production Research, 62*(7), 2522–2547. DOI: 10.1080/00207543.2023.2218947

Juliet, A. H. (2025, June). AI-Driven Smart Logistics Route Optimization Using IoT and Machine Learning for Efficient Supply Chain Management. In 2025 11th International Conference on Communication and Signal Processing (ICCSP) (pp. 925-930). IEEE.

Kamal, R., Kaur, M., Kaur, J., & Malhan, S. (2024). Artificial Intelligence-Powered Political Advertising: Harnessing Data-Driven Insights for Campaign Strategies. In *The Ethical Frontier of AI and Data Analysis* (pp. 100-109). IGI Global.

Kamal, R., & Malhan, S. (2024). Synchronizing Senses: Neuromarketing Techniques and the Marketing Mix. In *Sensible Selling Through Sensory Neuromarketing* (pp. 107-126). IGI Global.

Kamal, R., & Sofat, Y. (2024). Neurological Pathways to Impulse Buying in Virtual Reality. In *Sensible Selling Through Sensory Neuromarketing* (pp. 287–307). IGI Global. DOI: 10.4018/979-8-3693-4236-7.ch014

. Louis, F., & Hubert, K. (2024). The Impact of Artificial Intelligence on Logistics Decision Making.

Montoya-Torres, J. R., Muñoz-Villamizar, A., & Mejia-Argueta, C. (2023). Mapping research in logistics and supply chain management during COVID-19 pandemic. *International Journal of Logistics*, *26*(4), 421–441. DOI: 10.1080/13675567.2021.1958768

Nicoletti, B. (2025). AI Transformation of Logistics. In *Artificial Intelligence for Logistics 5.0: From Foundation Models to Agentic AI* (pp. 107–131). Springer Nature Switzerland. DOI: 10.1007/978-3-031-94046-0_4

Oriekhoe, O. I., Ashiwaju, B. I., Ihemereze, K. C., Ikwue, U., & Udeh, C. A. (2024). Blockchain technology in supply chain management: A comprehensive review. *International Journal of Management & Entrepreneurship Research*, *6*(1), 150–166. DOI: 10.51594/ijmer.v6i1.714

Oriekhoe, O. I., Omotoye, G. B., Oyeyemi, O. P., Tula, S. T., Daraojimba, A. I., & Adefemi, A. (2024). Blockchain in supply chain management: a systematic review: evaluating the implementation, challenges, and future prospects of blockchain technology in supply chains. *Engineering Science & Technology Journal*, *5*(1), 128–151. DOI: 10.51594/estj.v5i1.732

. Richards, G., & Grinsted, S. (2024). *The logistics and supply chain toolkit: over 100 tools for transport, warehousing and inventory management*. Kogan Page Publishers.

Shahzad, K., Zhang, Q., Ashfaq, M., Zafar, A. U., & Ahmad, B. (2024). Pre-to post-adoption of blockchain technology in supply chain management: Influencing factors and the role of firm size. *Technological Forecasting and Social Change*, *198*, 122989. DOI: 10.1016/j.techfore.2023.122989

. Soori, M., Jough, F. K. G., Dastres, R., & Arezoo, B. (2024). AI-Based Decision Support Systems in Industry 4.0, A Review. *Journal of Economy and Technology*.

. Suganda, U. K., Buchory, H. A., & Aripin, Z. (2024). ACCEPTANCE OF BLOCKCHAIN TECHNOLOGY IN SUPPLY CHAIN MANAGEMENT IN INDONESIA: AN INTEGRATED MODEL FROM THE PERSPECTIVE OF SUPPLY CHAIN PROFESSIONALS FOR SUSTAINABILITY. *KRIEZ ACADEMY: Journal of development and community service, 1*(2), 33-51.

Surabhi, S. N. R. D., & Buvvaji, H. V. (2024). The AI-Driven Supply Chain: Optimizing Engine Part Logistics For Maximum Efficiency. *Educational Administration: Theory and Practice, 30*(5), 8601–8608.

Ukato, A., Sofoluwe, O. O., Jambol, D. D., & Ochulor, O. J. (2024). Optimizing maintenance logistics on offshore platforms with AI: Current strategies and future innovations. *World Journal of Advanced Research and Reviews, 22*(1), 1920–1929. DOI: 10.30574/wjarr.2024.22.1.1315

Xu, Z., Guo, L., Zhou, S., Song, R., & Niu, K. (2024). Enterprise supply chain risk management and decision support driven by large language models. *Applied Science and Engineering Journal for Advanced Research, 3*(4), 1–7.

Yaiprasert, C., & Hidayanto, A. N. (2024). AI-powered ensemble machine learning to optimize cost strategies in logistics business. *International Journal of Information Management Data Insights, 4*(1), 100209. DOI: 10.1016/j.jjimei.2023.100209

Chapter 6
Deep Learning-Based Poly Cystic Ovarian Syndrome Disease Prediction

Santhi Selvaraj
http://orcid.org/0000-0002-3252-4728
Mepco Schlenk Engineering College, India

S. Selva Nidhyananthan
http://orcid.org/0000-0001-9131-8409
Mepco Schlenk Engineering College, India

G. Ananthi
http://orcid.org/0000-0003-3227-2134
Mepco Schlenk Engineering College, India

ABSTRACT

PCOS is a condition which leads to growth of ovarian cysts and prevalent endocrine disorder in child bearing women which can lead to infertility during the upcoming years. It causes hormonal imbalance and issues with metabolism thereby affecting the overall health and appearance. Some of the common symptoms include oily skin, darkened acne marks, weight gain, hypertension and irregular menstrual cycle. According to that the proposed work discloses a novel method to predict the PCOS disease based on external symptoms like pigmentation, patches and hair growth in face using camera sensors. This model is implemented by getting face images using the camera sensor and predicting PCOS using machine learning and deep learning techniques. Currently, diagnosis of PCOS is done only using ultrasound

DOI: 10.4018/979-8-3693-8327-8.ch006

scans, which are bound to produce several harmful effects on the internal organs. Moreover, many women are unaware of the presence of PCOS. As an alternative to the current method of diagnosis, this system will be an alternative to predict the PCOS based on external symptoms.

INTRODUCTION

The growing trend of PCOS is mostly seen in the women of age group 15-45 years. It is a hormonal disorder which requires prediction in advance. The existing techniques focus only on detection of PCOS disease rather than the advance predictions. Our ideology enlightens upon designing a system for predicting the disease in advance by analyzing the facial symptoms. PCOS is a condition which leads to growth of ovarian cysts and prevalent endocrine disorder in child bearing women which can lead to infertility. The growing inclination of PCOS is mostly perceived in the age group 15 to 45 years (Rani R et al, 2021). Stein and Leventhal first found PCOS in 1935 in Chicago and they observed some similar symptoms among groups of people like lack of menstruation, infertility, excess body hair, and hormonal abnormalities. A study conducted in All India Institutes of Medical Sciences shows that 20-25% Indian women of childbearing age are suffering from PCOS. It can lead to other problems like miscarriage, diabetes, high blood pressure, depression and anxiety, endometrial cancer, heart disease and obesity, etc. Today, the prevalence of PCOS is increasing in different countries, and it ranges from 4%-20% worldwide. The prevalence ranges will increase year by year and it will be reached as hidden Epidemic diseases in the future. In earlier days, most people were unaware of this disease and only went to the hospital if they had severe symptoms of PCOS. Several ultrasound tests and puncture or surgical treatment are required at this time to heal from PCOS. Following that, researchers focused on data mining, and machine and deep learning strategies for diagnosing and predicting PCOS from medical datasets like ultrasound images and symptom parameters. The present invention provides the system to predict the PCOS disease using external symptoms by applying Image Processing and Deep Learning techniques. One of the aspects of the present invention is using camera for capturing face images and processing these images for symptom analysis. Another aspect of the present invention includes image segmentation techniques for segmenting nose patches, pigmentation, hair growth in upper lip and from the captured image. It also deals with the feature extraction methods for extracting the features of segmented nose, cheek, upper lip images and then utilizing Convolutional Neural Networks for predicting whether PCOS disease is present or not by discriminating the features of normal and PCOS affected images.

BACKGROUND AND LITERATURE REVIEW

Most of the applications of PCOS disease prediction is based on ultrasound images and it was implemented using Local Gradient Hexa Pattern (LGHP), Feature Vector based algorithm, Convolutional Neural Networks etc., The clinical and metabolic parameters are considered as a valuable source for predicting PCOS disease in women. In addition to these features, the facial symptoms can also be used for predicting the PCOS with more accuracy and in less time.

A Facial Biometric System Soumendu et al (2020) proposed a client-server paradigm by using Raspberry Pi model running on local derivative pattern (LDP) algorithm. Initially, images of people were captured using Raspberry Pi camera sensor. Features were extracted from the image using ELGHP algorithm. These extracted features were then transferred to server for verification of image. The process was carried out to analyze the performance of both ELGHP and LGHP algorithms using the world class databases such as LFW, CMU-PIE, Color-FERET, Extended Yale B and Gallagher database. Owing to the higher accuracy and better performance of ELGHP algorithm, it is well suited for parallel processing.

Feature Vector based algorithms (Palak Mehrotra et al (2011), Yasmine Abu Adla et al (2021) and Guangxin et al (2020) were used to formulate the features. These algorithms detected the PCOS disease automatically based on the markers. Clinical and metabolic parameters acted as an early marker of PCOS. Based on four clinical features such as Follicle-Stimulating Hormone (FSH), Luteinizing Hormone (LH), Body Mass Index (BMI), and Cycle Length the probability for PCOS was predicted accurately. Features were classified by two classifiers Bayesian and Logistic Regression. Owing to the higher accuracy & better performance, Bayesian classifier is well suited and classified the Normal and PCOS groups.

A system has been proposed for an early detection and prediction of PCOS rather than the traditional method of performing clinical test and unnecessary radiological imaging procedures (Amsy et al, 2019 and Mehrotra et al, 2011). Initially, the following information were collected from the patient such as Physiological symptoms: skin darkening (neck), Metabolic symptoms: those observed after clinical tests, Ultrasound scans. The Machine Learning algorithms were used like Logistic Regression (LR), Linear Discriminant Analysis (LDA), K-nearest neighbors (KNN), Classification and Regression Trees (CART), Random Forest Classifier, Naïve Bayes Classifier, and Support Vector Machine. Several parameters like age, BMI, cycle length was analyzed. Accuracy measures were calculated for all the above-mentioned different machine learning algorithms.

Several data mining methods for PCOS prediction were published by Palvi Soni et al (2018). From the data's collected features, the PCOS was classified and predicted using the Naïve Bayes classifier, Decision Tree, and Support Vector machine.

The PCOS is detected by using Gaussian Naive Bayes, Logistic Regression, SVM, Random Forest and K-Nearest Neighbor in Kaggle which was done by (Vedpathak et al, 2020). Neetha Thomas et al, 2020 used clinical data from multiple clinics in the Thodupzha Municipality to predict PCOS.

Malik et al, 2020 diagnosed PCOS disease from clinical data of the patients using various classification algorithms and evaluated the efficiency of the algorithms using precision, recall, accuracy and Kappa coefficients. A mobile application based PCOS detection was done by Preeti et al, 2021 using machine learning algorithms with Gini measures. Selvaraj et al, 2022 recommended a diet for PCOS disease for Indian women using multi-attribute and multi-labeling classifiers. Khanna et al, 2023 proposed an explainable artificial intelligence framework for predicting PCOS in the Kaggle dataset. Alamoudi et al, 2023 proposed a deep-learning fusion approach for predicting PCOS from ultrasound images. Tiwari et al, 2022 proposed a SPOSDS system for diagnosing PCOS using a machine learning algorithm in the Kaggle dataset.

In all previous relevant works, the main research gap was exclusively focused on the Kaggle dataset or ultrasound pictures for predicting and detecting PCOS using machine and deep learning algorithms. However, using the Kaggle dataset's symptoms we collected the real time images from face and predict the PCOS based on face symptoms.

MAIN FOCUS OF THE CHAPTER

The idea of this work is to detect the PCOS disease using external face symptoms using various image processing and deep neural network techniques.

PROPOSED METHOLOGY

The proposed work aims in developing a deep learning model that can effectively diagnose PCOS. Image Collection, Image Segmentation, Feature Extraction, Image classification, PCOS Prediction and model evaluation are the stages involved in this process.

Figure 1. The flow of the proposed work

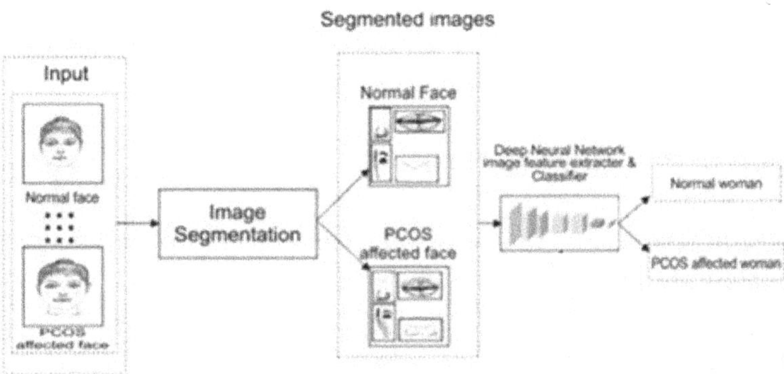

Figure 1 presents the flow of PCOS prediction. The proposed work involves different deep learning to classify and detect the PCOS from the image dataset.

1. Image Collection

The input to the system is a woman's face. The faces of women are taken and given as input to the system. The size of the image considered is 224 X 224 pixels. The person's face is captured using Raspberry Pi camera sensor. Since features have to be extracted from the face, high quality images of the person are captured and stored. The captured images are stored internally in the local storage of the computer for further processing

2. Image Segmentation

The captured images are passed for the image segmentation process. Here, the woman's face is segmented into various parts of face such as eyes, nose, cheeks and mouth. It uses Viola-Jones Algorithm. These segmented images are used for further processing.

The segmented parts are stored into their respective folders so as to proceed with further process of feature extraction.

Segmentation has basic functionality:

A. Face Detection
B. Detection of individual parts
C. Cropped parts extraction

A. Face Detection

The input for the process is the captured image from the previous process. In the image, full face of the person is detected using a function.

B. Detection of Individual Parts

After detecting the face, advancing towards the detection of various parts of face, Viola-Jones algorithm is used.

Functions Used

- Cascade Object Detector
  - The cascade object detector uses the Viola-Jones Algorithm for the detection of people's face, eyes, nose, and mouth
    vision.CascadeObjectDetector

    – creates a detector for detecting the objects using the algorithm

For parts of face, the object detection is done as follows:

- FDetect = vision.CascadeObjectDetector;
- EyeDetect = vision.CascadeObjectDetector('EyePairBig');
- NoseDetect = vision.CascadeObjectDetector('Nose','MergeThreshold',50);
- MouthDetect = vision. CascadeObjectDetector('Mouth','MergeThreshold',290);

C. Cropped Parts Extraction

To proceed further, after detection of the parts of face, they have to be cropped and retrieved. For this, the function imcrop() is used.
imcrop(I, rect) where:

- I is the image to be cropped
- rect is the crop rectangle

Functions Used

- isdir (dir_name): to determine if the input is a directory. It returns: logical 1 if dir_name is a directory; logical 0 otherwise
- fullfile(): to build full filename from the directories and filename specified

- step(Detector, I): returns the Bounding box values that contains [x,y,Width,Height] of the objects
- imread(filename): reads a grayscale or color image from the file specified by the string filename
- imwrite(image, filename): writes the image to the file specified by the filename
- imcrop(image, rect): crops an image to the specified rectangle
- size(X): returns the size of dimension of array X
- length(X): returns the length of the largest array dimension in X
- zeros(m,n): returns an m-by-n matrix of zeros

3. Feature Extraction

Feature Extraction is the process of retrieving the features from the segmented parts of face retrieved from the previous process. It involves the following processes:

- Creating an image datastore from the local storage
- Design/Load a Convolutional Neural Network
- Splitting Data as train and test
- Calculating accuracy of prediction
- Storing the output labels into an excel sheet.

i) Creating an image datastore from the local storage

As an initial step in this process, the image files stored in the local storage are converted to an image datastore. It is used to train the model in subsequent processes.

ii) Design/Load a Convolutional Neural Network

Out of the several pre-trained networks available, a network is loaded for proceeding towards training the model.

The following are the available pre-trained networks:

- VGG-16
- ResNet50
- Inceptionv3
- EfficientNet
- SqueezeNet
- GoogLeNet
- ResNet

- EfficientNet
- DarkNet
- ShuffleNet

Here, the network called ResNet-50 is used for feature extraction.

A. ResNet-50

One of the variants of the ResNet model is ResNet-50. It has 48 Convolution layers along with 1 MaxPool layer and 1 Average Pool layer. It is a convolutional neural network which is 50 layers deep. A pretrained version of the network trained on more than a million images from the ImageNet database can be loaded.

Figure 2. Resnet-50 Architecture

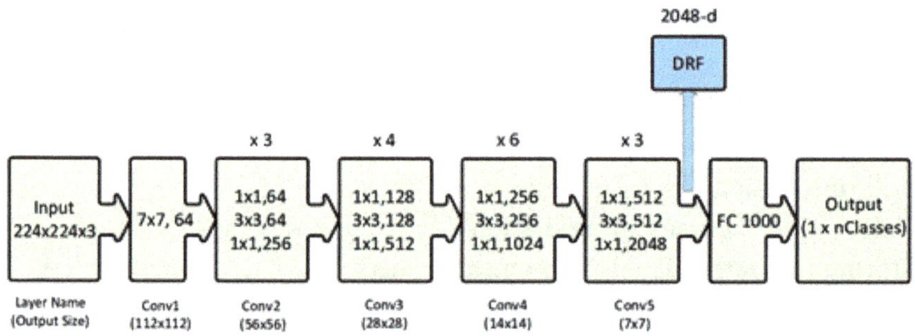

Figure 2 presents the architecture of ResNet-50. The pretrained network can classify images into 1000 object categories, such as keyboard, mouse, pencil, and many animals. As a result, the network has learned rich feature representations for a wide range of images. The network has an image input size of 224x224. The following are the layers involved in the ResNet-50 architecture:

- Image Input Layer
- Convolution2D Layer
- Batch Normalization Layer
- ReLU Layer
- Max Pooling Layer
- Addition Layer
- Global Average Pooling Layer
- Fully Connected Layer
- Soft Max Layer
- Classification Output Layer

iii) Split the data as Train & Test data

The data is split up into train data and test data by splitting up the image data-store. Later, the training and test sets are then changed to the required input size using augmentedImageDatastore() function.

iv) Calculating accuracy of prediction

The accuracy of the system is calculated by creating a confusion matrix between the test labels and the predicted labels. The prediction process shows an accuracy value of about 92%.

v) Storing the output labels into an excel sheet

Each and every feature considered for analysis has its own labels:

- Affected
- Normal

vi) Calculating accuracy of prediction

The accuracy of the system is calculated by creating a confusion matrix between the test labels and the predicted labels. The prediction process shows an accuracy value of about 92%.

4. Classification

The excel sheet containing the prediction labels for each and every feature is given as input for the classification process. Here, comparisons of the cell values using logical operators are done to classify the person as 'Affected' or 'Normal'.

RESULTS AND DISCUSSION

The results of PCOS Prediction System are explained in detail below. The images from the dataset are passed for process where the parts of the face are detected using Viola-Jones Algorithm.

Figure 3. Detection of face and its individual parts

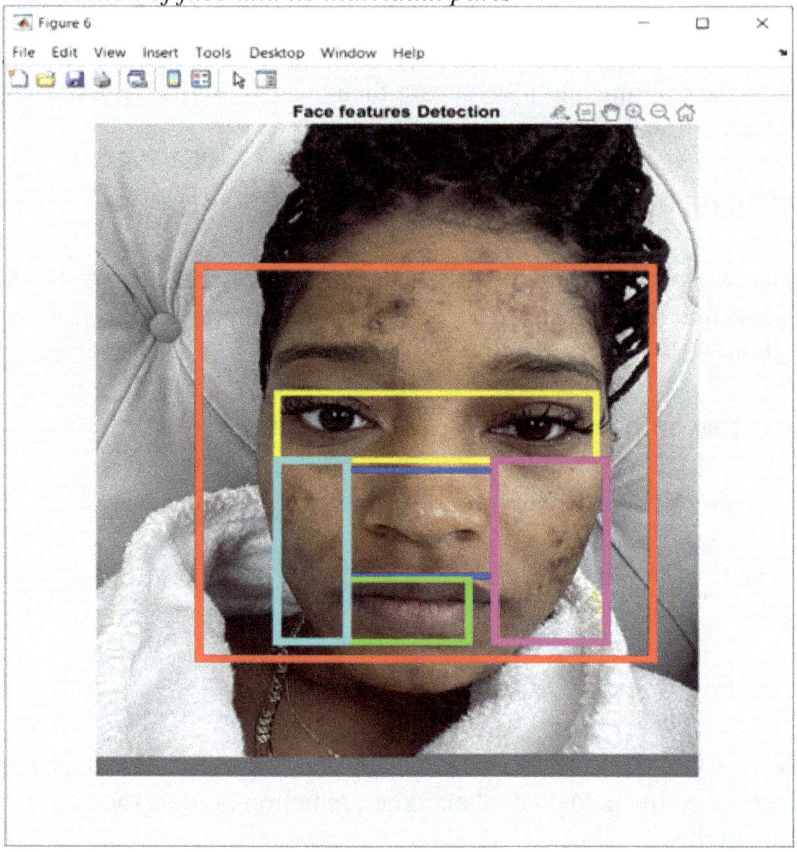

Figure 3 presents the result of applying the Viola-Jones algorithm on the input image. It detects the entire face and all the individual parts of the face such as eyes, nose, mouth, left and right cheek. The detected parts are shown with rectangular boxes in different colors.

The detected parts of the face are segmented using the image segmentation process.

Figure 4. Segmented Eyes

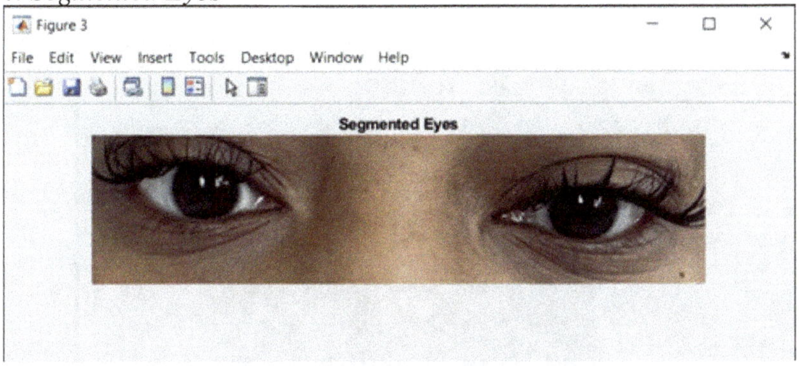

Figure 4 presents the result of segmented eyes.

Figure 5. Segmented Nose

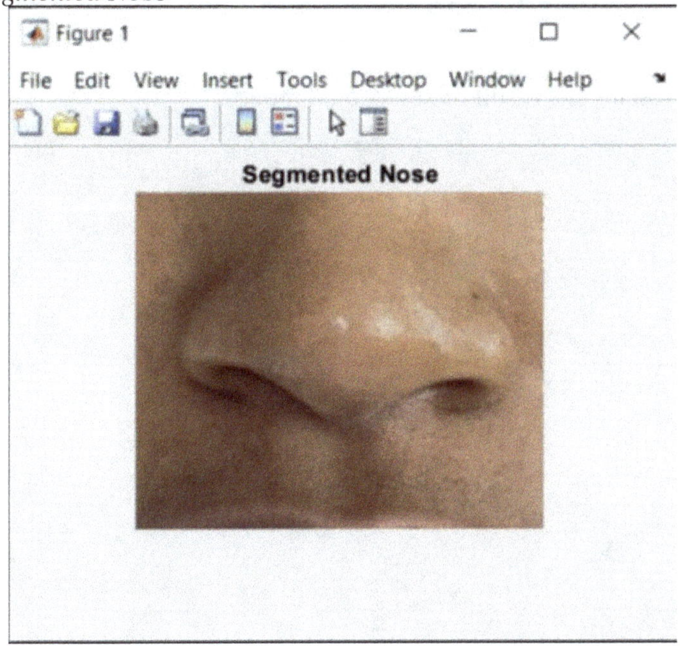

Figure 5 presents the result of segmented nose.

Figure 6. Segmented Mouth

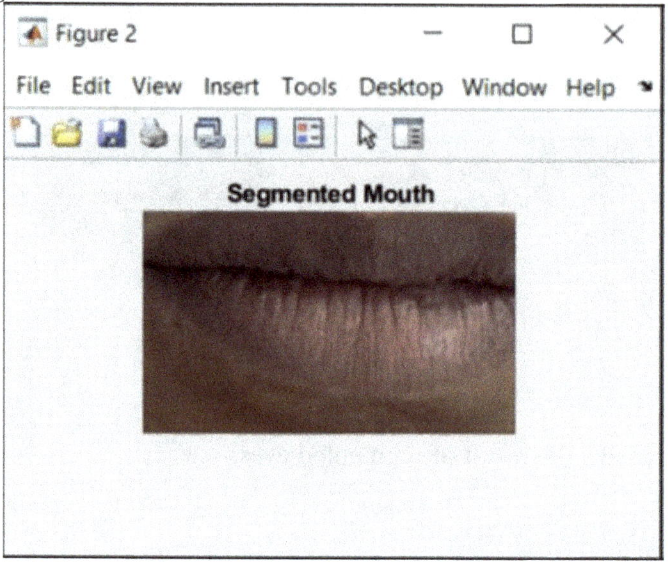

Figure 6 presents the result of segmented mouth.

Figure 7. Segmented Cheek

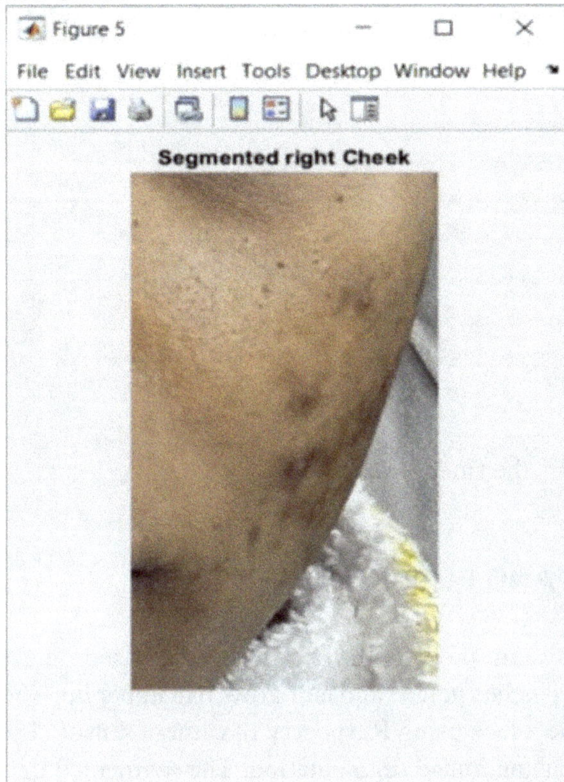

Figure 7 presents the result of segmented cheek.

The segmented images from the folders are passed through the CNN for analyzing the facial features and predicting the labels for each. Based on the values obtained for the presence/absence of the facial features, the final labels for the presence/ absence of PCOS in women are predicted.

Figure 8. Final predictions

Image	Acne	Facial Hair	Nose Darkness	Disease
1.jpg	0	1	1	Yes
10.jpg	1	0	0	Yes
13.jpg	1	0	1	Yes
16.jpg	1	0	1	Yes
29.jpg	1	1	0	Yes
3.jpg	0	1	0	Yes
30.jpg	0	0	0	No
31.jpg	1	0	0	Yes

Figure 8 presents the final predictions of CNN.

CONCLUSION AND FUTURE WORK

The proposed system predicts the PCOS disease based on external symptoms like pigmentation, patches in face and hair growth in upper lip. The system captures the image of people's face using Raspberry Pi camera sensor. The captured image is then segmented using image segmentation. The segmented images are stored in separate folder for feature extraction. The extracted features are then passed through CNN to predict whether the person is affected or not. Finally, the result from CNN is saved in the database. Thus it reduces the severity of disease by predicting the disease in advance and also it overcomes the effects of ultrasound scans.

In Future, the system can be implemented with multiple input CNN to predict the result more accurately. This will improve the accuracy of predicting the PCOS disease. Some additional features like darkness of neck can be analyzed for improving the prediction accuracy condition.

REFERENCES

Abu Adla, Y., Raydan, D., Charaf, M.-Z. J., Saad, R. A., Nasreddine, J., & Diab, M. O. (2021). Automated Detection of Polycystic Ovary Syndrome Using Machine Learning Techniques, *Sixth International Conference on Advances in Biomedical Engineering*, 1-5. DOI: 10.1109/ICABME53305.2021.9604905

Alamoudi, A., Khan, I., Aslam, N., Alqahtani, N., Alsaif, H., Al Dandan, M., Al Gadeeb, M., & Al Bahrani, R. (2023). A Deep Learning Fusion Approach to Diagnosis the Polycystic Ovary Syndrome. *Applied Computational Intelligence and Soft Computing*, *2023*, 1–15. DOI: 10.1155/2023/9686697

Khanna, V., Chadaga, K., Sampathila, N., Prabhu, S., Bhandage, V., & Hegde, G. (2023). A Distinctive Explainable Machine Learning Framework for Detection of Polycystic Ovary Syndrome. *Applied System Innovation*, *6*(2), 1–26. DOI: 10.3390/asi6020032

Mehrotra, P., Chatterjee, J., Chakraborty, C., Ghoshdastidar, B., & Ghoshdastidar, S. (2011). Automated screening of Polycystic Ovary Syndrome using machine learning techniques, *2011 Annual IEEE India Conference*, 1-5. DOI: 10.1109/INDCON.2011.6139331

Rani, R., Hajam, Y., Kumar, R., Bhat, R., Rai, S., & Rather, M. (2021). A Landscape Analysis of the Potential Role of Polyphenols for the Treatment of Polycystic Ovarian Syndrome. *Phytomedicine Plus : International Journal of Phytotherapy and Phytopharmacology*, *2*(1), 1–21.

Selvaraj, S., Nidhyananthan, S. S., Vanmathi, R., & Ramya, M. (2022). Diet Recommendation for Poly Cystic Ovarian Syndrome of Indian Patients Using Multi-Attribute and Multi-Labeling Classifier. *Journal of Pharmaceutical Negative Results*, •••, 13.

Soni, P., & Vashisht, S. (2018). Exploration on Polycystic Ovarian Syndrome and Data Mining Techniques, *Proceedings of the International Conference on Communication and Electronics Systems*. DOI: 10.1109/CESYS.2018.8724087

Thomas, N., & Kavitha, A. (2020). Prediction of polycystic ovarian syndrome with clinical dataset using a novel hybrid data mining classification technique. [IJARET]. *Int J Adv Res Eng Technol*, *11*(11), 1872–1881.

Tiwari, S., Kane, L., Koundal, D., Jain, A., Alhudhaif, A., Pola, K., Zaguia, A., Alenezi, F., & Althubiti, S. (2022). SPOSDS: A Smart Polycystic Ovary Syndrome Diagnostic System Using Machine Learning. *Expert Systems with Applications*, *203*, 203. DOI: 10.1016/j.eswa.2022.117592

Vedpathak, S., & Thakre, V. S. (2020). Pcocare: PCOS Detection and Prediction Using Machine Learning Algorithms. *Bioscience Biotechnology Research Communications*, •••, 240–244.

KEY TERMS AND DEFINITIONS

CNN: Convolutional Neural Networks are one of the deep learning architectures used for classification in various applications such as NLP, image and video processing.

Feature Extraction: The process of extracting a subset of features from the original images in order to minimize the feature space as much as possible while meeting predetermined criteria is known as feature extraction.

Image Processing: It is the process of transforming the images into digital representations and perform various operations for extracting the information from images.

Internet of Things: It describes the network of physical things embedded with software, sensors and communication technologies for the purpose of connecting and exchanging information with other systems over the internet.

PCOS: PCOS is a syndrome that causes ovarian cysts to form and is a common endocrine problem in childbearing women that can lead to infertility.

Chapter 7
Deep Learning in Medical Imaging:
Improving Diagnostics of Brain Tumors Using Neural Networks via Classification Task

Meenu Vijarania
http://orcid.org/0000-0003-0206-5927
K.R. Mangalam University, Gurugram, India

Swati Gupta
K.R. Mangalam University, Gurugram, India

Sagar Jain
K.R. Mangalam University, Gurugram, India

Shiomm Kumar
K.R. Mangalam University, Gurugram, India

ABSTRACT

Brain tumor is one of the most fatal diseases in the world. As per the WHO cancer is the 2nd leading cause of death globally and around 9.6 million people died in 2018. Tumors are of 2 types: Benign and malignant. Benign tumors are usually not dangerous as they do not spread to other parts of the body but malignant tumors are dangerous as they are fast growing and spread to other body parts and can be life threatening. In order to quickly and effectively start the brain tumor treatment, it is really important for the doctor to diagnose the patient to correctly identify the type of tumor the patient has. But manual diagnosis by the doctor is not the best way to proceed with a disease fatal like tumors as manual diagnosis is prone to

DOI: 10.4018/979-8-3693-8327-8.ch007

errors, time consuming and highly depends on the skill level of the doctor itself. In situations like this the deep learning models for Brain MRI image classification task can be quite useful as it gives better results with higher accuracy than the manual diagnosis and saves time. Prior researchers have done a lot of work in this field but still there is room for improvement. The proposed model utilize the dataset having 7022 Brain MRI images is a merger of 3 datasets: Br35H, figshare, SARTAJ which is publicly available on kaggle. The classification of the dataset is done into 4 categories namely: pituitary, no tumor, glioma and meningioma. The training and testing dataset comprises of 5712 and 1310 images respectively. The proposed Brain tumor classification model with test accuracy of 99.8% uses EfficientNetB3 pretrained model for extraction of powerful features and utilizes transfer learning in order to study the complex Brain MRI images patterns in depth. It is evident from the outcomes that the proposed method achieves higher accuracy compared with existing state of art techniques.

1. INTRODUCTION

The brain is a complex organ which carries out a wide range of tasks. It is crucial for basically all the things that happen in our body like controlling involuntary actions (i.e breathing, swallowing, beating of heart, digestion etc), interpretation of sensory information, cognitive processes like problem solving skill, critical thinking, decision making etc. But just like other organs, the brain is also prone to diseases. As already discussed, brain tumor is one of the most fatal diseases and as per the numbers of WHO around 10 million people died due to cancer worldwide in the year 2020 (Available from: https://www.who.int/news-room/fact-sheets/detail/cancer). The two terms namely: tumor and cancer are related but they are not the same. The uncontrolled growth or division of cells form an abnormal mass or lump which is called tumor. In medical terminology, mass or lump refers to the collection of cells or tissues that forms a distinct solid swelling like structure that can be seen or felt by touch or by imaging tests like X-rays, CT-scans or MRIs. Tumors are of 2 types: Benign and malignant. Benign tumors are usually not dangerous as they do not spread to other parts of the body but malignant tumors are dangerous as they are fast growing and spread to other body parts and can be life threatening. Malignant tumor is basically known as cancer. Into the bloodstream or in the lymphatic system the malignant tumors shed their cancer cells and these cells then travel to other parts of the body via bloodstream and there they form new tumors and this process by which the malignant tumors spread throughout the body is known as metastasis (Abdusalomov, A. B. et al., 2023).

Malignant tumors can penetrate and destroy neighboring tissues which can lead to various problems and harmful consequences (Mathivanan, S. K.et al., 2024):

(1) Organs improper functioning: When a malignant tumor spreads, it can interfere in the normal functioning of the organs and it can hamper their ability to carry out their tasks. Eg. improper filtering of blood in case of kidneys, improper production of hormones in case of endocrine glands.
(2) impaired bodily functions: malignant tumors can disturb the normal functioning of the bodily functions like respiration, digestion which can lead to development of symptoms like difficulty in breathing and difficulty in swallowing.
(3) Pain and discomfort: tumors can cause pain and discomfort as due to their abnormal growth, they may exert unwanted pressure on the nerves, bones, organs or cause inflammation there.
(4) compromised immune system: malignant tumors can slow down the immune system as they release certain substances which hinders the body's ability to recognize tumors and destroy them.
(5) Risk of organ failure: malignant tumors interfere in the normal functioning of the organs. Their abnormal growth puts unwanted pressure on vital organs, may obstruct blood flow and may produce harmful substances which increases the risk of organ failure.
(6) Potential for life-threatening complications: As malignant tumors spread throughout the body, disturbs the functioning of the organs greatly, may cause multiple organs failure and hence can potentially lead to death.

Benign tumor is not cancerous but it can still cause a wide range of problems especially benign brain tumors as the brain is rigid and does not have space for tumors to grow so brain tumors will exert unwanted pressure on brain nerves, glands etc. These are the common symptoms:

Weakness, difficulty in maintaining the balance of body, weakened memory, issues with the vision, difficulty in communication.

There are around 150 known brain tumors. There are 2 kinds of classification done in brain tumors: primary tumors and metastatic brain tumors. Primary tumors are the tumors that originally develop in the brain itself. Metastatic brain tumors are the tumors that first develop to some other body part and later spread and develop in the brain. Primary brain tumors are further classified into 2 categories: glial and non-glial. The word glial comes from the glial cells found in the brain and non glial means tumors found in brain nerves, brain glands and brain blood vessels. These are the names of some of benign brain tumors: Chordomas, Craniopharyngiomas,

Gangliocytomas, Meningiomas, Schwannomas, Pituitary adenomas etc and here are the examples of some of the malignant brain tumors: gliomas, Glioblastoma, Astrocytoma, Ependymomas.

As already mentioned in the abstract the early diagnosis of the brain tumor is really important so that the treatment can be started as soon as possible. But the correct identification of the type of tumor the patient has is highly dependent on the skill level of the Doctor as he has to understand the Brain MRI manually and has to take the decision (Celik, M.et al., 2024). Even if the decision was correct, then also it is a time consuming process and also prone to errors.

Many researches have been conducted in the similar domain. Various challenges are there in the classification of the brain MRI images:

- Developing a stable model is difficult as tumors occur in a wide range of shapes, locations & sizes.
- Highly Accurate models that can distinguish tumors and sub tumors are quite complex to develop.
- Availability of Labeled data especially in the medical imaging field is often limited and also different radiologists can label the data differently as per their understanding and expertise.

In the proposed model EfficientNetB3 pretrained model, Sequential model, Transfer learning capabilities, Ensemble learning and augmentation technique are utilized in order to build a robust model which can classify a wide range of unseen images both efficiently and accurately. Various hyperparameters like regularization strength, learning rate, dropout rate are tuned and also effective data preprocessing techniques are incorporated to increase the model's efficiency.

In order to extract useful features EfficientNetB3 is quite useful and transfer learning technique utilizes its preexisting learnings and helps speed up the process. Sequential model enables addition of different layers to prevent overfitting issues. Hyperparameters allow optimizing the overall model by tuning various parameters. The data augmentation brings variety to the input dataset which in return allows the model to classify more accurately new unseen dataset.

The major objectives of our proposed work are as follows:

- To assist health workers take critical decisions timely and accurately by eliminating human error.
- To address issues in classification that pose a substantial challenge like variability in different kinds of tumors in terms of tumor size, shapes and locations.
- To tackle limited data size issue via advanced data augmentation technique.

- To optimize the model's performance and to achieve relatively higher accuracy by incorporating better techniques like hyperparameter tuning.

Glioma, meningioma and pituitary tumors are considered to be primary brain tumors. Let's understand in brief about all 3.

Glioma tumor: Nervous system is a network of cells used for controlling various functions throughout our entire body. The 2 main parts of nervous system are: CNS (central) and PNS (peripheral). CNS consists of brian and spinal cord. PNS consists of nerves and clusters of nerve cell bodies called ganglia which are located outside the brain and spinal cord. PNS connects CNS with the rest of our body. 2 types of cells found in our nervous system are: neurons and glial cells. Transmission of electrical and chemical signals throughout our body is done by neurons whereas the glial cells support and protect neurons. Glial cells are around 10 times more than the neurons. The uncontrolled growth of the glial cells forms a tumor which is known as gliomas.

Meningioma tumor: It is also a primary brain tumor. The protective layer that provides cushioning and support to the brain and the spinal cord is called meninges. The abnormal growth of meninges cells results in the formation of the meningioma tumor.

Pituitary tumor: Pituitary tumor arises from the pituitary gland. Pituitary gland is also known as the master gland. This gland is located below the hypothalamus inside the brain. Pituitary gland releases a lot of hormones like: ACTH(responsible for maintaining blood pressure, blood glucose, inflammation etc), FSH(responsible for sperm production in male & estrogen in female), GH(responsible for growth and metabolism), TSH(responsible for thyroid hormone, metabolism), LH(responsible for testosterone in male & ovulation in female), Prolactin (responsible for lactation).

For this research paper the image dataset is taken from the kaggle and the data is divided into 4 classifications namely: Glioma, meningioma, no tumor and Pituitary. In total there are 7022 images in the dataset. The training dataset has 5712 images and the testing dataset has 1310 images. The figure 1 shows the kaggle image dataset used for training and testing. 3 codes using different models and techniques are written which are giving us remarkably high test accuracies as 99.8%, 99.2% and 96.7%. In 99.8% and 99.2% test accuracy code the EfficientNetB3 Pretrained model and Sequential model are used. In 96.7% test accuracy giving code the DenseNet169 pretrained model is used.

Figure 1. Brain MRI images sample

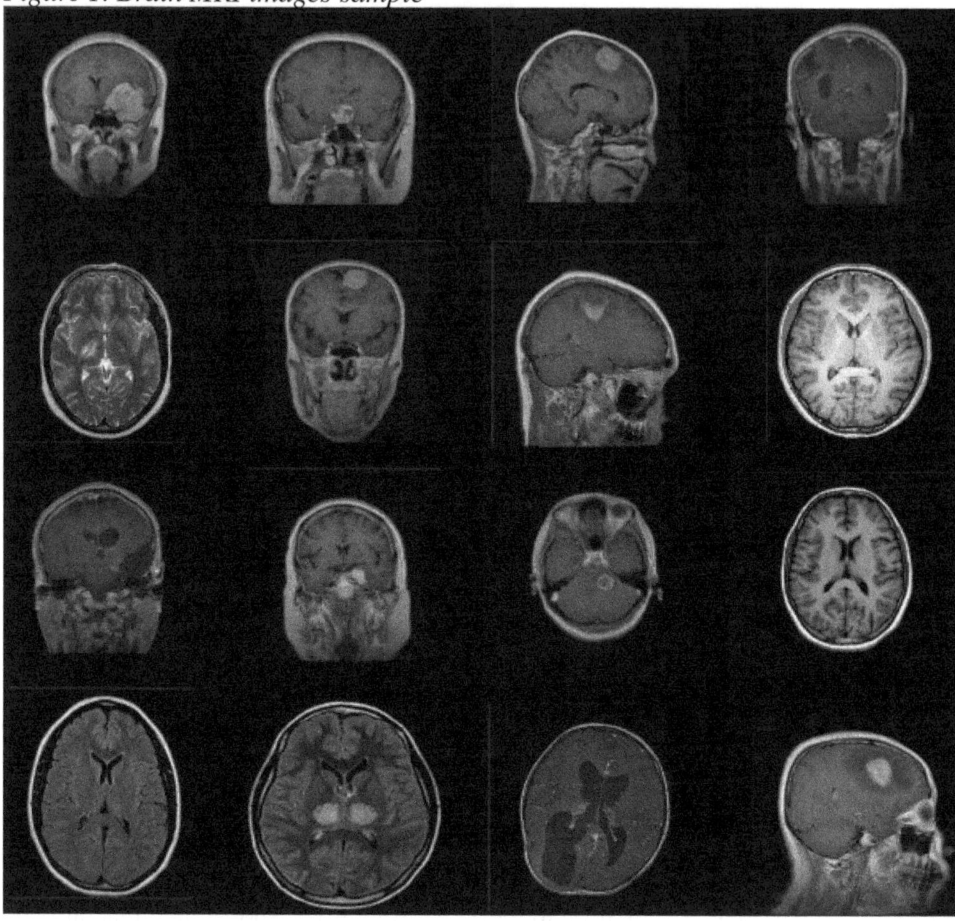

Figure 1 shows the sample of brain MRI images taken from the kaggle dataset: https://www.kaggle.com/datasets/masoudnickparvar/brain-tumor-mri-dataset/data

2. RELATED WORK

On the classification of brain tumors namely glioma, meningioma, no tumor, pituitary a lot of work has already been done. But our approach is giving us a remarkable test accuracy of 99.8%. In order to achieve it, a lot of related work was referred. So, in this section different papers are compared.

As per their paper (Celik, M., 2024) they have used the combination of Deep learning models with the ML algorithms in order to accurately do the brain MRI images classification task. They have used convolution neural network for feature extraction task whereas ML algorithms for feature classification task. They have used nine state-of-the-art CNN models to compare the performance. Their mean classification accuracies are as follow:

(i)DarkNet19-SVM= 95.01%

(ii) DarkNet53-SVM= 95.58%
(iii) DenseNet201-SVM= 96.87%
(iv) EfficientNetB0-SVM= 97.01%
(v) InceptionV3-SVM= 95.3%
(vi) NasNetMobile-SVM= 95.01%
(vii) ResNet50-SVM= 96.3%
(viii) ResNet101-SVM= 95.87%
(ix) Xception-SVM= 96.23%

The prime focus of this research paper was obtaining high accuracy and lesser computational time but they could have improved over other aspects of paper as well like interpretability of results and generalizability over other dataset. One of their proposed models i.e InceptionV3 could be improved as it took 370 minutes in completing the computational work. One of their hybrid models which used convolution neural network model for feature extraction and ML algorithm for feature classification got a high accuracy of 97.15%. Optimal hyperparameter values of ML algorithms were obtained by utilizing Bayesian optimization algorithm. One of their proposed hybrid models completed the classification process in just 67 minutes which can help doctors to take decisions timely. Among the 9 state-of-the-art CNN models used, the EfficientNetB0 model stands out and gives the highest efficiency.

Aamir et al. presented (Aamir et al., 2024) a model which first inputs the preprocessed enhanced brain MRI images via Optimal contrast and non-linear techniques and afterwards utilizes EfficientNet-B0 and one other pre-trained deep learning model in order to extract important features. Furthermore, the partial least squares (PLS) method is used so that the hybrid feature vector can be formed from the resulting feature vectors. Segmentation and Agglomerative clustering is then applied to identify the top tumor locations. The classification accuracy of 98.95% is achieved. The 2 main limitations that it may face are computational complexity and generalizability to diverse datasets.

A Deep Convolutional Neural Network model using Res net 152 Transfer Learning is presented by Kumar et al.(Kumar, K. A., et al., 2022). In order to classify the brain MRI images Transfer learning tactics are used. Otsu binarization method is used to increase the quality of the images while in the data preprocessing phase. Gray-Level

Co-Occurrence Matrix methods are utilized for extraction of image features like Correlation, Homogeneity, Entropy, contrast, Energy. ResNet 152 batch normalization layer is added. MATLAB platform is utilized for the simulation process. Their proposed method attained the highest accuracy of 99.57% which is their biggest advantage. Reliance on MATLAB for simulation is a drawback.

In this research (Aurna, N. F., 2022) a two-stage feature ensemble deep Convolutional Neural Network (CNN) model is used. It utilizes its proposed CNN model along with five pre-trained models in order to concatenate the best chosen model in 2 different stages for feature extraction. Among five different classifiers the best classifier is chosen based on their accuracy. Most important features are chosen using PCA and given to the classifier. Overall the proposed model is giving an average accuracy of 99.13%. The reliance on pre-trained models and PCA for feature extraction may introduce bias or limit the model's adaptability to new or diverse datasets.

Abdusalomov et al. presented (Abdusalomov, A. B., 2023) YOLOV7 model. Convolutional block attention module has been used for feature extraction. Multi scale feature fusion is being done via Bi-directional feature pyramid network. Data augmentation techniques are used. This paper achieved a really great accuracy of 99.5%. One of the limitations is that it may find it hard to detect small tumors.

This research (Mathivanan, S. K. et al., 2024) reported a model that uses deep transfer learning architectures like ResNet152, DenseNet169, MobileNetv3, VGG19. Various image enhancement techniques and neural networks for image analysis are used. Heavy computational costs along with greater training time is associated with the deep learning models. 99.75% accuracy with MobileNetv3 is achieved.

The authors in (ZainEldin, H., 2022) proposed a Convolutional Neural Network model. Inception-ResnetV2 which is a pre-trained model has been used. Adaptive Dynamic Sine-Cosine Fitness Grey Wolf Optimizer is used.

BRaTS 2021 Task 1 dataset has been used and with that it achieved a high accuracy of 99.99%. The limitation is that it needs labeled data for training. High computational power is needed for training purpose and there is complexity in optimization of the hyperparameters.

Mohsen et al. presented (Mohsen, H., 2018) a deep neural network model. For feature extraction, discrete wavelet transform is used. Principal component analysis is used for dimensionality reduction. It's advantage lies in the fact that it has used powerful feature extraction techniques and overall achieved a good performance. It got accuracy of 96.97% with DNN, For training it needs labeled data. Interpretability of results would be tough due to the black-box nature of DNNs.

As per this research (Chattopadhyay & Maitra, 2022) a convolution neural network model along with traditional classifiers and deep learning methods are used. SVM classifiers are applied and few activation algorithms like RMSProp, sigmoid, softmax, etc are used. Tensorflow and keras are used. High accuracy of 99.74% is achieved. It relies on the labeled Brain MRI dataset.

Zhang et al. presented (Zhang, Y., 2011) a neural network classifier model in which wavelet transform for feature extraction is used. For feature reduction principal component analysis is used. Back Propagation Neural Network with scaled conjugate gradient for classification is done. Computation time per image is only 0.0451 seconds and the most amazing thing is that it got 100% accuracy. It relies on MATLAB and the biggest limitation I found is that it has only used 66 images dataset which is really very less and thus the model will find it difficult to get the same accuracy with other images.

This research (Rahman, M. L., 2022) shows a system which tracks certain activities of the brain to detect the presence of Brain Tumors. Those certain brain activities are tracked by Mi band 2 which is a wristband device and Arduino-Uno sensors. 99.3% accuracy is claimed in this paper. It is a cost efficient and easier alternative as compared to the traditional methods where brain MRI images are utilized. The problem is that it can not detect the location and size of tumors. Their process is highly symptom dependent rather than direct tumor imaging and analysis.

This research (Yang, Y., 2018) reported a CNN model which specifically utilized AlexNet and GoogLeNet architectures on the brain MRI images dataset. In order to improve the performance they have made use of transfer learning and fine-tuning techniques . They managed to get an accuracy of 90.9% which is little less in comparison with other related works that has been done by other researchers in this domain.

In this research paper (Ghassemi, N., 2020) a Deep neural network model along with GAN is used to avoid overfitting issues. Data augmentation techniques like rotation of image, mirroring and dropout regularization techniques have been used. For actual implementation part keras 2.2.4 and python 3.6.6 were used. The specs of the system on which the implementation was done were given as Ryzen 1700 CPU, 8 GB RAM, 6 GB GTX 1060 GPU. A relatively smaller dataset of around 3000 images is used in comparison to what other researchers have used. Generative Adversarial Networks (GAN) has enhanced feature learning.

Techniques like data augmentation and dropout help prevent overtraining on the small dataset.They achieved 93.01% and 95.6% accuracy. Softmax classifier has been used. They used a relatively smaller dataset.

This research (Deepak & Ameer, 2019) reported a Deep Transfer learning model which made use of GoogleNet in order to extract relevant features from the Brain MRI images dataset. five-fold cross-validation process is done. Implementation of the model is done on the Matlab. Poor performance is seen in the transfer learned model and some wrong classification is there particularly from meningioma class. Overfitting problem is also there when the smaller training dataset is provided. Despite the limitations discussed it still managed to get the accuracy of 98%. Evaluation is done on various parameters like AUC, F-score, recall, precision.

Table 1. Comparative survey

Reference	Year	Author	Technology	Dataset	Highest Accuracy	Advantage	Limitations
2	2024	Celik et al.	Deep Convolutional Neural Network models with ML algorithms	Fighshare, SARTAJ, and Br35H https://www.kaggle.com/datasets/masoudnickparvar/brain-tumor-mri-dataset/data	97.07%	One of their proposed models got 67 minutes as computatio nal time which is quite less.	Lesser accuracy, difficulty in interpretability of results and generalizability
3	2022	Aamir et al.	EfficientNet-B 0 pre-trained deep learning model	Figshare https://figshare.com/articles/dataset/brain_tumor_dataset/1512427	98.95%	Usage of EfficientN et-B0 pretrained model with PLS method to achieve high accuracy	Computational complexity & generalizability to diverse datasets.
4	2022	Kumar et al.	Res net 152 Transfer learning DCNN Model	Brats MRI image dataset	99.57%	The proposed method achieves a high accuracy of 99.57%	reliance on MATLAB for simulation
5	2022	Aurna et al.	Two stage feature ensemble deep Convolutional Neural Network model	-	99.76%	Proposed model achieved high accuracy of 99.76%	The reliance on pre-trained models and PCA for feature extraction may introduce bias or limit the model's adaptability to new or diverse datasets
6	2023	Abdusalomov et al.	YOLOV7 Model	2548 gliomas images, 2658 pituitary images, 2582 meningioma images, 2500 non-tumors images	99.5%	Achieved high accuracy and can find the precise location of the tumors without human interpretati on.	Small tumors detection is difficult with the proposed method and the dataset is relatively smaller than other research
7	2024	Mathivanan et al.	ResNet152,DenseNet169, MobileNetv3, VGG19	Fighshare, SARTAJ, and Br35H https://www.kaggle.com/datasets/masoudnickparvar/brain-tumor-mri-dataset/data	99.75%	99.75% accuracy with MobileNet v3 is achieved	Heavy computational costs along with greater training time is associated with the proposed deep learning model. It did not check how well the model works on other dataset

continued on following page

Table 1. Continued

Reference	Year	Author	Technology	Dataset	Highest Accuracy	Advantage	Limitations
8	2022	ZainEldin et al.	Inception-Resn etV2 CNN Model	BRaTS 2021 Task 1 dataset of 1250 images	99.99%	It achieved a very high accuracy of 99.99% with the Inception-ResnetV2 model.	It needs labeled data, High computational power for training purpose and high complexity in optimization of the hyperparameter s
9	2018	Mohsen et al.	Deep neural network model	dataset of 66 brain MRIs from http:// med.ha rvard.edu/A ANLIB/	96.97%	Utilization of effective feature extracting methods like PCA & discrete wavelet transform which helped in achieve good accuracy and overall performan ce	black-box nature of deep neural networks limits Interpretability of result
10	2022	Chattopadhy ay et al.	SVM based convolutional neural network model	BRATS dataset	99.74%	Achieved high accuracy of 99.74% via CNN & traditional classifiers	Dependence on labeled data
11	2011	Zhang et al.	Neural network classifier model	66 Brain MRI images	100%	Achieved 100% accuracy	Dataset is quite less hence will have difficulty in classifying other unseen images.
12	2022	Rahman et al.	Mi band 2 wristband device & Arduino- Uno sensors	375 brain tumor patient's data collected from a Bangladesh' s hospital	99.3%	Cost efficient method via mi bands and arduino sensors	Can't detect size and location of tumors
13	2018	Yang et al.	CNN model with AlexNet and GoogleNet	-	90.9%	Effective use of transfer learning and fine-tuning techniques	Got relatively lower accuracy
14	2020	Ghassemi et al.	Deep neural network model with GAN	3064 Brain MRI images From Nanfang Hospital, Guangzhou, China and General Hospital	95.6%	Using GAN improved overfitting issues and feature learning as well.	Used relatively smaller dataset
15	2019	Deepak et al.	Deep Transfer learning model with GoogleNet	figshare	98%	Utilization of Google net helped a lot in extraction of valuable features and hence improved accuracy.	some wrong classifications are there particularly from meningioma class

Manual diagnosis is time consuming, prone to errors and also highly dependent on the skill level of the doctor itself. These factors put a patient's life at great risk. Numerous researches have already been done on the Brain Tumor domain but after going through so many papers some scope of improvements could be seen. For this research paper our main objective is to work on those areas of improvements that were identified by using different models and techniques in order to increase the accuracy of brain tumor classification even more. A relatively smaller dataset was used by prior researchers which brings the difficulty in generalizing new unseen images accurately and also as technological advancement has been seen, new models and techniques are available to be used in order to improve the performance of the models.

3. MATERIALS AND METHODS

3.1 Overall architecture

The usage of correct models, techniques and procedures is quite important so that the model can effectively learn from the provided data and thus can later on classify the unseen Brain MRI images correctly. Many researches have been conducted in the past with various proposed methods in order to correctly identify the tumors. The challenge with the tumors is that they are available in many different shapes, sizes, and locations which makes the analysis quite difficult.

3 models with test accuracies as follows: 99.8%, 99.2%, 96.7% are proposed. Here explanation of the working of the highest test accuracy giving model through various diagrams is given.

The figures 2, 3,4 clearly show the procedures taken in order to achieve the high accuracy of 99.8%.

Figure 2. Procedures taken to get highest accuracy

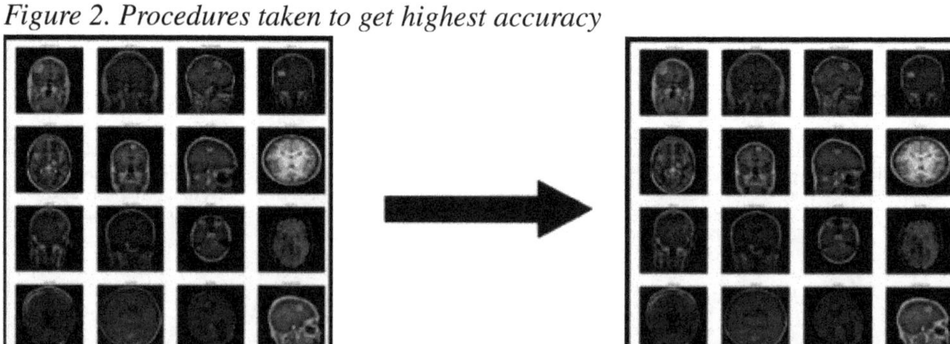

5712 Brain MRI dataset from Figshare, Sartaj, Br35H fetched from training folder & stored in a dataframe called train _df

Augmentation is applied & stored in a dataframe called train_gen. These augumented images will be used for training the model

Figure 3. Procedures taken to get highest accuracy

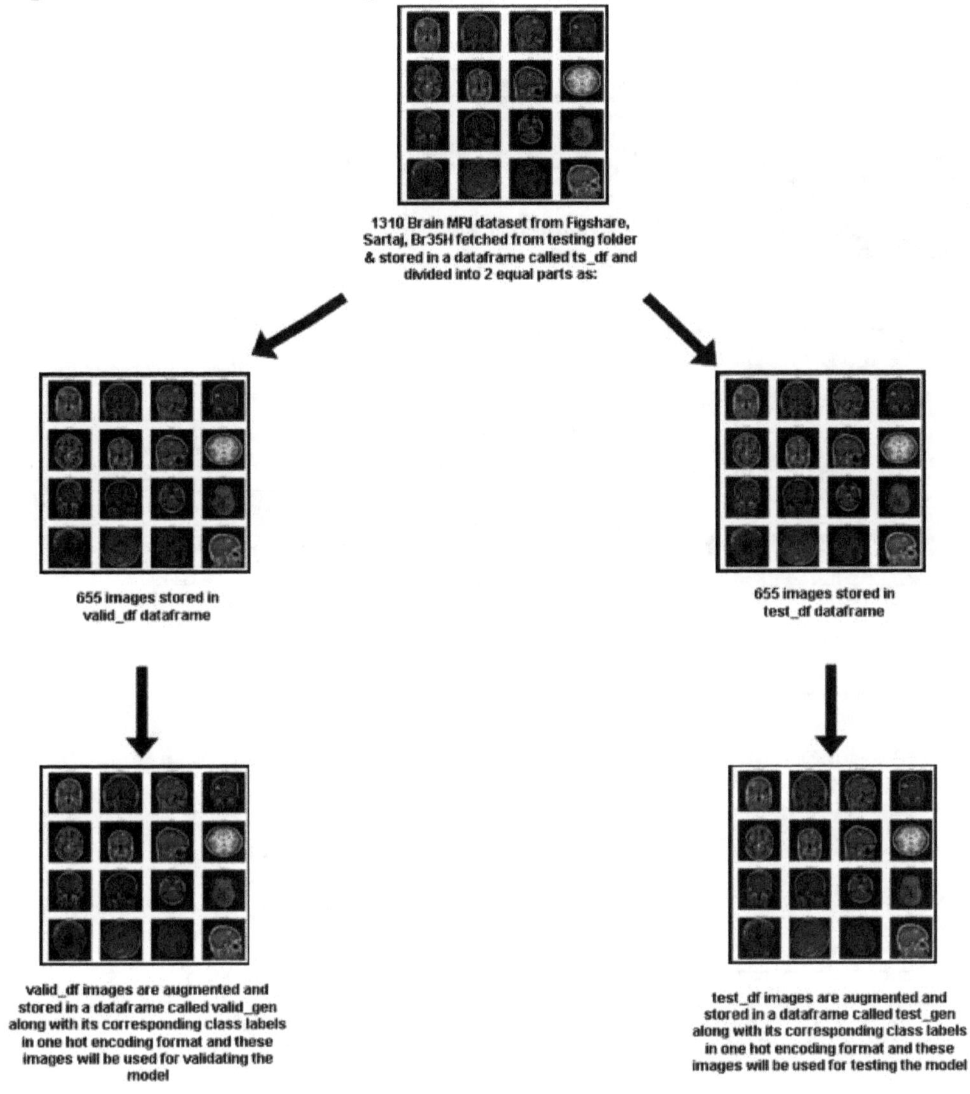

The below diagram explains the overall procedure taken in order to achieve the highest accuracy of 99.8%.

Figure 4. Procedures taken to get highest accuracy

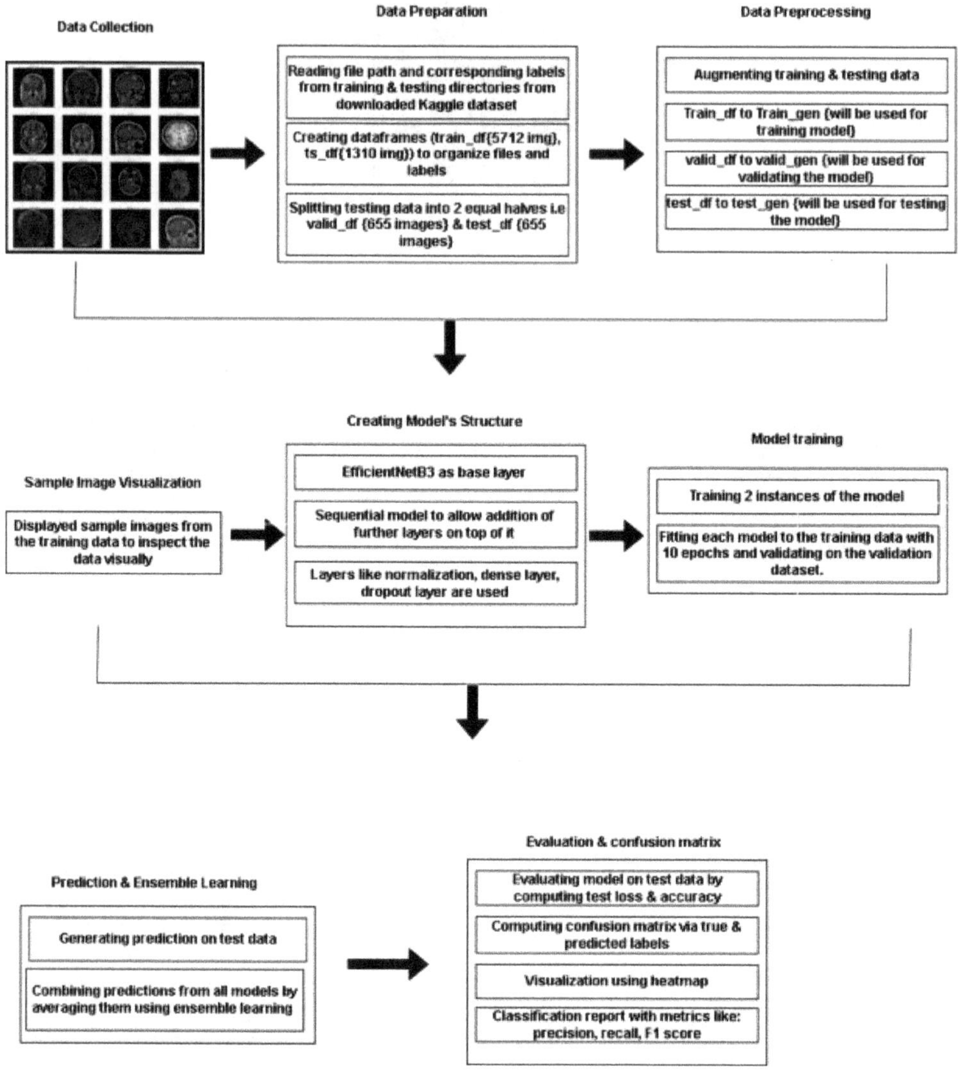

Pretrained EfficientNetB3 and Sequential models were selected due to their demonstrated efficacy. EfficientNetB3 is used as the base layer. Sequential model enabled the addition of multiple layers on top of it like batch normalization layer, dense layer, dropout layer in order to avoid overfitting issues. Sequential models are widely used as they are versatile and can be used for achieving various kinds of tasks like classification, regression etc.

EfficientNetB3 belongs to the EfficientNet family which is a neural network architecture developed by Google. It has the ability to uniformly scale various dimensions like resolution, height, width of the given images. And this pretrained model is designed by Google in such a way that it is efficient in both memory usage and processing speed while still delivering high performance.

3.2 Dataset collection

[1] The Brain MRI images are collected from the kaggle dataset (https://www.kaggle.com/datasets/masoudnickparvar/brain-tumor-mri-dataset/data)

It consists of 7022 labeled images in total. The data is divided into 4 categories namely: gliomas, meningioma, no tumor, pituitary. The dataset is catego rized into 2 directories: Training dataset and Testing dataset. Training dataset comprises of 5712 images while the testing dataset comprises of 1310 images. 5712 images are used for training the model, 655 images are used for validating the model and another 655 images dataset are used for testing the model. All 3 sets of images which were used for different purposes (i.e training, validation, testing) were first augmented then they were used in order to train the model to generalize well to a wide set of new unseen brain MRI images. Below figure 5 shows the dataset distribution.

Figure 5. Dataset Distribution

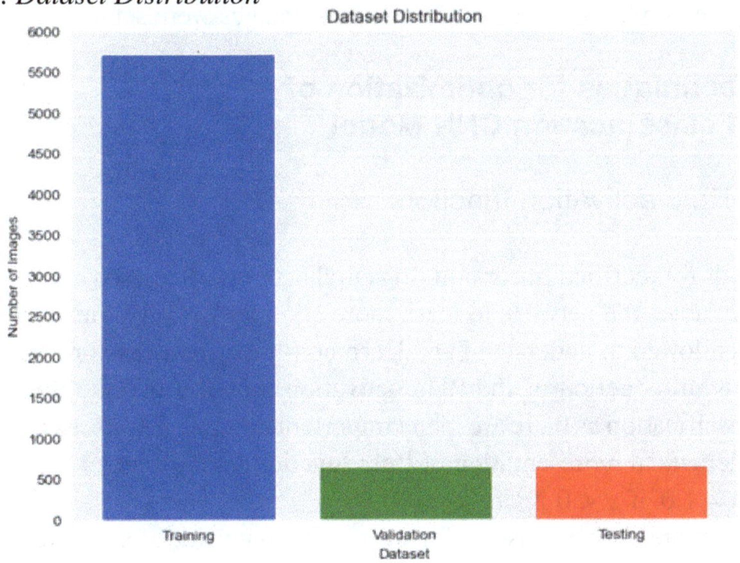

3.3 Data Preprocessing and Augmentation

These both are one of the many crucial steps in order to increase the performance of the overall model. Once the kaggle's dataset was downloaded to the local system, 5712 brain MRI images were fetched from the training directory and stored in a dataframe called train_df. Later on augmentation is applied on the train_df dataset and stored in a new dataframe called train_gen. The augmented dataset contained in the train_gen dataframe was used to train the model. 1310 brain MRI images were fetched from the testing directory and stored in a dataframe called ts_df. The dataframe ts_df was divided into 2 equal parts. 655 brain MRI images were stored in a dataframe called valid_df and another set of 655 brain MRI images were stored in a dataframe called test_df.

Later on, the augmentation technique was applied on both the dataframes. After augmentation valid_df dataframe changed to valid_gen and test_df changed to test_gen. The augmented images dataset contained in the valid_gen dataframe was used for validating the model in order to check whether the model can classify the data correctly or not. And the augmented images dataset contained in the test_gen dataframe was used for testing the model.

For augmentation the batch size was set to 16 and images size was set to 224 * 224 pixels. The number of channels in the input images were set to 3.

3.4 Key Techniques for optimization of Brain MRI classification CNN Model

3.4.1 The Relu activation function:

Relu stands for rectified linear unit. In neural networks it is used as an activation function. It enables the network to learn more complex data. By introducing Relu the model is allowed to understand and learn non-linear relationships between the features. This introduction of the Relu activation function is quite important for tasks like classification as there are many important non linear features in the image pixels. Mathematical representation of Relu function is represented as:

$ReLU(x) = \{ 0, \text{if } x < 0\ X, \text{if } x>=0 \}$

The above expression means that for any given input value of x, the Relu function will give the maximum of 0 and x.

3.4.2 Dense layer:

In a neural network, the dense layer is a layer in which every neuron is connected with all the neurons of the previous layer. In order to learn the complex patterns this layer is used. Dense layer is used in tasks like classification and regression.

Mathematically, the output Oi can be represented as:

$O_i = \text{ReLU} (\sum^{n}_{j=1} \text{Input}_j * \text{Weight}_{ij} + \text{Bias}_i)$

The above expression shows a mathematical formula representing the calculations done in dense layer. Oi stands for output of neuron i.

Oi is calculated by using an activation function like ReLU on the sum of the weighted inputs along with an addition of the bias.

3.4.3 Batch normalization:

It is one of the many techniques used in neural networks. It is used to normalize the activation of each layer and thus speeds up the training process.

Batch normalization for an input x is calculated as:

$BN (x) = (x\text{-Mean}(x)) / (Var(x) + \in)$

In order to decrease the covariate shift, the mean of the input batch is subtracted from the input. To bring the activations to similar scales, the value is then divided by the standard deviation.

3.4.4 Dropout Regularization:

In neural networks to avoid overfitting issues dropout regularization technique is used. It prevents the network from relying too much on a particular set of features.

The mathematical expression for dropout regularization can be represented as:

$\text{Output}_i = \text{Input}_i * \text{Mask}_i * 1/1\text{-p}$

Output(i) refers to output of neuron i Input (i) refers to the input of the neuron i

Mask (i) refers to randomly setting of neuron's output to zero with p as a probability P refers to the dropout rate with a value ranging between 0.2 to 0.5

3.4.5 Categorical Cross-Entropy Loss function:

To measure the difference between the predicted probability distribution and the actual probability distribution a loss function called categorical cross-entropy is used.

Mathematical expression of Categorical Cross-Entropy Loss function:

For a single sample: $L(y,y\char`^) = - \Sigma i yi \,.\, \log(y\char`^_i)$

For a batch of samples: $L(Y, Y\char`^) = - 1/N \, \Sigma^{N}_{j=1} \Sigma_i Y_{ji} \,.\, \log(Y\char`^_{ji})$

Where Y is the true distribution(one-hot encoded), Y^ is the predicted distribution, N is the batch size, and i iterates over the classes.

3.4.6 Adamax optimization:

It is used for training the neural network. In order to allow the model to learn better from the data, the adamax optimizer helps the model by making adjustments in the weights and biases of the network.

Overall it helps the model to learn more effectively and efficiently from the provided dataset. Mathematical expression of Adamax optimization:

1. Exponential Moving Average of Gradients (m): $M_t = \beta_1.m_{t-1} + (1-\beta_1).gt$
2. Exponential Moving Average of Squared Gradients (v):

$$\nu_t = \max(\beta_2 . \nu_{t-1}, |gt|^2)$$

3. Bias-Corrected Estimates: $m\hat{}_t = m^t/1-\beta^t_1$

$$\nu\hat{}_t = \nu_t / 1-\beta^t_2$$

4. Update Rule for Parameters (θ):

$$\triangle\theta_t = - \eta/\nu\hat{}_t .m\hat{}_t$$

mt and vt represents the first and second estimates of gradients at time t. β1 and β2 are exponential decay rates

gt is the gradient at time t. Learning rate is denoted by n.

m^t and v^t are the bias corrected estimates

θt represents the parameters (weights and biases) of the neural network at time *t*.

4. EVALUATION METRICS

(1) Confusion Matrix:

To evaluate the performance of the overall classification model a matrix or a table is made which is known as confusion matrix. It compares the actual labels associated with the provided dataset with the predicted labels that are given by the model. It provides a summary of the model's predictions and their accuracy. It consists of four values: True Positives (TP), True Negatives (TN), False Positives

(FP), and False Negatives (FN). It helps calculate metrics like accuracy, precision, recall, and F1 score.

The figure 6 shows the confusion matrix of the 99.8% accuracy giving code:

Figure 6. Confusion Matrix

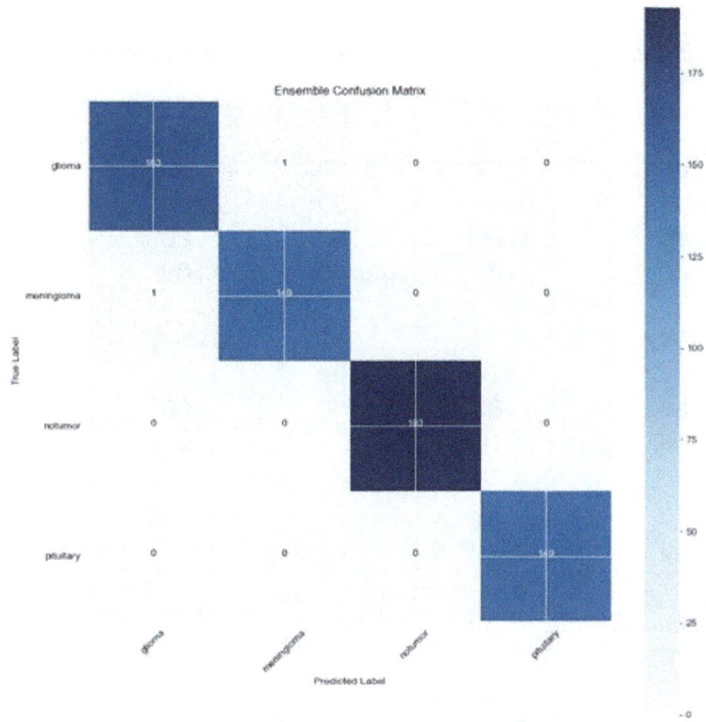

(2) Classification report:

It is a report that shows the summary of many evaluation metrics like Precision, Recall, F1 Score, and accuracy for a classification model. Below is the mathematical representation of metrics:

Precision = TP/(TP+FP) Recall = TP/(TP+FN)

F1 Score = 2* (Precision * Recall) / (Precision + Recall) Accuracy = (TP+TN)/(TP+TN+FP+FN)

Precision measures how many of the mode's positive predictions were correct. Accuracy measures the overall correctness of the mode's prediction.

Recall measures how many of the actual positive cases the model correctly identified Error rate measures the proportion of incorrect predictions made by the mode.

Figure 7 shows the comprehensive classification report of the 99.8% accuracy giving code and Figure 8 shows the precision, recall, f1 score of 99.8% accuracy giving code by class via graph.

Figure 7. showing comprehensive classification report with metrics

	precision	recall	f1-score	support
glioma	0.99	0.99	0.99	164
meningioma	0.99	0.99	0.99	150
notumor	1.00	1.00	1.00	193
pituitary	1.00	1.00	1.00	149
accuracy			1.00	656
macro avg	1.00	1.00	1.00	656
weighted avg	1.00	1.00	1.00	656

Figure 8. Precision, Recall, F1 Score by Class

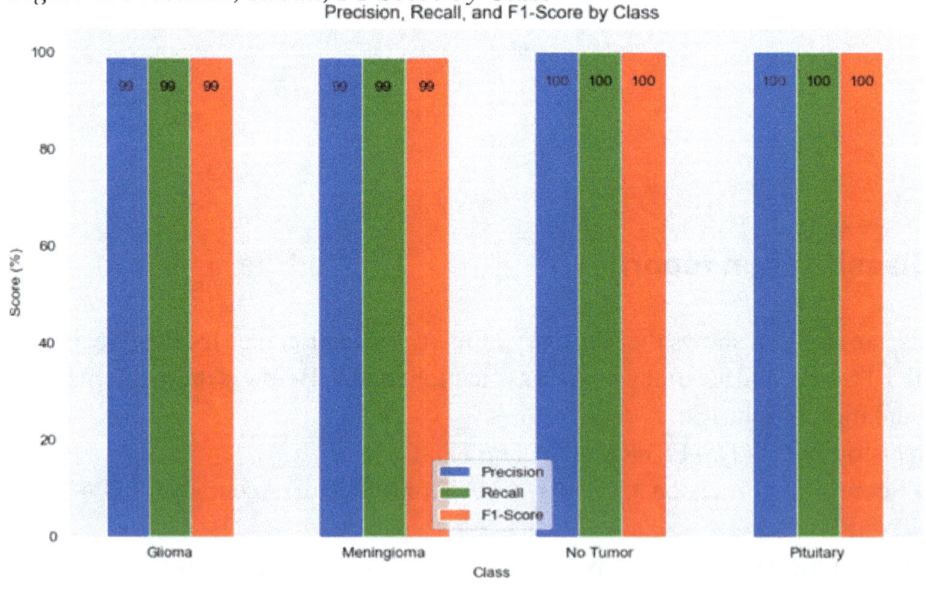

5. RESULT

In this particular section, the results are presented which were achieved using various models and techniques. As already told earlier, 3 codes in total were written which gave us following test accuracies: 99.8%, 99.2% and 96.7%. For the highest test accuracy giving code pretrained EfficientNetB3 model and Sequential model along with the ensemble learning technique was primarily used. For 99.2% test accuracy giving code EfficientNetB3 and Sequential model was utilized which was trained only once unlike the code with highest test accuracy. And for 96.7% test accuracy code the DenseNet169 model was utilized.

The below line graph and dot graph depicts the same.

Figure 9. Comparison of 3 models as line graph

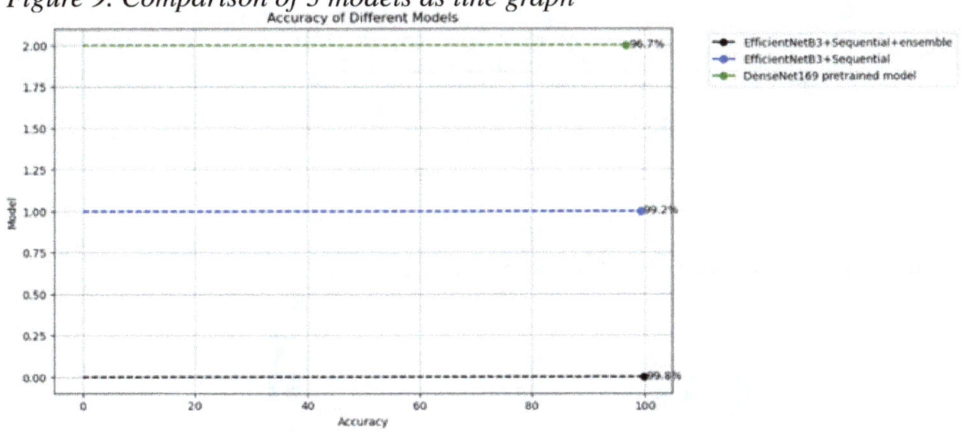

Figure 10. Comparison of 3 models as dot graph

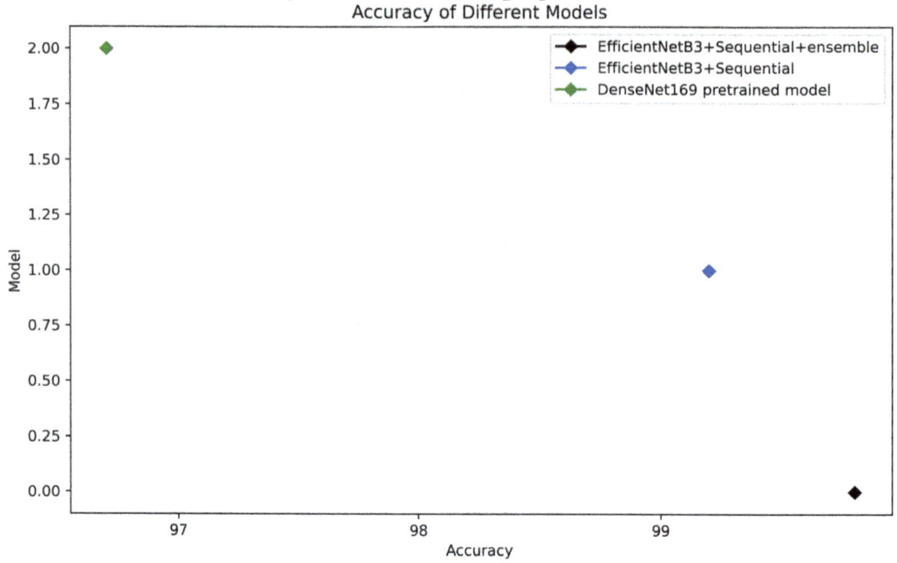

Figure 11. Confusion matrix of 99.8% test accuracy code

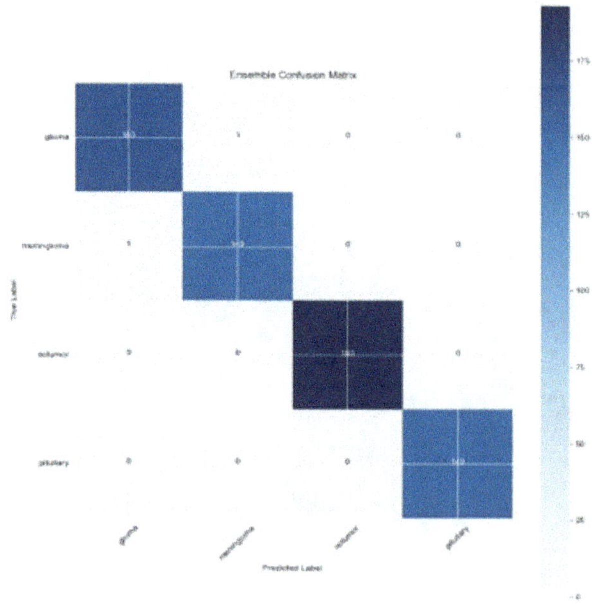

The below graph depicts the training and validation metrics over Epochs for the code giving 99.8% test accuracy.

Figure 12. Training and validation metrics over Epochs

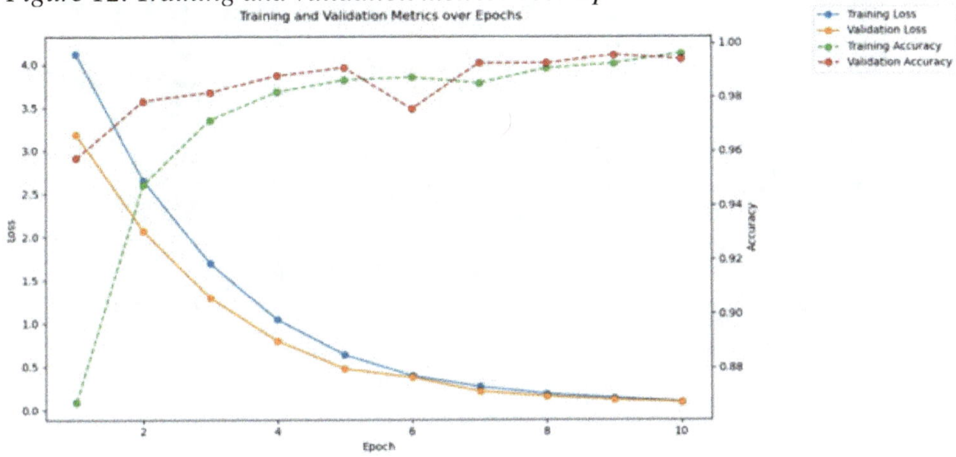

Table 2. Following are the systems on which the models were trained and tested on.

Model used	Accuracy achieved (%)	Specs of System utilized
EfficientNetB3 + Sequential + Ensemble learning technique	99.8	8 GB RAM 3 GHz CPU, NVIDIA Geforce 2 GB RTX 3050 TI
EfficientNetB3 + Sequential	99.2	8 GB RAM 3 GHz CPU, NVIDIA Geforce 2 GB RTX 3050 TI
DesneNet169	96.7	8 GB RAM 3.6 GHz CPU, NVIDIA Geforce 2GB MX 230 Graphics

The below 2 graphs (Figure 14 and 15) clearly depicts the comparison between our work and prior researchers' work.

Figure 13. Comparison of our work with prior researches (test accuracy vs researchers)

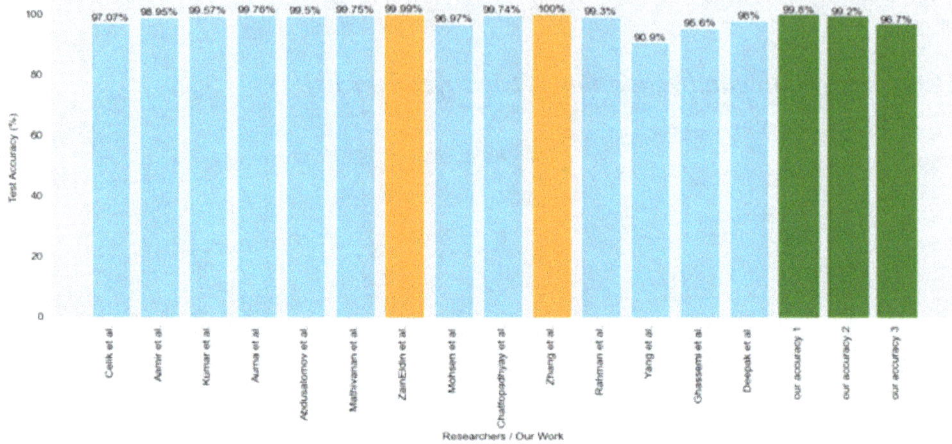

Figure 14. Comparison of our work with prior researches (test accuracy vs models used by researchers)

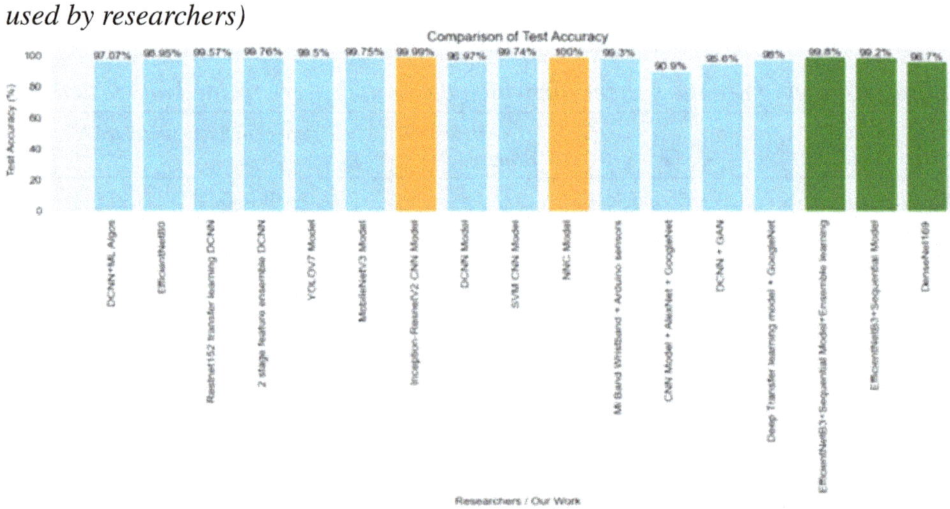

In figure 13 and 14, the 3 green colored bars represent our works. As clearly shown among our 3 works the highest of 99.8% accuracy is achieved. Whereas the 2 orange colored bars represent those researches which got higher than our 99.8% accuracy.

After analyzing their works, it was noticed that both of them used a relatively smaller dataset. To be precise the one with the 100% accuracy used only 66 Brain

MRI images and the one with 99.99% accuracy used 1250 Brain MRI images. The major issue while using a smaller dataset is that as the model is trained on a smaller dataset so it becomes difficult for the model to generalize or classify the new unseen brain MRI images accurately.

To elaborate more, the model used in the code with 99.99% accuracy was trained on 850 images, validated on 250 images and tested on 150 images. Whereas our model which gave 99.8% accuracy was trained on a much larger dataset i.e trained on 5712 images, validated on 655 images, tested on another set of 655 images. Hence our model is more robust as it is trained on a larger dataset so it can classify well to unseen Brain MRI images.

6. CONCLUSION

There are around 150 kinds of brain tumors identified so far. Our area of focus is on 3 kinds of tumors. The Brain MRI dataset was collected from the kaggle which had 7022 images in total. They are divided into 4 categories namely: glioma, meningioma, no tumor, pituitary. Training and testing part comprises of 5712 and 1310 images respectively. 3 codes using different models and techniques were written which gave us the following test accuracies: 99.8%, 99.2% and 96.7%.

The highest accuracy giving code particularly uses sequential model, pretrained EfficientNetB3 model and ensemble learning approach along with the layers like batch normalization layer, dense layer, dropout layer in order to avoid overfitting issues. Techniques like: augmentation, regularization, adamax optimization etc were also used to enhance the results.

Many similar researches were analyzed. Most of them use a relatively smaller dataset which potentially can bring the problems in classifying new unseen images in real world scenarios. Few of the researches indeed used the same dataset as used by us but they achieved a little less accuracy than what is achieved by our model. And computationally also our model is quite efficient. So it is concluded that our proposed model definitely uses improved methods and techniques.

7. FUTURE WORK

As per the WHO cancer is the 2nd leading cause of death globally and around 9.6 million people died in 2018 and around 10 million people died in 2020. The number of deaths can be reduced if the treatment can be started early and that can only happen if a doctor diagnoses the patient to correctly identify the type of tumor the patient has. Manual diagnosis is prone to errors, time consuming and highly depends on the skill level of the doctor itself. Our model is using a large dataset of 7022 images and that is currently giving remarkable accuracy of 99.8% which is quite practical to use in the real world healthcare domain. As high accuracy with a large dataset means that the model can correctly classify the new unseen Brain MRI images of the patients.

As per the future work, in order to increase the generalization and performance of the model combining predictions from multiple models with diverse architectures using ensemble learning could be done. And adding more advanced data augmentation techniques can help increase model's accuracy and overall robustness.

REFERENCES

Aamir, M., Rahman, Z., Dayo, Z. A., Abro, W. A., Uddin, M. I., Khan, I., Imran, A. S., Ali, Z., Ishfaq, M., Guan, Y., & Hu, Z. (2022). A deep learning approach for brain tumor classification using MRI images. *Computers & Electrical Engineering*, *101*, 108105. DOI: 10.1016/j.compeleceng.2022.108105

Aamir, M., Rahman, Z., Dayo, Z. A., Abro, W. A., Uddin, M. I., Khan, I., Imran, A. S., Ali, Z., Ishfaq, M., Guan, Y., & Hu, Z. (2022). A deep learning approach for brain tumor classification using MRI images. *Computers & Electrical Engineering*, *101*, 108105. DOI: 10.1016/j.compeleceng.2022.108105

Abdusalomov, A. B., Mukhiddinov, M., & Whangbo, T. K. (2023). Brain tumor detection based on deep learning approaches and magnetic resonance imaging. *Cancers (Basel)*, *15*(16), 4172. DOI: 10.3390/cancers15164172 PMID: 37627200

Aurna, N. F., Yousuf, M. A., Taher, K. A., Azad, A. K. M., & Moni, M. A. (2022). A classification of MRI brain tumor based on two stage feature level ensemble of deep CNN models. *Computers in Biology and Medicine*, *146*, 105539. DOI: 10.1016/j.compbiomed.2022.105539 PMID: 35483227

Celik, M., & Inik, O. (2024). Development of hybrid models based on deep learning and optimized machine learning algorithms for brain tumor Multi-Classification. *Expert Systems with Applications*, *238*, 122159. DOI: 10.1016/j.eswa.2023.122159

[] Chattopadhyay, A., & Maitra, M. (2022). MRI-based brain tumour image detection using CNN based deep learning method. Neuroscience informatics, 2(4), 100060.

Deepak, S., & Ameer, P. M. (2019). Brain tumor classification using deep CNN features via transfer learning. *Computers in Biology and Medicine*, *111*, 103345. DOI: 10.1016/j.compbiomed.2019.103345 PMID: 31279167

Ghassemi, N., Shoeibi, A., & Rouhani, M. (2020). Deep neural network with generative adversarial networks pre-training for brain tumor classification based on MR images. *Biomedical Signal Processing and Control*, *57*, 101678. DOI: 10.1016/j.bspc.2019.101678

Haq, A., Li, J. P., Khan, S., Alshara, M. A., Alotaibi, R. M., & Mawuli, C. B. (2022). DACBT: Deep learning approach for classification of brain tumors using MRI data in IoT healthcare environment. *Scientific Reports*, *12*(1), 15331. DOI: 10.1038/s41598-022-19465-1 PMID: 36097024

Kumar, K. A., Prasad, A. Y., & Metan, J. (2022). A hybrid deep CNN-Cov-19-Res-Net Transfer learning architype for an enhanced Brain tumor Detection and Classification scheme in medical image processing. *Biomedical Signal Processing and Control, 76*, 103631. DOI: 10.1016/j.bspc.2022.103631

Mathivanan, S. K., Sonaimuthu, S., Murugesan, S., Rajadurai, H., Shivahare, B. D., & Shah, M. A. (2024). Employing deep learning and transfer learning for accurate brain tumor detection. *Scientific Reports, 14*(1), 7232. DOI: 10.1038/s41598-024-57970-7 PMID: 38538708

Mohsen, H., El-Dahshan, E. S. A., El-Horbaty, E. S. M., & Salem, A. B. M. (2018). Classification using deep learning neural networks for brain tumors. *Future Computing and Informatics Journal, 3*(1), 68–71. DOI: 10.1016/j.fcij.2017.12.001

Rahman, M. L., Reza, A. W., & Shabuj, S. I. (2022). An internet of things-based automatic brain tumor detection system. *Indonesian Journal of Electrical Engineering and Computer Science, 25*(1), 214–222. DOI: 10.11591/ijeecs.v25.i1.pp214-222

Yang, Y., Yan, L. F., Zhang, X., Han, Y., Nan, H. Y., Hu, Y. C., Hu, B., Yan, S.-L., Zhang, J., Cheng, D.-L., Ge, X.-W., Cui, G.-B., Zhao, D., & Wang, W. (2018). Glioma grading on conventional MR images: A deep learning study with transfer learning. *Frontiers in Neuroscience, 12*, 804. DOI: 10.3389/fnins.2018.00804 PMID: 30498429

ZainEldin, H., Gamel, S. A., El-Kenawy, E.-S. M., Alharbi, A. H., Khafaga, D. S., Ibrahim, A., & Talaat, F. M.ZainEldin. (2022). Brain tumor detection and classification using deep learning and sine-cosine fitness grey wolf optimization. *Bioengineering (Basel, Switzerland), 10*(1), 18. DOI: 10.3390/bioengineering10010018 PMID: 36671591

Zhang, Y., Dong, Z., Wu, L., & Wang, S. (2011). A hybrid method for MRI brain image classification. *Expert Systems with Applications, 38*(8), 10049–10053. DOI: 10.1016/j.eswa.2011.02.012

Chapter 8
Presenting the Methodologies, Challenges, and Opportunities in Underwater Target Recognition

Rashid Nadeem
http://orcid.org/0009-0008-4163-7282
Pondicherry University, India

V. Uma
http://orcid.org/0000-0002-7257-7920
Pondicherry University, India

ABSTRACT

This chapter explains the significance of Underwater Target Recognition (UTR) for marine research, defence, and exploration, focusing on the challenges posed by the unique underwater environment. It begins by examining the difficulties of underwater sensing and introduces Reinforcement Learning (RL) as a promising approach to improve UTR systems. RL enhances decision-making in uncertain, variable conditions. The chapter provides an overview of RL principles, explaining how they can be adapted to address underwater challenges, and discusses key RL algorithms with relevant modifications. By integrating RL into UTR, the chapter highlights how traditional limitations can be overcome, significantly advancing target recognition technologies in marine environments. Additionally, the potential

DOI: 10.4018/979-8-3693-8327-8.ch008

of Deep Reinforcement Learning (Deep RL), which leverages deep neural networks for more robust solutions, is explored as a future direction, showcasing RL potential to optimize UTR processes in complex underwater conditions.

INTRODUCTION

Sound Navigation and Ranging (SONAR) systems have been instrumental in the advancement of underwater exploration and research. Since their inception in the early 20th century, these systems have evolved considerably, establishing themselves as indispensable tools for navigation, communication, and object detection in underwater environments. The evolution of SONAR technology has paralleled advancements in oceanographic studies, driven by the strategic necessity of effective UTR. This chapter aims to provide a comprehensive introduction to the complex world of SONAR systems, exploring their development, applications, and the challenges they face, particularly in the context of UTR. The primary function of SONAR systems is to utilize sound waves to navigate, communicate, and detect objects beneath the water's surface. These systems operate by emitting sound pulses and analysing the echoes that return from objects. This method allows for the detection, localization, and characterization of underwater objects, making SONAR a critical technology in both military and civilian applications. Over the decades, SONAR technology has undergone significant advancements, enhancing its capabilities and expanding its applications. From early rudimentary devices to sophisticated modern systems, SONAR has continually evolved to meet the growing demands of underwater exploration and research.

One of the primary applications of SONAR systems is UTR. This involves identifying and locating objects beneath the water's surface, a task that is vital for various fields, including naval defence, marine biology, and environmental monitoring. The process of UTR is inherently complex due to the unique and variable characteristics of underwater environments. Factors such as water temperature, salinity, and pressure can affect the propagation of sound waves, making it challenging to accurately detect and identify targets (Steiniger et al., 2021). Moreover, the dynamic nature of oceanic noise adds another layer of complexity to this process. Oceanic noise originates from a multitude of sources, both natural and anthropogenic. Biological activities, such as the sounds produced by marine life, geological phenomena contribute to the acoustic landscape of the ocean. This diverse array of noise sources can interfere with SONAR signals, complicating the detection and recognition of underwater targets (Xiao et al., 2021). As a result, one of the primary challenges in UTR is distinguishing relevant signals from background noise.

Despite these challenges, the strategic importance of UTR has driven extensive research and innovation in this field. The ability to accurately detect and identify underwater objects is crucial for a variety of applications, from ensuring naval security to studying marine ecosystems (Zhufeng et al., 2022). Over the years, researchers have explored numerous techniques to enhance the performance of SONAR systems in challenging underwater environments. Among these techniques, RL has emerged as a promising approach. RL is a type of Machine Learning (ML) where an agent learns to make decisions by interacting with its environment. In the context of SONAR systems, RL can be used to improve the accuracy and efficiency of target recognition by enabling the system to adapt to changing underwater conditions (Cao et al., 2019). By continuously learning from its interactions with the environment, an RL-based SONAR system can develop strategies to mitigate the effects of noise and other environmental factors, thereby enhancing its performance.

The application of RL in UTR, however, is not without its challenges. One of the primary difficulties is the need for large amounts of training data to effectively train the RL models. Collecting this data in underwater environments can be logistically challenging and expensive. Additionally, the dynamic and unpredictable nature of underwater conditions means that RL models must be capable of adapting to new and unforeseen situations. This requires sophisticated algorithms and computational resources, which can pose significant challenges for researchers. Despite these challenges, the potential benefits of using RL in SONAR systems are substantial (Szepesvari, 2010). RL offers the possibility of creating more robust and adaptive systems that can perform effectively in a wide range of underwater conditions. By leveraging the capabilities of ML, researchers can develop SONAR systems that are not only more accurate but also more efficient, reducing the time and resources required for UTR.

Despite significant progress in SONAR technology and Deep Learning (DL) methods, achieving consistent and reliable recognition performance under highly dynamic underwater acoustic conditions remains a persistent challenge.

The evolution of SONAR technology has been driven by the strategic importance of UTR, a task that is both complex and challenging due to the unique characteristics of underwater environments and the presence of diverse noise sources. As RL continues to advance, the potential to overcome these challenges becomes more apparent. Despite these obstacles, advancements in RL offer promising solutions for improving the accuracy and efficiency of SONAR systems. By addressing the inherent challenges of underwater environments, researchers can develop more effective and reliable systems for UTR, paving the way for new discoveries and innovations in oceanographic studies.

The objectives of chapter:

- Explain the background of the Physics of Underwater Acoustics and Fundamental Principles of SONAR.
- Discuss the various sources of noise in the ocean that impact the effectiveness of SONAR systems.
- Highlight the strategic importance and ongoing research efforts in UTR.
- Explore the application of RL techniques in UTR to improve decision-making processes.
- Address the challenges associated with using RL for UTR and suggest potential solutions.

BACKGROUND KNOWLEDGE

The underwater environment is highly dynamic, with factors like salinity, pressure, and temperature impacting sound propagation. Acoustic SONAR systems are vital in such environments for navigation, communication, and target detection since sound waves travel efficiently underwater, unlike electromagnetic waves. However, ocean ambience, including background noise from marine life, water movement, and human activities, can introduce noise that disrupts SONAR performance. These complexities must be addressed when designing effective underwater systems for tasks like surveillance and exploration.

Underwater Environment

The underwater environment encompasses a range of complex physical and acoustic characteristics that significantly impact sonar and underwater communication systems. Understanding these aspects is crucial for effective design and operation of such systems (Kaur & Vijay, 2023).

Physical Properties of the Ocean

The physical properties of the ocean include its temperature, salinity, and pressure, which collectively influence its density and, consequently, its sound propagation characteristics. Ocean temperature varies with depth and latitude, creating layers with distinct thermal gradients. The upper layer, or the mixed layer, experiences fluctuations due to surface heating, wind mixing, and seasonal changes. Below this, the thermocline is a zone where temperature decreases sharply with depth. Salinity, which is the concentration of dissolved salts in seawater, also affects density and sound speed. Higher salinity increases the water's density, enhancing sound transmission. Pressure, which increases with depth, further affects sound speed and density.

Collectively, these factors create a dynamic and stratified medium through which sound waves travel, influencing their speed, direction, and attenuation.

Channel Characteristics

The channel characteristics of the underwater environment describe how sound waves interact with the water column and the seabed. The oceanic channel can be viewed as a layered medium where sound waves encounter different acoustic impedances due to variations in water density and temperature. Sound propagation is also influenced by the sea floor and any objects or features it contains, such as underwater mountains or sediment layers (Pushpa Mala et al., 2024). The seabed can reflect, absorb, or scatter sound waves, affecting the signal quality and detection range. Additionally, the presence of biological organisms, such as schools of fish or marine mammals, can introduce noise and variability into the acoustic environment. Understanding these channel characteristics is essential for predicting how sound will travel and for designing systems to compensate for or leverage these effects.

Propagation of Sound in the Marine Environment

Sound propagation in the marine environment is governed by the principles of wave physics, with speed, direction, and attenuation being key factors. The speed of sound in seawater is influenced by temperature, salinity, and pressure, with warmer water increasing sound speed, while higher salinity and pressure also contribute to faster propagation. Sound waves can refract, or bend, due to changes in the speed of sound with depth, creating phenomena such as sound channels where sound waves can travel long distances with minimal attenuation. Attenuation, or the reduction in sound intensity, occurs due to absorption by the water, scattering by particles, and interaction with the seabed. The marine environment also presents challenges such as varying background noise levels from natural and anthropogenic sources, which can mask or distort the desired signals. Understanding these propagation characteristics is critical for optimizing sonar performance and ensuring reliable underwater communication and detection.

Underwater environment presents a complex interplay of physical properties, channel characteristics, and sound propagation dynamics. A comprehensive understanding of these factors is essential for effectively designing and deploying underwater acoustic systems.

Underwater Acoustics

Underwater acoustics is the study of sound propagation through water, a field crucial for various marine applications, including SONAR systems (Ahmad et al., 2024). Underwater sound waves travel significantly faster in air approximately 1500m/s due to the higher density and elasticity of water. The speed of sound in water is influenced by several factors, including temperature, salinity, and depth. As temperature increases, the water becomes less dense and more elastic, leading to an increase in sound speed (Yao et al., 2023). Conversely, salinity affects the water's density and elasticity, altering sound velocity. Depth impacts the pressure, which also affects the speed of sound.

Sound absorption in water is another important consideration. As sound waves propagate, they lose energy primarily due to the conversion of sound energy into heat. This absorption is frequency-dependent, with higher frequencies being absorbed more quickly than lower frequencies. Additionally, sound waves undergo refraction when they pass through layers of water with different temperatures or salinities. Refraction causes the sound waves to bend, which can alter their direction and range. Reflective and scattering phenomena also play a role; sound waves can reflect off objects or surfaces, and scatter due to irregularities in the water or objects within it (Siddhartha et al., 2023). These effects can influence the accuracy of sonar systems by altering the perceived location and characteristics of underwater objects.

The mathematical foundation for determining the distance to an object using sonar involves calculating the time it takes for a sound pulse reach the object and travel back. The fundamental formula used is:

$$\text{Distance} = \frac{\text{Speed of sound} \times \text{travel time}}{2} \dots \qquad (1)$$

SONAR System

A SONAR system generally includes a sensor or a set of sensors, known as hydrophones, which function as underwater microphones or transducers (Korkmaz et al., 2023). These hydrophones convert acoustic pressure in the water into electrical voltage. Sonar can be classified into two main types: active sonar and passive sonar.

Active Sonar

Active sonar is a technique used to detect and identify underwater objects by emitting sound waves and analysing the echoes from those objects (Ashok & Latha, 2023). The process begins with a sonar system emitting a pulse of sound into the water using hydrophone. These sound waves shown in figure 2 travel through the water and bounce off from objects, creating echoes. The sonar system then receives these echoes and processes them to determine the location, size, and characteristics of the objects. Active sonar is particularly useful for navigation, mapping, and object detection in underwater environments.

The main drawback with active sonar is that it sends out signals, which can be picked up by enemies. This lets them figure out where the sonar is and how fast moving. In such situations usually better to use passive sonar, which listens for sounds without giving away its position.

Figure 1. Active Sonar Mechanics

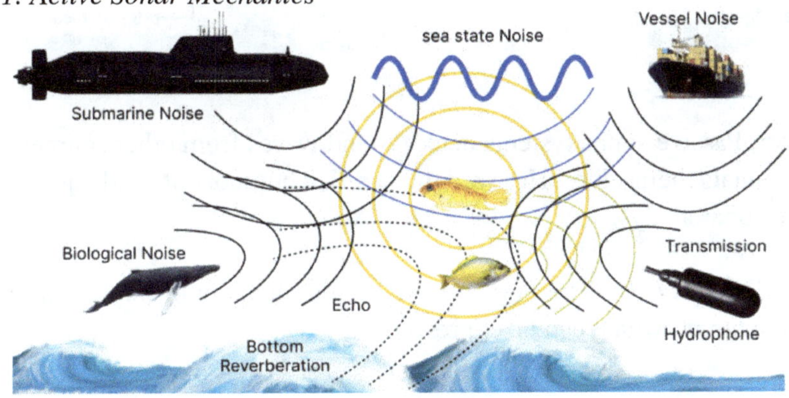

Passive Sonar

Passive sonar is a technique used to detect underwater objects by listening for sounds that are naturally emitted or reflected by those objects (Kamal, & Supriya, 2021). Unlike active sonar, which sends out sound pulses and analyses their echoes, passive sonar relies on detecting the sounds that are already present in the environment. This method involves hydrophones or other sensors in picking up acoustic signals from various sources, such as marine life, vessels, or underwater machinery. By analysing these sounds, passive SONAR systems can identify and track objects without actively transmitting any signals themselves. This approach is often used for stealth operations and monitoring purposes, as it does not reveal the presence of the sonar system to potential targets the processes illustrated in Figure 3.

Figure 2. Passive Sonar Mechanics

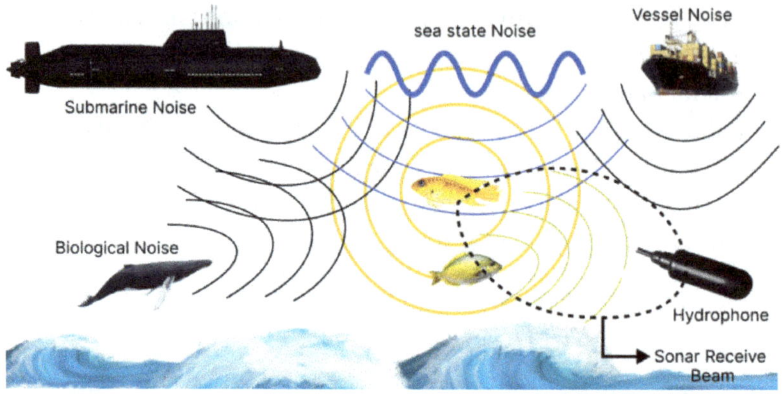

In short, Passive sonar systems detect sound waves from other sources without emitting signals themselves. Here are the detailed components and equations used in passive sonar analysis:

- *Source Level (SL):* The Source Level is the intensity of the sound produced by the target, which can be expressed as:

$$SL = 10\log_{10}\left(\frac{I}{I_0}\right) \ldots \tag{2}$$

Where, I = Intensity of the sound at 1 meter from the source.
I_0 = Reference intensity, typically 10^{-12} W/m^2 in water.

- *Transmission Loss (TL):* Transmission Loss accounts for the reduction in sound intensity as it travels through the water. It can be estimated using:

$$TL = 20\log_{10}(R) + \alpha R \ldots \tag{3}$$

Where, R = Range or distance between the source and the receiver, measured in meters.
α =Absorption coefficient, which depends on the frequency of the sound and the properties of the water, measured in decibels per meter (dB/m).

- *Noise Level (NL):* The Noise Level in the environment can be influenced by various factors, Viz. Ambient noise and Self-noise. The total noise level is usually expressed in decibels (dB). It is generally expressed by the following equation:

$$NL = 10\log_{10}\left(\frac{I_{signal}}{I_0}\right) \ldots \quad (4)$$

Where, I_{signal} = Power of the signal in the desired direction.

- *Directivity Index (DI):* The Directivity Index represents the ability of the sonar system to focus on sounds coming from a particular direction, reducing the influence of noise from other directions. It is calculated as:

$$DI = 10\log_{10}\left(\frac{I_{signal}}{I_{noise}}\right) \ldots \quad (5)$$

Where, I_{signal} = Power of the signal in the desired direction.
I_{noise} = Power of the noise in the same direction.

- *Signal-to-Noise Ratio (SNR):* The SNR for passive sonar is given by:

$$SNR = SL - TL - NL + DI \ldots \quad (6)$$

- *Detection Threshold (DT):* The Detection Threshold is the minimum SNR required for a sonar system to detect a target. It is typically determined experimentally and depends on the sonar equipment and environmental conditions.

To detect a target, the SNR must be greater than or equal to DT,

$$SNR \geq DT \ldots \quad (7)$$

This equation helps determine whether a target can be detected given the source level, transmission loss, noise level, and directivity index of the sonar system.

Signal Preprocessing

The passive sonar signal processing system begins with a hydrophone array to capture underwater acoustic signals, as illustrated in Figure 4. These signals are then amplified and converted from analog to digital form by an Analog-to-Digital(A/D) Converter. This conversion is essential for enabling the digital processing of the signals.

After conversion, the digital signals are input into a beamformer. The beamformer analyses the signals to determine the direction of object arrival (such as a submarine, marine life, or underwater structure). This analysis involves calculating SNR using the Equation (6). Once the SNR is determined, the system can perform several functions, such as selecting beams, analysing bearing times, detecting, classifying, and tracking signals. For a target to be reliably detected, the SNR must be greater than or equal to DT Equation (7).

Figure 3. Basic steps in passive sonar signal processing

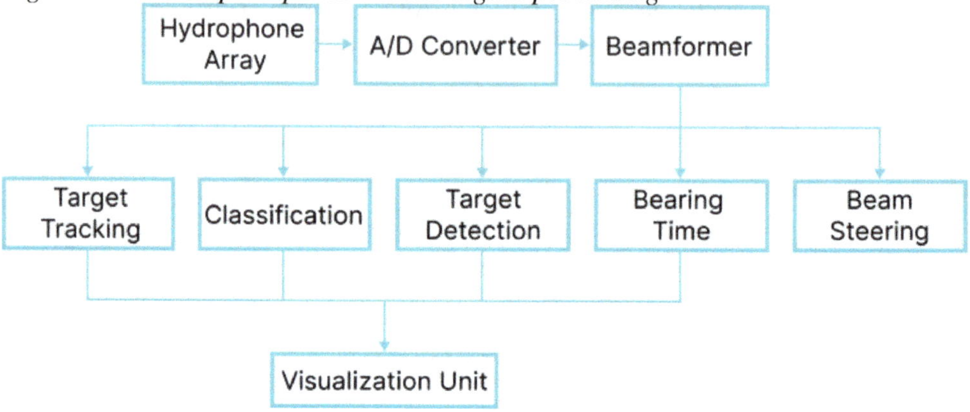

Finally, the processed results are displayed for interpretation and decision-making, enabling operators to effectively respond to the information gathered from underwater acoustic data. As these systems operate in the complex and dynamic oceanic ambiance, they must contend with a variety of environmental factors that influence sound propagations.

Ocean Ambience

Oceanic ambience, encompasses the background sounds present in the marine environment, primarily generated by natural and anthropogenic sources. This ambient noise significantly impacts underwater acoustic communications and SONAR systems by introducing varying levels of interference that can mask or distort signals. Understanding the characteristics and sources of oceanic ambient noise is crucial for improving the detection and classification of underwater targets, optimizing sonar performance, and mitigating the ecological impacts of human activities on marine life.

Natural Noise: Natural ocean noise as detailed in Table 2, encompasses sounds produced by natural phenomena and processes within the marine environment. These sounds arise from biological activities, physical interactions, and geological events (Kumar, & Bhaumik, 2022).

- *Biological Noise:* Includes sounds made by marine organisms such as whales, dolphins, fish, and invertebrates. These noises serve purposes like communication, navigation, and mating.
- *Geophysical Noise:* Results from natural physical processes, including the interaction of wind with the sea surface, rainfall impacts, and thermal noise from molecular agitation in water.
- *Seismic and Geological Noise:* Comprises low-frequency sounds generated by seismic activities such as underwater earthquakes, volcanic eruptions, and underwater landslides.

Table 2. Natural Noise in Ocean Environments

Source	Definition	Frequency Range
Marine Mammals	Sounds produced by whales, dolphins, and seals for communication, navigation, and echolocation	10 Hz to 200 kHz
Fish	Acoustic signals generated by fish for mating calls, territorial displays, and communication	50 Hz to 5 kHz
Invertebrates	Noises made by shrimp, crabs, and other invertebrates through activities	2 kHz to 20 kHz
Wind and Waves	Noise generated by the interaction of wind with the sea surface, including breaking waves and bubble formation	100 Hz to 50 kHz
Rain	Acoustic impact of raindrops hitting the ocean surface	Above 100 kHz
Earthquakes	Low-frequency sounds produced by underwater seismic activity	1 Hz to 20 Hz
Volcanic Eruptions	Acoustic emissions from underwater volcanic activities and hydrothermal vents	1 Hz to several hundred Hz
Underwater Landslides	Sounds from shifting underwater sediments and geological movements	Below 100 Hz

Anthropogenic Noise: Anthropogenic noise as detailed in Table 3, refers to sounds introduced into the ocean as a result of human activities. These noises can have significant effects on marine life and ecosystems (Kumar, & Bhaumik, 2022).

- *Shipping Noise:* Arises from the operation of commercial and fishing vessels, including noises from engines, propellers, and other machinery.
- *Industrial Noise:* Includes sounds from activities related to oil and gas exploration, such as seismic surveys and drilling operations, as well as noise from offshore construction projects.
- *Military Noise:* Consists of acoustic emissions from naval sonar systems, underwater explosions, and other military operations.

- *Recreational Noise:* Generated by recreational activities such as boating, jet skiing, and scuba diving.
- *Other Human Activities:* Encompasses noise from scientific research equipment and harbor operations, including activities like loading and unloading.

Table 3. Anthropogenic Noise in Ocean Environments

Source	Definition	Frequency Range
Commercial Shipping	Continuous noise from the engines, propellers, and machinery of large commercial vessels	10 Hz to 1 kHz
Fishing Vessels	Noise generated by smaller boats and their fishing equipment	100 Hz to 10 kHz
Oil and Gas	Exploration Acoustic disturbances from seismic surveys, drilling operations, and platform activities	5 Hz to 300 Hz (seismic surveys) 10 Hz to 1 kHz (drilling)
Construction	Noise from building offshore structures such as wind farms, oil rigs, and underwater pipelines	10 Hz to 10 kHz
Active Sonar	Powerful sound pulses emitted by naval sonar systems for detection and navigation	Below 1 kHz (low-frequency); 1 kHz to 10 kHz (mid-frequency); Above 10 kHz (high-frequency)
Explosions	Noise from underwater detonations used in military exercises, testing, or demolition	Few Hz to several kHz
Boating	Sounds from recreational boats, jets skis, and other watercraft	100Hz to 10 kHz

The underwater environment is characterized by various factors which collectively influence the propagation of sound. These characteristics create a distinct oceanic ambience that affects how acoustic signals are transmitted and received. Understanding these acoustic conditions is essential for developing effective UTR systems, as directly impact the clarity and accuracy of sonar detection.

UNDERWATER TARGET RECOGNITION

UTR is a crucial area in marine research and defence applications, where identifying and classifying objects submerged in water is essential for navigation, environmental monitoring, and security. The complexity of the underwater environment, characterized by factors such as light absorption, scattering, and noise, presents significant challenges for traditional image processing techniques. Advancements in DL and RL have opened new avenues for enhancing the accuracy and reliability of UTR systems. DL, with its ability to model complex patterns and features, has proven effective in processing sonar images and underwater video feeds, enabling the identification of objects ranging from marine life to underwater mines (Yang, Li, Shen, & Xu, 2019). RL on the other hand, optimizes the decision-making process by learning from interactions with the environment, making it particularly suitable for dynamic and unpredictable underwater conditions. By leveraging these technologies, modern UTR systems can achieve higher precision and adaptability, paving the way for more effective underwater exploration and surveillance.

Manual Target Classification

Manual target classification in underwater environments involves human operators analyzing sonar images or underwater video footage to identify and categorize objects. This process relies heavily on the expertise and experience of the operators, who use visual cues and domain knowledge to distinguish between different types of targets, such as fish, rocks, or man-made objects. While manual classification can be accurate, it is time-consuming, labor-intensive, and prone to human error, especially in challenging conditions with poor visibility or high noise levels. Furthermore, the reliance on subjective judgment can lead to inconsistencies in classification results.

The advent of ML and DL technologies has provided an opportunity to automate and enhance the accuracy of target classification. By training algorithms on large datasets of labeled underwater images, DL models can learn to recognize complex patterns and features that may be difficult for human operators to discern. This shift towards automated classification not only reduces the workload of human operators but also improves the consistency and reliability of UTR systems.

Need for Automated Target Recognition

The need for Automated Target Recognition (ATR) in underwater environments arises from the limitations and challenges associated with manual classification. The vastness of the ocean, coupled with the dynamic and often hostile underwater conditions, makes manual target classification impractical for large-scale or real-time applications. ATR systems, powered by advanced ML algorithms, offer several advantages over manual methods. Firstly, they can process and analyse large volumes of data much faster than human operators, enabling real-time monitoring and decision-making. Secondly, automated systems can operate continuously without fatigue, ensuring consistent performance over extended periods (Luo & Zhang, 2021). Thirdly, the use of sophisticated algorithms allows for the detection and classification of subtle and complex features that may be overlooked by human operators. Furthermore, automated systems can be deployed in remote or hazardous environments where it may be unsafe or impractical for humans to operate. By addressing these challenges, ATR systems enhance the efficiency and effectiveness of underwater exploration, surveillance, and monitoring activities.

Automated Target Recognition

ATR in underwater environments leverages the power of DL and RL to accurately identify and classify objects submerged in water as shown in figure 6. DL algorithms, particularly CNN, have shown great promise in processing sonar images and underwater video feeds. These algorithms can automatically extract and learn hierarchical features from raw data, enabling them to distinguish between different types of targets with high precision (Luo & Zhang, 2021). For instance, a CNN trained on a dataset of underwater images can learn to identify characteristics such as shape, texture, and size, which are crucial for distinguishing between various objects.

Figure 4. Basic ATR System

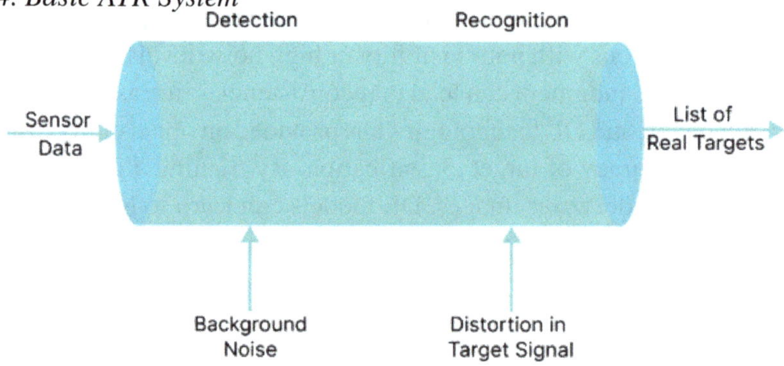

RL further enhances the capabilities of ATR systems by enabling adaptive decision-making. In a RL framework, an agent interacts with the underwater environment, receiving feedback in the form of rewards or penalties based on its actions (Yang, Li, Shen, & Xu, 2019). Through this process, the agent learns to optimize its actions to achieve the best possible outcome, such as correctly identifying a target. This approach is particularly useful in dynamic and unpredictable underwater conditions, where the agent can continuously learn and adapt to changes in the environment. By integrating DL and RL, ATR systems can achieve high levels of accuracy, robustness, and adaptability, making them invaluable tools for underwater exploration, defence, and environmental monitoring.

Practical Challenges in Real Deployments

For instance, field experiments conducted by NOAA (2022) and NPOL (India) have highlighted frequent SONAR detection failures resulting from ambient shipping noise and thermocline-induced signal distortions. Such findings emphasize the pressing need for adaptive, learning-based models that can perform real-time environmental compensation and maintain robust detection accuracy under dynamic acoustic conditions.

RELATED WORKS IN UTR

UTR has garnered significant research interest due to its vital applications in maritime surveillance, environmental monitoring, and underwater robotics. The advent of DL and RL techniques has revolutionized the approaches to UTR, providing enhanced accuracy and robustness compared to traditional methods. One notable advancement is the MFF-MDNN method proposed for underwater acoustic target recognition (Miao et al., 2021). This approach leverages multi-dimensional fusion features, combining Gammatone Frequency Cepstral Coefficient (GFCC) and Modified Empirical Mode Decomposition (MEMD) with a Gaussian Mixture Model (GMM) to enhance the deep neural network (DNN) structure (Wang, Liu, Zhang, & Xue, 2019). This method achieved a recognition accuracy of 94.3%, significantly outperforming previous techniques and demonstrating strong adaptability to diverse underwater acoustic environments.

Further innovation in UTR is demonstrated by the ADCNN model (Yang, Li, Shen, & Xu, 2019), which is inspired by auditory perception mechanisms. This model introduces deep filter sub-networks, fusion layers, and decision layers to efficiently decompose, model, and classify ship-radiated noise signals as illustrated in Table 1. The ADCNN method achieved an impressive 81.96% classification accuracy in experiments, highlighting its efficacy in UTR tasks (Yang, Li, Shen, & Xu, 2019). In addition to these methods, the integration of Convolutional Neural Networks (CNN) (Hu et al., 2018) and Extreme Learning Machine (ELM) (Nsalo Kong et al., 2024) has shown promise in underwater target classification and recognition. This hybrid approach utilizes deep CNNs for feature extraction from underwater sound signals, followed by ELM for classification. This combination has been proven to improve recognition rates significantly, achieving a 93.04% recognition rate in experiments, thus outperforming traditional classification methods.

Table 1. Summary of underwater object detection technique

Author's	Datasets	Method used	Techniques	Issues	Results
(Alkhonaini & S, 2024)	droneRF and CardRF datasets	HRL-based UAV detection	REINFORCE algorithm, Entropy regularisation	Lack of comparison with traditional methods; Limited detection exploration	Achieves 99.7% detection accuracy; Improved cumulative return and reduced loss
(Walia & K, 2024)	UIDEF and TrashCan for trash detection	Review of DL frameworks	Fast R-CNN, YOLOv8n, YOLOv8x, YOLOv5s	Lack of benchmarks; Challenges in maritime environments for Mask R-CNN	YOLOv8-nano and YOLOv8-XLarge achieve real-time localization; High F1 scores and mean-average precision
(Steiniger, Kraus, & Meisen, 2022)	SSS and SAS data for ATR tasks	Review of DL in sonar imagery	CNNs, FCN, YOLOv1, ResNet-50, VGG-16, AlexNet	Lack of public benchmark dataset; Absence of investigation on recent detectors	Identifies research gaps and state-of-the-art methods; Advances in feature extraction and classification
(Doan, Huynh-The, & Kim, 2022)	UA signals dataset (70% training, 30% testing)	Dense CNN for UA signal classification	CNN with dense	Lack of comparison with traditional sonar systems; Limited exploration of real-time applications	UATC-DenseNet outperforms existing models with high accuracy; Larger kernel size enhances classification
(Luo & Zhang, 2021)	ShipsEar database	UATR method based on ResNet	MWSA, cDCGAN for data augmentation	Lack of real-time application; Limited window lengths exploration	High classification accuracy; Effective feature extraction and data augmentation
(Nayak & Ravindran, 2020)	MIT-Adobe FiveK dataset	ObjectRL for image preprocessing	Proximal Policy Optimization (PPO), SSD, YOLO-v3	Lack of user preferences focus; Absence of region exploration	ObjectRL improves detection through digital transformations; Underperforms grid-search in some cases
(Yang, Li, Shen, & Xu, 2019)	Ship-radiated noise signals (Cargo, Passenger ship, Tanker, Ocean)	ADCNN model for UATR	Deep filter sub-networks, fusion layers, and decision layer	Lack of comparison with non-DL methods; Limited hyperparameter exploration	ADCNN achieves 81.96% classification accuracy; Enhances UATR classification performance

continued on following page

Table 1. Continued

Author's	Datasets	Method used	Techniques	Issues	Results
(Wang, Liu, Zhang, & Xue, 2019)	Underwater acoustic signals (20 hours, divided into six categories)	MFF-MDNN for UTR	GFCC, MEMD, GMM for DNN modification	Single feature limitations; GMM's shallow recognition model; Redundant features in DNN	MFF-MDNN achieves 94.3% accuracy; Outperforms other methods
(Khishe & Mohammadi, 2019)	Sonar dataset (70% training, 30% testing)	SSA for training MLP networks	Salp swarm algorithm (SSA)	Limited dataset characteristics exploration	MLP-SSA outperforms other classifiers; Best convergence rates and avoids local minima

The Dense CNN (Doan, Huynh-The, & Kim, 2022) model also presents a significant contribution to UTR. This model employs a dense architecture specifically designed for classifying underwater acoustic signals. Evaluations under various SNR have demonstrated the superior performance of the UATC-DenseNet model, which not only outperforms existing models but also enhances classification accuracy through the use of larger kernel sizes. A comprehensive review (Luo et al., 2021) of DL applications in sonar imagery for UTR tasks reveals that CNNs, Gabor CNNs, Fully Convolutional Networks (FCN), and YOLO-based architectures have been instrumental in feature extraction and classification tasks. This review (Steiniger, Kraus, & Meisen, 2022) identifies significant research gaps and underscores the advancements in these methods, emphasizing the potential of DL in addressing the complexities of underwater environments. Lastly, the use of RL (Alkhonaini & S, 2024), particularly through algorithms has been explored to enhance object detection and UTR performance. The ObjectRL algorithm, which optimizes pre-processing techniques to maximize object detection performance, exemplifies the integration of deep RL in digitally transforming images for better detection outcomes. Despite its potential, ObjectRL's performance is sometimes hindered by the inability to recover from full-scale distortions (Nayak & Ravindran, 2020).

Although these models achieve high accuracy in controlled datasets, most lack generalization to dynamic underwater conditions, highlighting the need for adaptive reinforcement frameworks explored in this chapter.

Over recent years, RL has emerged as a powerful tool for improving the accuracy and efficiency of detecting and classifying underwater objects, as shown in Figure 1.

Figure 5. Year-wise advancements in DL and RL for underwater object detection

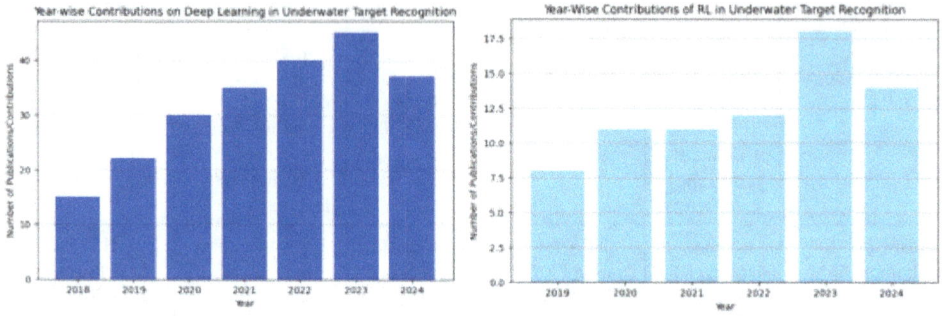

The integration of DL and RL techniques has significantly advanced the field of UTR. These methods have demonstrated superior accuracy, adaptability, and performance, marking a substantial improvement over traditional UTR approaches. The continuous development and refinement of these techniques hold promise for further enhancing UTR capabilities in various applications. The conceptual framework illustrates how environmental input is processed through RL-based adaptive models to achieve improved target recognition accuracy. This study bridges these gaps by integrating RL for adaptive decision-making, providing a foundation for future UTR research and defence applications.

BASICS OF REINFORCEMENT LEARNING

In this section, we explore the formulation of RL problems, where an agent makes decisions in an environment to achieve specific goals as indicated by reward functions as illustrated in Figure 7. Key characteristics of RL include: managing sequential decision-making, operating without direct supervision performing with feedback provided only in the form of scalar rewards, and experiencing significantly delayed feedback.

Initially, the agent perceives the current state S_t of the environment, which includes all relevant information about the underwater surroundings and potential targets. Based on this state, the agent takes an action A_t, which could involve moving a certain way, adjusting its sensors, or employing specific recognition algorithms (Wang et al., 2024).

Figure 6. Basic Reinforcement Learning Mechanics (Sutton & Barto, 2018)

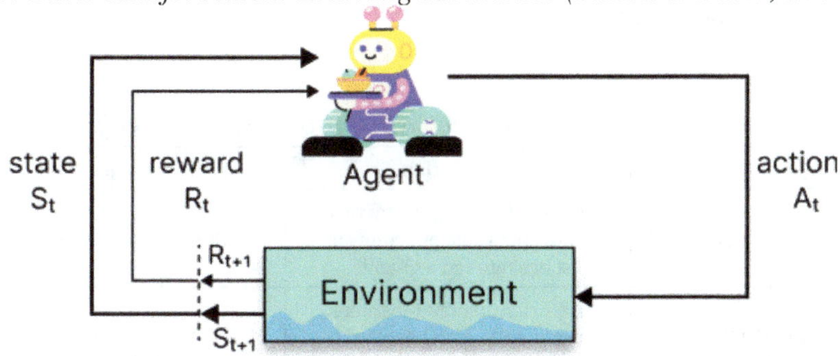

Once the action is executed, it impacts the environment, resulting in a new state S_{t+1}. The environment provides feedback to the agent in the form of a reward R_t, indicating the success or failure of the action in terms of target recognition. For instance, a successful identification might yield a positive reward, whereas an incorrect identification or a miss might result in a negative reward or no reward. This feedback loop continues iteratively, enabling the agent to learn optimal strategies for target recognition. Over time, through trial and error, the agent refines its actions to maximize cumulative rewards, improving its ability to accurately and efficiently recognize underwater targets. The iterative process is visually represented in the Figure 7, where the agent continually interacts with the environment, updates its state based on received rewards, and adjusts its actions to enhance performance. This cycle embodies the core mechanism of RL, facilitating adaptive and intelligent decision-making for UTR tasks.

Table 4 summarizes various RL approaches and their specific applications to underwater object detection tasks. This table provides an overview of different RL methodologies employed in the field, highlighting their effectiveness and adaptation to the unique challenges posed by underwater environments. By categorizing these approaches and their applications, Table 4 illustrates the diverse strategies used to enhance the accuracy and efficiency of underwater object detection through RL. The insights presented in this table underscore the evolving nature of RL techniques and their growing relevance in addressing complex underwater detection problems. Deep RL enhances traditional RL by incorporating DL techniques to improve an agent decision-making in complex underwater environments. By utilizing deep neural networks, the agent can process high-dimensional sonar data, identifying intricate patterns that signal potential targets. This approach allows the agent to learn from both immediate and delayed rewards, refining its strategies over time to boost accuracy and efficiency in target recognition. Ultimately, Deep RL effectively addresses the unique challenges of underwater object detection, enabling the agent to adapt to dynamic conditions.

Table 4. Summary of various RL and Deep RL approaches and specific applications

Approach	Description	Applications
Q-Learning (Deraj et al., 2023)	A model-free algorithm that learns the value of actions in states through a Q-table.	Path Following Control of a Ship
Deep Q-Network (DQN) (Wang, Zhou, & Tang, 2023)	An extension of Q-learning using deep neural networks to approximate Q-values for continuous state spaces.	UAV Autonomous Navigation and Collision Avoidance.
Policy Gradient Methods (Geng & Hui, 2024)	Directly optimizes the policy by updating the parameters of a policy network.	Power allocation in complex underwater where the action space is continuous.
Proximal Policy Optimization (PPO) (Camponogara, & Farinelli, 2024)	An advanced policy gradient method that uses clipped objective functions to stabilize training.	Aquatic navigation in non-stationary and unpredictable environments
Actor-Critic Methods (Hadi, Khosravi, & Sarhadi, 2023)	Combines policy gradient and value function approaches to optimize both policy and value functions.	End-to-End Motion Planning and Control of Autonomous Underwater Vehicles (AUVs) for Formation and Obstacle Avoidance
Deep Deterministic Policy Gradient (DDPG) (Zhao et al., 2023)	A policy gradient method for continuous action spaces using DL.	Path Planning and Obstacle Avoidance in Complex Environments
Twin Delayed Deep Deterministic Policy Gradient (TD3) (Castelli et al., 2016)	An enhancement of DDPG that reduces function approximation errors and overestimation bias.	UAV navigation in environments with moving obstacles.
Soft Actor-Critic (SAC) (Weng et al., 2024)	A method that incorporates entropy maximization to improve exploration and stability.	Optical Link Alignment for AUVs

WORKFLOW OF UTR USING RL

The Data Collection phase is a vital and foundational aspect of the entire process. Its primary objective is to gather relevant data that will be used for the purpose of training the model. This involves a series of critical steps, starting with the identification of reliable and diverse data sources. The quality and variety of the data will have a significant impact on the model's ability to generalize and perform accurately in real-world scenarios. Once the sources are identified, the next step is data acquisition, which may involve various methods such as collecting data from sensors, databases, or manual observations as shown in Figure 8. Acquiring a substantial amount of high-quality data is crucial, as it forms the backbone of the model's learning process. After acquisition, the data must be carefully labelled (Xue et al., 2022). Data labeling is the process of annotating the data with the correct answers, which is essential for supervised learning tasks. In the context of UTR, this might involve labeling different underwater objects, such as marine life, submerged structures, or other entities, to provide the model with clear and precise examples to learn from.

Figure 7. Comprehensive Workflow of Underwater Target Recognition Using RL

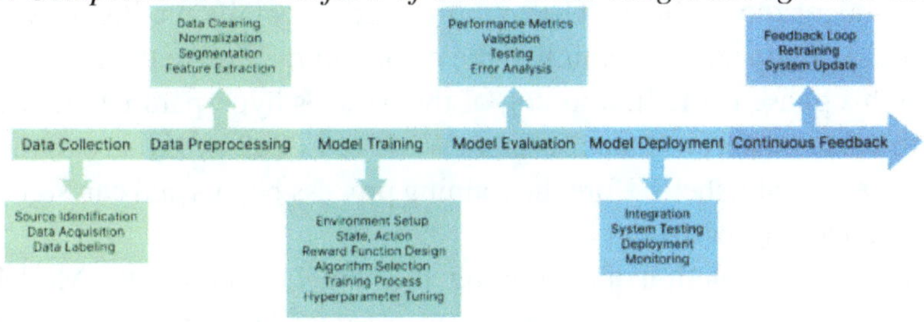

Following the data collection phase, the subsequent critical process is Data Preprocessing. Raw data, particularly in intricate environments such as underwater scenarios, often contains noise, inconsistencies, and irrelevant information that can impede the model's learning progress. Data preprocessing overcomes these challenges through a series of steps designed to sanitize and prepare the data for training. Data cleaning is a crucial step where erroneous or corrupt data points are removed or corrected, guaranteeing the dataset's accuracy and dependability (Xu et al., 2024). Normalization is another essential step, in which data is scaled to a standard range, typically between 0 and 1, to ensure that each feature contributes equally to the model's learning process. Segmentation is particularly important in underwater applications, where images or sensor readings need to be divided into meaningful segments to isolate targets from the background. Feature extraction follows, where significant attributes or characteristics are identified and extracted from the data. These features are the inputs that the model will learn from, so careful extraction is vital to ensure that the most informative aspects of the data are utilized (Bach et al., 2021).

Once preprocessing of the data has been completed, the subsequent phase of Model Training commences. This phase is the site of actual learning, and it encompasses the tasks of establishing the environment, defining the states and actions, devising reward functions, selecting appropriate algorithms, executing the training process, and fine-tuning the hyperparameters for optimal performance. The initial step in this phase involves the creation of a controlled environment where the model can operate. This may involve constructing simulated underwater environments that replicate real-world conditions. Defining states and actions is a critical element of RL, whereby the model learns to take actions based on its current state to maximize the reward. The state signifies the model's present situation, such as the position and attributes of an underwater target, while actions represent the potential moves the model can undertake. Designing the reward function is another indispensable step, as it evaluates the model's actions and must be carefully crafted to encourage the model to make correct identifications and to discourage incorrect ones. The next step is the selection of the most appropriate RL algorithm based on the specific requirements and constraints of the problem. The training process entails the iterative updating of the model's parameters to minimize the error and maximize the reward. The final step in this phase is the fine-tuning of the model's hyperparameters, which are adjusted to enhance performance further (Walia & L, 2024). Hyperparameters are settings that are established before the training process begins and can significantly impact the model's effectiveness.

Following the completion of its training, the model undergoes the Model Evaluation phase, which is designed to assess its accuracy and reliability (Pushpa Mala et al., 2024). Evaluation entails utilizing performance metrics to quantify the model's performance on unseen data, with common metrics such as accuracy, precision, recall, and F1 score providing different insights into its performance. Validation techniques are employed to ensure that the model can generalize well to new data and is not prone to overfitting. Testing then follows, where the model is evaluated on a separate test set that was not utilized during training or validation. This provides an unbiased estimate of the model's performance in real-world scenarios. Error analysis is a crucial component of evaluation, where the model's mistakes are analysed to understand where and why it fails. This can offer valuable insights into areas where the model needs improvement and guide further development efforts. Once the model has proven to be effective and reliable, it proceeds to the Model Deployment phase (Tian et al., 2021). Deployment involves integrating the model into the target system where it will be utilized. This could involve embedding the model into underwater drones, autonomous vehicles, or other systems designed to operate in underwater environments. System testing is an essential aspect of deployment, where the integrated system is thoroughly tested to guarantee that it functions correctly and that the model performs as anticipated in the operational environment. Monitoring is another critical element, where the system is continuously monitored to detect any issues or performance degradation. Deployment also entails setting up mechanisms for updating the model as new data becomes available or as the environment changes.

The final phase is Continuous Feedback, which is essential for maintaining and improving the model over time. This involves establishing a feedback loop where the model's performance is regularly assessed, and new data is collected to retrain and update the model. This is particularly important in dynamic environments such as underwater, where conditions can change rapidly, and new types of targets may need to be recognized (Sutton & Barto, 2018). Retraining the model with new data ensures that it remains effective and adapts to new challenges. System updates are also part of this phase, where both the model and the overall system may need adjustments to incorporate new features or improvements based on the feedback received (Alkhonaini & S, 2024). In summary, this structured approach ensures a systematic and thorough development process, leading to robust and reliable RL models for UTR. By meticulously following each phase data collection, data pre-processing, model training, model evaluation, model deployment, and continuous feedback developers can create models that are not only accurate and effective but also adaptable to changing conditions and capable of continuous improvement. This holistic workflow is essential for tackling the unique challenges posed by underwater environments and achieving high performance in UTR tasks. The evaluation scale was developed based on key performance metrics such as accuracy, F1 score, and SNR, derived from existing literature (Miao et al., 2021 & Xu et al., 2024). These indicators formed the basis for comparative analysis across RL.

APPLICATIONS OF RL IN UNDERWATER TARGET RECOGNITION

UTR is pivotal for various applications including defence, environmental monitoring, and resource management. Traditional methods often struggle with the complexities of underwater environments, such as variable acoustic properties and limited visibility. RL an advanced subset of ML, has shown promise in addressing these challenges. This section provides an in-depth exploration of how RL enhances UTR across several key applications.

Sonar-Based Detection and Classification

Sonar systems are essential for detecting and classifying underwater targets. RL can significantly enhance the performance of sonar-based detection in the following ways:

Adaptive Thresholding

Sonar systems rely on threshold settings to distinguish between signals from actual targets and background noise. Setting these thresholds optimally is critical for accurate target detection. RL algorithms can dynamically adjust these thresholds based on ongoing environmental feedback and historical data. By continuously learning from detection outcomes, RL models can refine threshold settings to balance sensitivity and specificity, reducing false positives and negatives. This adaptability is crucial in fluctuating underwater environments where acoustic conditions can vary widely.

Feature Selection

Sonar data can be complex and high-dimensional, containing numerous features that may or may not be relevant for target classification. RL can automate the process of feature selection, identifying the most significant attributes of sonar signals for classification purposes. By learning which features contribute most to accurate classification, RL models can reduce the dimensionality of the data, which simplifies the classification task and enhances overall system performance. This process helps in focusing computational resources on the most pertinent features, improving efficiency and accuracy.

Classification Models

RL-based models can be trained to classify underwater targets based on their acoustic signatures. Traditional classification methods might use fixed models or heuristics, but RL allows for the development of adaptive classification systems. RL agents can learn from a variety of target signatures and environmental conditions to develop robust classification strategies. Over time, these models improve their ability to distinguish between different types of underwater objects, such as submarines, fish, or underwater debris, by adapting to new data and evolving target characteristics.

Autonomous Underwater Vehicles (AUVs)

AUV play a critical role in underwater exploration, research, and surveillance. RL offers several enhancements to AUV operations:

Navigation and Path Planning

Navigating underwater environments presents challenges due to obstacles, variable currents, and complex terrain. RL algorithms can optimize navigation strategies for AUVs by learning from past experiences and real-time environmental feedback. RL can enable AUVs to plan and adjust their paths dynamically, avoiding obstacles and reaching target locations more efficiently. This adaptive navigation capability is vital for AUVs performing tasks in cluttered or unpredictable environments.

Target Following

Tracking underwater targets requires continuous adjustments in response to dynamic conditions. RL can be utilized to develop sophisticated strategies for following and monitoring targets. By learning from interactions with moving targets and varying environmental factors, RL models can devise optimal tracking strategies. This capability allows AUVs to maintain focus on moving targets, such as marine animals or underwater vehicles, even as conditions change.

Decision Making

RL enhances the decision-making capabilities of AUVs by allowing them to adapt their behaviours based on real-time data. Traditional systems might rely on predefined rules or scripts, but RL enables AUVs to make decisions in a more flexible and intelligent manner. This adaptability is crucial for handling unforeseen circumstances or adjusting mission strategies based on new information, such as changes in target behaviour or environmental conditions.

Marine Biological Research

Marine biology benefits from improved methods for understanding and monitoring aquatic life. RL can contribute in the following areas:

Species Classification

Accurate classification of marine species is essential for biodiversity studies and conservation efforts. RL models can classify species based on sonar or visual data, leveraging learned patterns and features. By training on diverse datasets, RL can improve classification accuracy and handle the variability in marine species appearances. This capability helps in monitoring species distribution and behaviour, which is crucial for ecological research.

Behaviour Analysis

Understanding the behaviour of marine animals can provide insights into their habits and interactions within ecosystems. RL can analyse patterns in animal behaviour and predict future actions based on historical data. This predictive capability aids in studying migration patterns, feeding behaviours, and social interactions among marine species, supporting conservation and management efforts.

Naval Defence and Security

In naval defence, UTR is crucial for identifying and managing potential threats. RL applications in this domain include:

Threat Detection

RL can improve threat detection systems by adapting to various acoustic and environmental conditions. Traditional systems might struggle with distinguishing between threats and benign objects, especially in noisy or complex environments. RL models can continuously learn and adapt their detection algorithms based on new data, enhancing the accuracy of threat identification.

Countermeasure Strategies

Developing effective countermeasure strategies in response to identified threats is essential for naval defence. RL-based systems can simulate various scenarios and learn optimal countermeasures based on past interactions and evolving threat profiles. This capability allows for the development of adaptive strategies that can respond to diverse and sophisticated threats.

Surveillance Systems

Surveillance systems are vital for monitoring underwater areas and detecting unusual activities. RL can enhance surveillance performance by optimizing data analysis and target tracking. RL models can learn to focus on suspicious activities and adjust tracking strategies based on real-time information, improving the overall effectiveness of surveillance operations.

Results demonstrate that RL-based frameworks can dynamically adapt to environmental variations, a capability not achievable with static DL models. This adaptive behaviour underpins the model's robustness in real-world maritime surveillance.

CHALLENGES IN SONAR SIGNAL PROCESSING AND TARGET RECOGNITION SYSTEMS

The challenges associated with sonar signal and ATR systems for UTR, particularly when utilizing RL, are multifaceted and significant. One major issue is the constraints imposed by the inherent hardware limitations, which restrict the frequency bandwidth available for underwater communications, making efficient data transmission challenging. Another critical challenge is the dynamic parameter reconfiguration, which is complicated due to the rapidly varying nature of underwater channels that makes dynamic power control difficult. Additionally, the busy terminal problem in acoustic modems poses obstacles to effective spectrum sharing schemes (Luo et al., 2014).

The limited availability of large datasets also hampers the development and training of robust algorithms. Although synthetic sonar images and PCA-based classifiers offer some solutions, the scarcity of high-quality real sonar images remains a significant barrier. This is compounded by the difficulty can sad by the low quality of collecting sonar images, which negatively impacts the reliability and applicability of sonar-based algorithms (Pailhas et al., 2010). Current side-scan technology also faces limitations in coverage and resolution, with identification performance reaching its threshold at 10-20 cm resolution.

The use of Generative Adversarial Networks (GANs) for realistic sonar image simulation shows promise but is still limited by the quality of the input data. Furthermore, there is a notable scarcity of sonar data available for training DL models, which affects the accuracy and effectiveness of ATR systems. Comparisons between models highlight uncertainties, particularly in the localization accuracy of smaller CNN compared to more robust models like YOLOv3 (Sung et al., 2019). These combined challenges underscore the complexity of developing reliable UTR systems using RL.

Given these challenges, there is a critical necessity for Deep RL analysing in sonar signals and ATR systems for UTR. Deep RL can address the limitations of traditional algorithms by utilizing large neural networks to extract salient features from sparse and frequently noisy sonar data. This capability is particularly crucial in dynamic underwater environments, where the variability of conditions can significantly affect performance. Through the implementation of Deep RL, an agent can acquire the ability to adapt its strategies in real time. Moreover, Deep RL algorithms can enhance their performance through continuous learning, even with limited datasets, by effectively generalizing from existing examples and synthesizing new scenarios. This adaptability is essential for overcoming the inherent challenges of sonar signal processing and target recognition, ultimately leading to more robust and efficient UTR systems.

FUTURE RESEARCH DIRECTIONS

In future research on UTR, the integration of Deep RL presents a promising direction. Deep RL combines the perceptual capabilities of DL with the decision-making framework of RL, enabling systems to learn optimal actions in complex and dynamic environments. By leveraging Deep RL, underwater autonomous vehicles can enhance their target recognition capabilities through continuous learning and adaptation. This approach facilitates handling diverse and uncertain underwater conditions, thereby improving the robustness and accuracy of target identification. Furthermore, Deep RL enables real-time decision-making, minimizing the need for human intervention and increasing operational efficiency. The ongoing advancements in computational power and the development of more sophisticated Deep RL algorithms are expected to drive significant improvements in UTR systems, rendering them more reliable and effective across various applications, including environmental monitoring, defence, and exploration.

In addition to Deep RL, other RL techniques, such as multi-agent reinforcement learning (MARL), could be investigated to enhance collaboration between multiple underwater autonomous systems. MARL enables diverse agents to cooperate, thereby improving the overall efficiency and coverage of underwater operations. Furthermore, Hierarchical RL can be utilized to decompose complex underwater tasks into simpler sub-tasks, potentially leading to accelerated learning and improved target recognition accuracy. Lastly, the integration of RL with transfer learning may facilitate the leveraging of knowledge from one underwater environment to another, potentially reducing the learning time for novel environments.

CONCLUSION

This chapter has discussed the significant advancements that RL brings to UTR, an important area in marine research, defence, and exploration. RL helps solve key challenges like signal loss, background noise, and changing underwater conditions, making decision-making and adaptability in UTR systems more effective. We have shown how optimized reward functions and advanced algorithms can improve the accuracy and reliability of these systems, overcoming traditional limitations. Furthermore, combining RL with multi-modal data and neural network models can further boost system performance. Looking to the future, Deep RL combines DL for recognizing patterns with RL for making decisions, offers great potential to handle the complexities of underwater environments. Continued research in RL and Deep RL will be crucial for improving UTR systems, making them more efficient and accurate. This work highlights the significant impact RL and Deep RL can have in advancing underwater acoustic sensing technologies.

REFERENCES

Ahmad, F., Ansari, M. Z., Anwar, R., Shahzad, B., & Ikram, A. (2024). Deep learning based classification of underwater acoustic signals. *Procedia Computer Science*, *235*, 1115–1124. DOI: 10.1016/j.procs.2024.04.106

AlKhonaini, A., Sheltami, T., Mahmoud, A., & Imam, M. (2024). UAV Detection Using Reinforcement Learning. *Sensors (Basel)*, *24*(6), 1870. DOI: 10.3390/s24061870 PMID: 38544131

Ashok, P., & Latha, B. (2023). Absorption of echo signal for underwater acoustic signal target system using hybrid of ensemble empirical mode with machine learning techniques. *Multimedia Tools and Applications*, *82*(30), 47291–47311. DOI: 10.1007/s11042-023-15543-2

Bach, N. H., Vu, L. H., & Nguyen, V. D. (2021). Classification of surface vehicle propeller cavitation noise using spectrogram processing in combination with convolution neural network. *Sensors (Basel)*, *21*(10), 3353. DOI: 10.3390/s21103353 PMID: 34065910

Cao, X., Zhang, X., Togneri, R., & Yu, Y. (2019). Underwater target classification at greater depths using deep neural network with joint multiple-domain feature. *IET Radar, Sonar & Navigation*, *13*(3), 484–491. DOI: 10.1049/iet-rsn.2018.5279

Castelli, T., Sharghi, A., Harper, D., Tremeau, A., & Shah, M. (2016). *Autonomous navigation for low-altitude UAVs in urban areas.* In arXiv preprint (arXiv:1602.08141).

Deraj, R., Kumar, R. S., Alam, M. S., & Somayajula, A. (2023). Deep reinforcement learning-based controller for ship navigation. *Ocean Engineering*, *273*, 113937. DOI: 10.1016/j.oceaneng.2023.113937

Doan, V.-S., Huynh-The, T., & Kim, D.-S. (2022). Underwater Acoustic Target Classification Based on Dense Convolutional Neural Network. *IEEE Geoscience and Remote Sensing Letters*, *19*, 1–5. DOI: 10.1109/LGRS.2020.3029584

Geng, X., & Hui, X. (2024). Power allocation based on multi-agent deep deterministic policy gradient for underwater acoustic communication networks. *Electronics (Basel)*, *13*(2), 295. DOI: 10.3390/electronics13020295

Hadi, B., Khosravi, A., & Sarhadi, P. (2023). *Adaptive formation motion planning and control of autonomous underwater vehicles using deep reinforcement learning.* In IEEE Journal of Oceanic Engineering.

Hu, G., Wang, K., Peng, Y., Qiu, M., Shi, J., & Liu, L. (2018). Deep Learning Methods for Underwater Target Feature Extraction and Recognition. *Computational Intelligence and Neuroscience*, *2018*, 1–10. DOI: 10.1155/2018/1214301 PMID: 29780407

Kamal, S., Chandran, C. S., & Supriya, M. H. (2021). Passive sonar automated target classifier for shallow waters using end-to-end learnable deep convolutional LSTMs. *Engineering Science and Technology, an International Journal*, *24*(4), 860–871. DOI: 10.1016/j.jestch.2021.01.014

Kaur, M., & Vijay, S. (2023). Deep learning with invariant feature-based species classification in underwater environments. *Multimedia Tools and Applications*, *83*(7), 19587–19608. DOI: 10.1007/s11042-023-15896-8

Khishe, M., & Mohammadi, H. (2019). Passive sonar target classification using multi-layer perceptron trained by salp swarm algorithm. *Ocean Engineering*, *181*, 98–108. DOI: 10.1016/j.oceaneng.2019.04.013

Korkmaz, B. N., Diamant, R., Danino, G., & Testolin, A. (2023). Automated detection of dolphin whistles with convolutional networks and transfer learning. *Frontiers in Artificial Intelligence*, *6*, 1099022. DOI: 10.3389/frai.2023.1099022 PMID: 36776422

Kumar, K., Bhaumik, S., & Arulampalam, S. (2022). Tracking an underwater object with unknown sensor noise covariance using orthogonal polynomial filters. *Sensors (Basel)*, *22*(13), 4970. DOI: 10.3390/s22134970 PMID: 35808465

Luo, X., Feng, Y., & Zhang, M. (2021). An underwater acoustic target recognition method based on combined feature with automatic coding and reconstruction. *IEEE Access : Practical Innovations, Open Solutions*, *9*, 63841–63854. DOI: 10.1109/ACCESS.2021.3075344

Luo, X., Zhang, M., Liu, T., Huang, M., & Xu, X. (2021). An Underwater Acoustic Target Recognition Method Based on Spectrograms with Different Resolutions. *Journal of Marine Science and Engineering*, *9*(11), 1246. DOI: 10.3390/jmse9111246

Luo, Y., Pu, L., Zuba, M., Peng, Z., & Cui, J.-H. (2014). Challenges and opportunities of underwater cognitive acoustic networks. *IEEE Transactions on Emerging Topics in Computing*, *2*(2), 198–211. DOI: 10.1109/TETC.2014.2310457

Miao, Y., Zakharov, Y. V., Sun, H., Li, J., & Wang, J. (2021). Underwater acoustic signal classification based on sparse time–frequency representation and deep learning. *IEEE Journal of Oceanic Engineering*, *46*(3), 952–962. DOI: 10.1109/JOE.2020.3039037

Nayak, S., & Ravindran, B. (2020). Reinforcement Learning for Improving Object Detection. arXiv:2008.08005.

Nsalo Kong, D. F., Shen, C., Tian, C., & Zhang, S. R. (2024). *Underwater acoustic monitoring: A comprehensive approach to enhance MFCC robustness and classification accuracy. Preprints.*

Pailhas, Y., Petillot, Y., & Capus, C. (2010). High-resolution sonars: What resolution do we need for target recognition? *EURASIP Journal on Advances in Signal Processing*, *2010*(1), 205095. DOI: 10.1155/2010/205095

Pushpa Mala, S., Prajwal Raju, P., Poojashree, B., Hebbar, R., Bedre, V., & Manasa, K. R. (2024). *Underwater fleck detection using convolutional neural network.* Journal of The Institution of Engineers (India): Series B, 105(2), 365–373.

Siddhartha, J. B., Jaya, T., & Rajendran, V. (2023). RDNN for classification and prediction of rock/mine in underwater acoustics. *Materials Today: Proceedings*, *80*, 3221–3228. DOI: 10.1016/j.matpr.2021.07.216

Steiniger, Y., Groen, J., Stoppe, J., Kraus, D., & Meisen, T. (2021). *A study on modern deep learning detection algorithms for automatic target recognition in sidescan sonar images.* In Proceedings of the 6th Underwater Acoustics Conference and Exhibition (Virtual Meeting, p. 070010). DOI: 10.1121/2.0001470

Steiniger, Y., Kraus, D., & Meisen, T. (2022). Survey on deep learning based computer vision for sonar imagery. *Engineering Applications of Artificial Intelligence*, *114*, 105157.

Sung, M., Kim, J., Kim, J., & Yu, S.-C. (2019). Realistic sonar image simulation using generative adversarial network. *IFAC-PapersOnLine*, *52*(21), 291–296. DOI: 10.1016/j.ifacol.2019.12.322

Tian, S., Chen, D., Wang, H., & Liu, J. (2021). Deep convolution stack for waveform in underwater acoustic target recognition. *Scientific Reports*, *11*(1), 9614. DOI: 10.1038/s41598-021-88799-z PMID: 33953232

Walia, J. S., & K, P. L. (2024). Deep Learning Innovations for Underwater Waste Detection: An In-Depth Analysis. arXiv:2405.18299.

Wang, W. A. N. G., Zhou, Z. H. U., Zhou, Z. H. O. U., & Tang, T. A. N. G. (2024). Deep-reinforcement-learning-based UAV autonomous navigation and collision avoidance in unknown environments. *Chinese Journal of Aeronautics*, *37*(3), 237–257. DOI: 10.1016/j.cja.2023.09.033

Wang, X., Liu, A., Zhang, Y., & Xue, F. (2019). Underwater Acoustic Target Recognition: A Combination of Multi-Dimensional Fusion Features and Modified Deep Neural Network. *Remote Sensing (Basel), 11*(16), 1888. DOI: 10.3390/rs11161888

Wang, Y., Xiao, J., Cheng, X., Wei, Q., & Tang, N. (2024). Underwater acoustic signal classification based on a spatial–temporal fusion neural network. *Frontiers in Marine Science, 11*, 1331717. DOI: 10.3389/fmars.2024.1331717

Weng, Y., Chun, S., Ohashi, M., Matsuda, T., Sekimori, Y., Pajarinen, J., Peters, J., & Maki, T. (2024). *Autonomous underwater vehicle link alignment control in unknown environments using reinforcement learning*. In Journal of Field Robotics. DOI: 10.1002/rob.22348

Xiao, X., Wang, W., Ren, Q., Gerstoft, P., & Ma, L. (2021). Underwater acoustic target recognition using attention-based deep neural network. *JASA Express Letters, 1*(10), 106001. DOI: 10.1121/10.0006299 PMID: 36154215

Xu, Q., Jiang, J., Xu, K., Dou, Y., Gao, C., Zhu, B., You, K., & Zhu, Q. (2024). Self-supervised learning for underwater acoustic signal classification with mixup. *IEEE Journal of Selected Topics in Applied Earth Observations and Remote Sensing, 17*, 3530–3542. DOI: 10.1109/JSTARS.2023.3325921

Xue, L., Zeng, X., & Jin, A. (2022). A novel deep-learning method with channel attention mechanism for underwater target recognition. *Sensors (Basel), 22*(15), 5492. DOI: 10.3390/s22155492 PMID: 35897996

Yang, H., Li, J., Shen, S., & Xu, G. (2019). A Deep Convolutional Neural Network Inspired by Auditory Perception for Underwater Acoustic Target Recognition. *Sensors (Basel), 19*(5), 1104. DOI: 10.3390/s19051104 PMID: 30836716

Yao, Q., Wang, Y., & Yang, Y. (2023). Underwater acoustic target recognition based on data augmentation and residual CNN. *Electronics (Basel), 12*(5), 1206. DOI: 10.3390/electronics12051206

Zhao, S., Wang, W., Li, J., Huang, S., & Liu, S. (2023). Autonomous navigation of the UAV through deep reinforcement learning with sensor perception enhancement. *Mathematical Problems in Engineering, 2023*(1), 3837615. DOI: 10.1155/2023/3837615

Zhufeng, L., Xiaofang, L., Na, W., & Qingyang, Z. (2022). Present status and challenges of underwater acoustic target recognition technology: A review. *Frontiers in Physics (Lausanne), 10*, 1044890. DOI: 10.3389/fphy.2022.1044890

ADDITIONAL READING

Domingos, L. C. F., Santos, P. E., Skelton, P. S. M., Brinkworth, R. S. A., & Sammut, K. (2022). A survey of underwater acoustic data classification methods using deep learning for shoreline surveillance. *Sensors (Basel), 22*(6), 2181. DOI: 10.3390/s22062181 PMID: 35336352

Er, M. J., Chen, J., Zhang, Y., & Gao, W. (2023). Research challenges, recent advances, and popular datasets in deep learning-based underwater marine object detection: A review. *Sensors (Basel), 23*(4), 1990. DOI: 10.3390/s23041990 PMID: 36850584

Hong, F., Liu, C., Guo, L., Chen, F., & Feng, H. (2021). Underwater acoustic target recognition with a residual network and the optimized feature extraction method. *Applied Sciences (Basel, Switzerland), 11*(4), 1442. DOI: 10.3390/app11041442

Jian, M., Liu, X., Luo, H., Lu, X., Yu, H., & Dong, J. (2021). Underwater image processing and analysis: A review. *Signal Processing Image Communication, 91*, 116088. DOI: 10.1016/j.image.2020.116088

Le, N., Rathour, V. S., Yamazaki, K., Luu, K., & Savvides, M. (2022). Deep reinforcement learning in computer vision: A comprehensive survey. *Artificial Intelligence Review, 55*(4), 2733–2819. DOI: 10.1007/s10462-021-10061-9

Sarkar, P., De, S., & Gurung, S. (2022). A survey on underwater object detection. In Bhattacharyya, S., Das, G., & De, S. (Eds.), *Intelligence Enabled Research* (Vol. 1029, pp. 91–104). Springer Singapore. DOI: 10.1007/978-981-19-0489-9_8

Srividhya, K., & Ramya, M. M. (2017). Accurate object recognition in underwater images using learning algorithms and texture features. *Multimedia Tools and Applications, 76*(24), 25679–25695. DOI: 10.1007/s11042-017-4459-6

Sutton, R. S., & Barto, A. G. (2018). *Reinforcement Learning: An Introduction* (2nd ed.). MIT Press.

Szepesvari, C. (2010). *Algorithms for Reinforcement Learning*. Morgan & Claypool Publishers. DOI: 10.1007/978-3-031-01551-9

Valente, J., António, J., Mora, C., & Jardim, S. (2023). Developments in image processing using deep learning and reinforcement learning. *Journal of Imaging, 9*(10), 207. DOI: 10.3390/jimaging9100207 PMID: 37888314

Chapter 9
Towards Secure Smart Contracts:
An AI-Enhanced Framework for Vulnerability Detection

Shankar Gugulothu
http://orcid.org/0009-0001-6001-5701
Department of Computer Science, Pondicherry University, India

M. Nandhini
http://orcid.org/0000-0001-5151-6216
Pondicherry University, India

ABSTRACT

Smart contracts, serving as self-executing programs on blockchain platforms, have emerged as a key innovation for enhancing data security. Despite advancements in both blockchain technology and smart contracts (SCs), Ethereum-based SCs remain vulnerable to security breaches. Exploitation of these vulnerabilities can result in substantial financial losses for both service providers and users. Consequently, the detection and mitigation of security vulnerabilities in smart contracts are critical to ensuring the security and reliability of blockchain platforms. Machine learning approaches are emerging as effective alternatives to traditional vulnerability detection methods, though many rely heavily on expert knowledge and primarily target familiar vulnerabilities. This chapter explores the creation of an AI-driven framework for detecting vulnerabilities in smart contracts, aimed at reducing risks and improving the reliability of blockchain systems. By incorporating advanced Machine Learning (ML) and Deep Learning (DL) techniques, the framework seeks to improve the accuracy and efficiency of vulnerability detection, addressing the shortcomings of traditional static and dynamic analysis methods. The proposed approach not only

DOI: 10.4018/979-8-3693-8327-8.ch009

strengthens the security of smart contracts but also contributes to the broader goal of building more resilient and reliable blockchain ecosystems. Through an in-depth analysis of methodologies and case studies, this chapter highlights the essential role of AI in advancing the secure development and deployment of smart contracts.

INTRODUCTION:

Smart contracts have emerged as a pivotal innovation in the development of blockchain technology, tracing their conceptual roots back to the late 1990s when Nick Szabo first introduced the idea. These digital contracts, self-executing by design, embed the terms of an agreement directly into code, offering a revolutionary approach to contractual governance in the modern era. With the advent of blockchain, smart contracts have gained renewed significance, forming the foundation of a wide range of decentralized applications (dApps) across various industries including finance, supply chain management, healthcare, e-voting, insurance, real estate and beyond(Farao et al., 2024; Neloy et al., 2023; Raj & Prakash, 2022; Rawashdeh, 2024; Ullah & Al-Turjman, 2023; Valencia-Payan et al., 2024).

Smart contracts are blockchain-based protocols accessible to anyone. They automatically execute when predefined conditions are met, eliminating the need for a trusted third party. Figure 1 illustrates an example of a smart contract. Typically developed in high-level programming languages such as Vyper (Marchuk et al., 2023) and Solidity (Dannen, 2017), these contracts also leverage the blockchain's tamper-resistant features, rendering them immutable once deployed. The immutable and open nature of smart contracts makes them vulnerable to attacks. These vulnerabilities pose a significant risk, making smart contracts a prime target for malicious hackers, as evidenced by numerous successful attacks. Moreover, even in the absence of an external threat, the risk of financial loss due to systemic failures remains a serious concern. A notable incident is the DAO event, where attackers exploited a reentrancy vulnerability in The DAO smart contract, resulting in the theft of 3.6 million Ether. This significant breach has intensified research focus on the security analysis of smart contracts. Lendf.Me is a decentralized finance (DeFi) application that leverages smart contracts to provide instant, decentralized lending services. On April 19, 2020, the platform experienced a significant security breach, resulting in the loss of $25 million in cryptocurrency.

Fig. 1. Smart Contract architecture

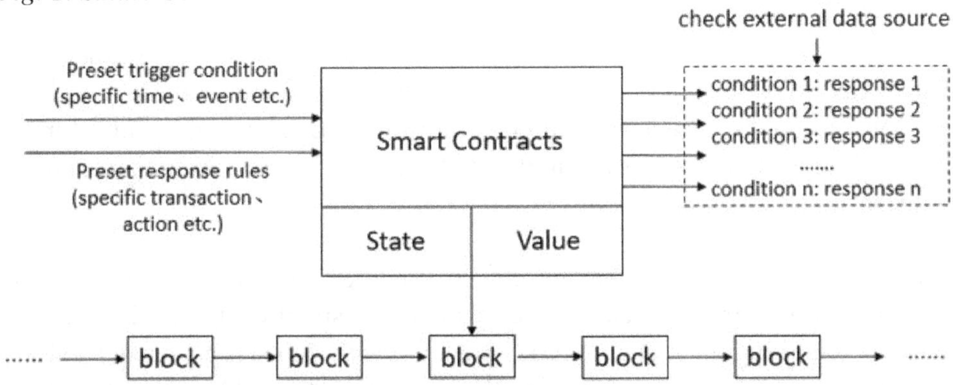

To mitigate the substantial losses caused by security vulnerabilities in smart contracts, several effective methods have been developed for vulnerability detection. These include formal verification, fuzz testing, symbolic execution, intermediate representation, machine learning and deep learning techniques. Common sources of smart contract vulnerabilities include insecure coding practices, flawed system architecture, improper implementation, insufficient security measures, and dependence on third-party libraries. Unlike traditional agreements, smart contracts are typically centered around the management of monetary assets. The immutable nature of blockchain technology means that once these contracts are deployed, any errors they contain cannot be corrected.

The primary causes of smart contract vulnerabilities can be attributed to several key factors:

1. **Transparency and Immutability of Source Code**: Smart contract source code is publicly accessible and immutable once deployed on the blockchain. This transparency, while promoting trust, also lowers the barriers for attackers, as they can easily analyze the code to identify and exploit vulnerabilities. The inability to apply patches to a deployed smart contract exacerbates this issue, making it easier for attackers to target known flaws within the blockchain ecosystem.
2. **Developer Oversight**: The creation of smart contracts typically involves high-level programming languages like Solidity. However, errors in the design patterns or coding practices can lead to significant vulnerabilities. Common issues include failure to account for potential flaws, such as integer overflows, uninitialized variables, or improper handling of arbitrary address writes. These errors often stem from developer oversight or a lack of rigorous testing, leaving the contract susceptible to exploitation.

3. **EVM Design-Level Vulnerabilities**: The Ethereum Virtual Machine (EVM) itself can be a source of vulnerabilities due to its bytecode structure and design specifications. One well-known issue at the EVM design level is the segment address attack, where attackers exploit weaknesses in how the EVM handles contract addresses. Such vulnerabilities are inherently tied to the architecture of the EVM, making them particularly challenging to mitigate through traditional means.

Various approaches have been developed to address and mitigate these vulnerabilities, ensuring greater security and resilience in smart contracts. The current approach to auditing smart contract code predominantly depends on manual reviews conducted by experts. However, this method is both costly and inefficient, making it challenging for auditors to comprehensively identify and extract vulnerability features within each contract. Existing research often simplifies the code into natural language or relies on the specialized knowledge of experts to identify code features. This simplification process, however, tends to be overly reductive, leading to potential loss of crucial information. Moreover, experts frequently rely on heuristic rule-based models that are often overly complex, lacking scalability, and not universally applicable, which in turn results in low accuracy and inefficiency in detecting vulnerabilities. Given the security challenges associated with smart contracts, developing effective techniques for extracting vulnerability features is essential (Ma et al., 2023)

Dynamic analysis techniques used for detecting vulnerabilities in smart contracts face significant challenges, including path explosion, difficulties in accurately modeling the execution environment, and scalability limitations. These issues often lead to incomplete analyses. Similarly, fuzz testing struggles with limited code coverage, inefficiency, and challenges in targeting specific vulnerabilities, which can result in both false positives and false negatives. Both methods are computationally intensive and may fail to identify critical vulnerabilities when used independently. Therefore, integrating these approaches with additional techniques is essential to achieve a more comprehensive security analysis.

Recently, the application of machine learning techniques to detect vulnerabilities in smart contracts has gained significant traction. These approaches have notably enhanced the efficiency of vulnerability detection. However, current research encounters several obstacles: (1) Machine learning models generally demand extensive labeled datasets for training, but a substantial portion of real-world data remains unlabeled. The process of manual labeling is both labor-intensive and time-consuming, posing a significant challenge. (2) Some research depends on pre-existing classification tools for labeling data, but this can lead to a high occurrence of false positives and false negatives, reducing the overall accuracy of the training models. (3) Additionally, in some studies, experts are tasked with defining particular defect patterns or setting explicit rules for detecting vulnerabilities. This approach can restrict the model's generalizability and effectiveness (Sun et al., 2023).

Current deep learning approaches that leverage sequence embedding often regard source code as a linear sequence, akin to natural language, and utilize conventional natural language processing techniques (e.g., RNN, BiLSTM, TextCNN, BERT) for vulnerability detection. However, these approaches overlook the intrinsic structural properties of source code, such as control flow graphs, data flow graphs, and abstract syntax trees, leading to suboptimal performance. In contrast, graph-based deep learning methods typically use models like Word2Vec and Doc2Vec to generate representations for individual nodes within the code. These models, however, suffer from out-of-vocabulary issues, which present significant challenges in token embedding. Additionally, many existing approaches tend to overlook the semantic information embedded within the individual statements of a node, further limiting their effectiveness in vulnerability detection(Tang et al., 2023).

This paper introduces an AI-based framework designed to improve the detection of vulnerabilities in smart contracts. The subsequent chapter section 2, provides a comprehensive background study on smart contracts, focusing on their inherent vulnerabilities and the associated financial impacts. Section 3 delves into various techniques for detecting vulnerabilities, including traditional methods, machine learning approaches, deep learning strategies, and graph learning techniques. Section 4 explores the challenges involved in effectively identifying and mitigating these vulnerabilities. Finally, Section 5 discusses potential future directions for advancing smart contract vulnerability detection methodologies, flagging the way for more robust and secure systems.

2. BACKGROUND

This section presents a background and overview of vulnerabilities in smart contracts and their associated financial losses. It begins by examining some common vulnerabilities in Solidity code and the root causes behind these issues. This is followed by a detailed account of notable attacks, outlining the financial damages they have caused.

A smart contract is a protocol that operates on the blockchain, accessible to anyone. It executes automatically when predefined conditions are met, eliminating the need for a trusted third party. Smart contract vulnerabilities refer to flaws or weaknesses in smart contracts' code that can lead to unintended behavior, exploitation, or security risks. Common types include logic errors, unsafe type inference, reentrancy, and improper handling of external calls. These vulnerabilities can result in financial loss or contract failure and highlight the importance of thorough testing and secure coding practices.

The Decentralized Application Security Project (DASP), launched by the private organization NCC Group in 2018, highlights ten categories of smart contract vulnerabilities. The DASP top 10 list highlights the most critical security vulnerabilities affecting smart contracts. These include: Integer Overflow and Underflow, Reentrancy Attacks, Access Control Vulnerabilities, Timestamp Dependence, Front-running Attacks, Logic Errors, Denial of Service (DoS) Attacks, Insecure Randomness, Unchecked External Calls, Gas Limit Vulnerabilities.

According to data present in slow mist, Blockchain hackers have collectively caused losses of approximately $33.47 billion across 1,684 hacking events. This significant figure highlights the vulnerabilities present in blockchain technologies and the need for improved security measures. Some of the notable attacks are listed down, among list reentrancy caused more damage to financial losses.

In July 2017, the popular Parity digital wallet experienced a major security breach, leading to the freezing of more than 280 million dollars (Palladino, 2017). In April 2022, Deus Finance experienced a significant security breach that resulted in the loss of approximately $13.4 million. The attackers exploited a zero-day reentrancy vulnerability, leveraging flash loan manipulations to execute the exploit effectively. List of all the hack with their vulnerabilities are listed in below table 1.

Table 1. Types of vulnerabilities and their financial losses

Year	Name of the event and Vulnerability type	Financial Loss	SWC and CWE
2016	DAO hack, reentrancy vulnerability	$3.6 million Ether	107 & 841
2017	Parity Multisig Bug, delegatecall	$270 million	104 & 252
2017	BatchOverFlow, integer overflow vulnerability	$3.5 millions	115 & 477
2020	Lend.me, reentrancy vulnerability	$25 million	SWC-107 &
2020	Cover Protocol, logic flaw	$5 million	SWC-132 & CWE-841
2021	bZx, reentrancy vulnerability	$ 8 millions	SWC-107 & CWE-290
2021	Compound, logic error	$68.8 millions	-
2021	THORChain1 &2, logic flaw	$7.6 millions and $ 8 millions	SWC-124 and CWE-703
2022	DeFi hacks, reentrancy vulnerability	$2.32 billion	107 & 841 ^3
2022	Fei Protocol, reentrancy vulnerability	$80 millions	107 & 841
2022	BasketDAOOrg, unauthorized access	$1.2 millions	114 & 362

- Means not applicable

Smart contract vulnerabilities pose a significant threat to the advancement of blockchain technology. Due to the inherent immutability of smart contracts, developers are unable to modify existing contracts to address detected vulnerabilities. As awareness surrounding smart contract security intensifies, the volume of scientific research dedicated to this field continues to grow.

2.1 Reentrancy Vulnerability

Reentrancy vulnerability is among the most critical issues in smart contracts, allowing attackers to drain funds by recursively invoking the target's withdrawal function. This flaw has led to substantial financial losses, notably in the DAO attack, where 3.6 million Ether (equivalent to $60 million) was stolen due to a reentrancy exploit. As a result, addressing and mitigating this vulnerability has become a focal point for researchers in the field. Sample code of showed in Fig. 2.

Fig. 2. Reentrancy vulnerability sample

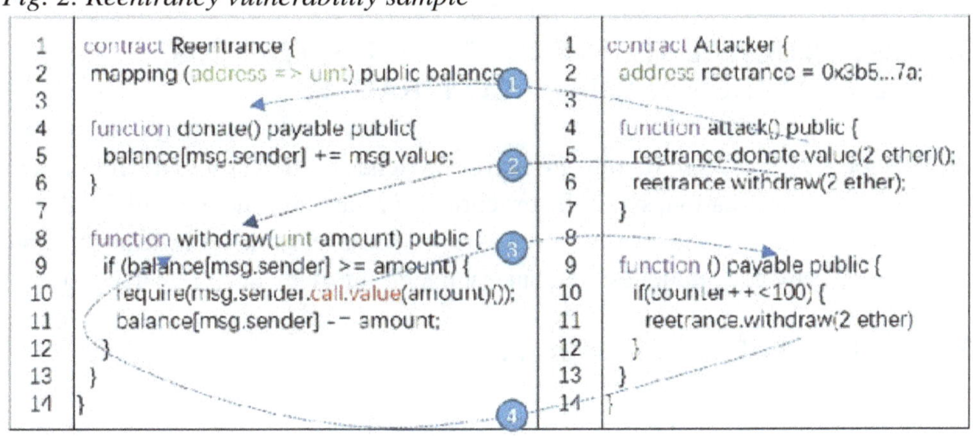

2.2 Timestamp vulnerability

Timestamp-based vulnerabilities arise when a smart contract depends on the time information provided by the blockchain network. This presents a potential issue, as malicious actors can manipulate the blockchain's time, which may result in incorrect contract execution. To mitigate this risk, developers should incorporate alternative time sources, such as oracles, or implement safeguards to prevent tampering with the time data supplied by the blockchain.

2.3 Integer underflow

Integer underflow occurs when the outcome of an arithmetic operation falls below the minimum value that can be represented, potentially resulting in unexpectedly large balances. Attackers can exploit these vulnerabilities to manipulate balances or quantities for personal gain. Preventing such issues involves using secure arithmetic libraries, appropriate data types, or implementing checks that prevent both underflow and overflow.

2.4 Logic flaws

A logic flaw vulnerability in a smart contract arises when the contract's code fails to perform as intended due to design errors or missteps in the sequence of operations. These vulnerabilities can have significant consequences, potentially allowing unauthorized access, mismanagement of funds, or improper execution of processes.

3. CONVENTIONAL TECHNIQUES FOR IDENTIFYING VULNERABILITIES IN SMART CONTRACTS

This section reviews four conventional approaches for detecting vulnerabilities, namely formal verification, symbolic execution, fuzz testing, and dynamic analysis. It will then examine the benefits of leveraging machine learning, deep learning, and graph neural network techniques to enhance vulnerability detection in smart contracts.

3.1 Formal verification methods

This approach uses mathematical reasoning and formal specifications to determine whether a smart contract adheres to defined security properties. Formal verification can be done in two ways those are theorem proving and model checking.

ZEUS, an automated formal verification tool, converts Solidity source code into Low-Level Virtual Machine (LLVM) intermediate language and employs eXtensible Access Control Markup Language (XACML) for writing verification rules. It then applies the SeaHorn verifier for formal validation.

Formal verification involves translating program code into a formal language and then validating it through mathematical proofs. Bhargavan et al. developed a formal verification framework to assess both the runtime safety and functional correctness of Ethereum contracts. Tools like ZEUS [18] utilize formal verification to automatically audit smart contracts. However, despite its precision, formal verification is grounded in complex mathematical logic, making it challenging to apply broadly for vulnerability detection(Wu et al., 2022). *Bhargavan et al., 2016* propose a formal verification framework using F* to analyze and verify Ethereum smart contracts. The framework ensures both runtime safety and functional correctness by translating Solidity code and EVM bytecode into F*, allowing for the detection of vulnerabilities such as reentrancy and gas limit issues through formal methods, Fig.3 shows formal verification core framework. Summary of all Formal verification methods are formulated in table 2.

Fig. 3 Formal verification framework

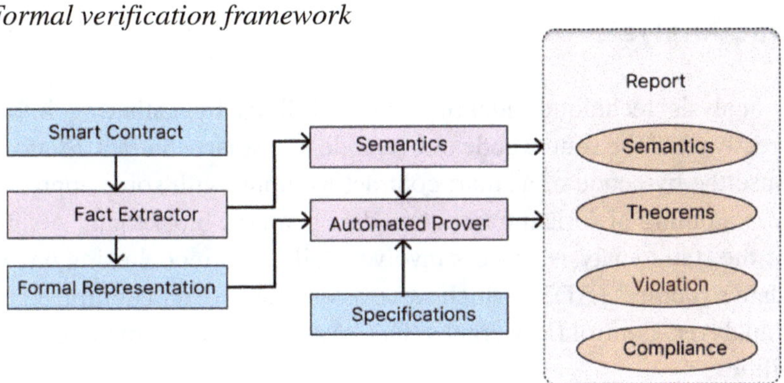

Table 2. Formal verification methods

Author, Year	Name of tool	Name of the model	Method used
Bhargavan et al., 2016	F*	Program verification	Functional programming language, existing verification languages
Bigi et al., 2016	PRISM	Model checking	Temporal logic specification and validation through game theory
Amani et al., 2018	Isabelle/HOL	Theorem proving	Mathematical logic, formal semantic(meta-theory) of low programming languages
Kalra et al., 2018	LLVM/ ZEUS	Program verification	Abstract interpretation and symbolic model checking, LLVM bitcode
Albert et al., 2019	SeaHorn, SAFEVM,	Program verification	Existing verification engines developed for C programs to verify low-level EVM code
Jiao et al., 2019	K framework	Program verification	Semantic-level(correct and secure high-level execution behavior) security properties

Despite strengths of current formal verification methods may not address all types of smart contract vulnerabilities, and some complex vulnerabilities can still be challenging to detect through formal verification alone(Zhen et al., 2024).

However, formal verification relies on complex mathematical logic, which limits its practical applicability for widespread vulnerability detection. Nonetheless, existing formal verification techniques may not address every type of vulnerability in smart contracts, and some complex vulnerabilities may still be challenging to detect using these methods.

3.2. Static Analysis

Static analysis techniques identify vulnerabilities by gathering information (facts) directly from the source code or bytecode of a smart contract. Static analysis methods use the bytecode of a smart contract as input, with some approaches additionally examining historical transaction data from the blockchain. A significant portion of the static analysis process involves building a model using one or more abstract data structures (ADS), which serve as an effective and optimized input for the static analyzer. Control flow graphs (CFGs) are frequently employed to identify vulnerabilities.

Vandal static analysis techniques process the bytecode of a smart contract, converting it into semantic logic relationships defined in the Soufflé language. This approach excels in performance, detecting vulnerabilities in just 4.15 seconds and surpassing current state-of-the-art methods. Slither converts the bytecode of a Solidity smart contract into an intermediate representation called SlithIR. This representation employs Static Single Assignment (SSA) form and a simplified instruction set to preserve semantic details that might otherwise be lost during the transition from Solidity to bytecode. EthIR converts EVM bytecode into a high-level control and data flow representation by reconstructing the high-level control and data flow from the low-level encoding in the control flow graphs (CFGs) generated by Oyente.

Traditional static detection methods like slither, vandal, primarily rely on static analysis theory and predefined matching rules. These approaches heavily depend on developer expertise, making them less effective at identifying unknown vulnerabilities. Consequently, their performance tends to be suboptimal in real-world applications. Summary of all static analysis tools are formulated in table 3.

Table 3. Static analysis tools

Author, Year	Name of tool	Solidity code/ EVM bytecode	Language & Academic/Non-Academic	Methodology and Time taken for detection	Vulnerability detects
2018	Slither	Source code	Python	Taints tracking approaches and data flow analysis	20 bugs like uninitialized variables, shadowing, re-entrancy, locked ether, suicidal contracts
2018	Vandal	EVM bytecode	Python(souffle) Academic	EVM bytecode to semantic logic(scrapper, disassembler, decompiler, and extractor), 4.15 seconds	Destroyable, Reentrancy, Unchecked Send, Unsecured Balance, Use of origin
2018	EthIR	EVM bytecode	Python, Academic	Rule-based intermediate representation(SACO)	-

Conventional static detection methods slither, vandal and ethIR are grounded in static analysis theory and rely heavily on predefined matching rules, which depend extensively on the expertise of developers. This reliance makes it challenging to identify unknown vulnerabilities, leading to suboptimal performance in real-world application environments (Tang et al., 2023).

3.3 Symbolic Execution

Symbolic execution techniques simulate the execution of a smart contract by substituting actual inputs with unique, traceable symbolic parameters, which allows to prove or disprove some presumptions about smart contracts. Symbolic execution is particularly useful for determining whether a specific code block can be executed (reachability), whether a particular execution path can be invoked, or if certain conditions can be met. Summary of all Symbolic execution with their methodology and vulnerability detected are formulated in table 4.

Table 4. Symbolic execution with their methodology and vulnerability detected

Year	Name of tool	Solidity code/ EVM bytecode	Language & Academic/Non-Academic	Methodology and Time taken for detection	Vulnerability detects
2016	Oyente	EVM bytecode	Python, Academic	Analyses program code path by a path, 350 seconds	Mishandled exceptions, Transaction-ordering dependence, Reentrancy Handling 19, 366 contracts,
2017	Mythril	EVM bytecode	Python, Non-academic (ConsenSys)	Symbolic execution, SMT solving and taint analysis	Detects 7 vulnerabilities
2018	Osiris	EVM bytecode	Python, Academic	CFG representing the individual path conditions and emphasizing the basic blocks, 35 seconds	signedness bugs, truncation bugs and arithmetic bugs,
2019	HONEYBADGER	EVM bytecode	Python, Academic	Loop continues until basic block of CFG complete, 142 seconds	Balance Disorder, Straw Man Contract, Inheritance Disorder, Type Deduction Overflow, Skip Empty String Literal, Uninitialised Struct, Hidden Transfer, Hidden State Update,

3.3. Dynamic Analysis

Dynamic analysis is a technique used to evaluate a software application during its execution. This method mirrors the approach attackers often take to identify potential vulnerabilities, as it operates without requiring access to the application's source code or internal architecture. By observing the program's behavior in real-time, dynamic analysis aims to uncover security flaws that might be exploited in practice.

Ivica Nikolić et al. (2018) present Maian, a tool that uses symbolic analysis and concrete validation to detect vulnerabilities like greedy, prodigal, and suicidal contracts across multiple invocations on Ethereum. Chao Liu et al. (2018) propose ReGuard, a fuzz testing tool designed to detect reentrancy bugs in Ethereum smart contracts by generating random transactions and analyzing runtime traces. Grossman et al. (2018) introduce ECFChecker, a framework for dynamically and statically checking if a smart contract is effectively callback-free (ECF), helping detect vulnerabilities like reentrancy and other callback-related issues. Summary of all Dynamic analysis methods are formulated in table 5.

Table 5. Dynamic analysis methods

Author, Year	Name of tool	Input	Language & Academic/ Non-Academic	Methodology and Time taken for detection	Bugs detected
Nikolić et al., 2018	Maian	Bytecode	Python, Academic	EVM semantic and traces, liveness violation, safety violation, *10 seconds per contract*	Greedy, Prodigal, Suicidal contracts
Liu et al., 2018	ReGuard	Smart contract	Python, Academic	Fuzz testing with runtime trace analysis	Reentrancy bugs
Grossman et al., 2018	ECFChecker	-	GO language, Academic	Dynamic and static ECF checking	Reentrancy, Callback-related issues

3.4 Fuzzy Testing

Fuzz testing, an automated software testing method, involves introducing invalid or unexpected inputs into a program to identify potential vulnerabilities. This process generates and inputs large volumes of random data, aiming to trigger unexpected behaviors or flaws in the software's functionality.

Jiang et al. (2018) propose *ContractFuzzer*, a tool that uses fuzzing techniques to detect vulnerabilities in Ethereum smart contracts. It has successfully identified key vulnerabilities such as reentrancy, exception handling issues, and timestamp dependencies by analyzing smart contracts' runtime behavior and ABI interfaces. Grieco et al. (2020) introduced *Echidna*, a smart contract fuzzer that focuses on user-defined properties and assertion checking, known for its ability to uncover vulnerabilities like gas usage inefficiencies in a fast and efficient manner. He et al. (2019) proposed *ILF*, a fuzzer that leverages imitation learning from symbolic execution to efficiently detect vulnerabilities in smart contracts, outperforming traditional fuzzers with its fast input generation. Summary of all Fuzzy testing methods are formulated in Table 6.

Table 6. Fuzzy testing methods

Author, Year	Name of tool	Input	Methodology	Type of vulnerability detected	Time
Jiang et al., 2018	Contrafuzzer	ABI specifications	Fuzzing, Test Oracles, Runtime Monitoring	Reentrancy, Gasless Send, Exception Disorder, Timestamp Dependency	-
Grieco et al., 2020	Echidna	User-defined properties, Contracts	Fuzzing, Property-based testing, Assertion checking	Gas Usage, Reentrancy, Assertion Failures	13.9 seconds
He et al., 2019	ILF	Smart contract ABI		Leaking Ether, Transaction-based issues	148 transactions per second

While traditional methods have demonstrated efficacy in vulnerability detection, they are accompanied by several limitations. These constraints include a high false positive rate, challenges in scalability, increased complexity, limited coverage of novel or evolving threats, and the necessity for expert knowledge. These drawbacks underscore the imperative for more advanced and adaptive approaches in smart contract security.

3.5. AI-Based Advanced Techniques for Smart Contract Vulnerability Detection

Traditional vulnerability detection methods have shown promise in identifying security issues within smart contracts; however, they present several challenges, such as being time-consuming, relying heavily on expert-crafted rules, and lacking scalability. To address these limitations, researchers have turned to AI-based models for smart contract vulnerability detection.

3.5.1. Classical Machine Learning models

Machine learning has proven highly effective for vulnerability detection, particularly in Ethereum smart contracts, where it enables real-time identification of various vulnerabilities. The selection of appropriate data representation and model architecture is crucial in optimizing detection accuracy and ensuring the model's ability to generalize across different contract types.

Xing et al. (2020) present a vulnerability detection model using a new feature extraction technique called slicing matrix, applied to smart contract bytecode. They achieved the best performance using a Random Forest model to detect vulnerabilities like short address, flows, and greedy contracts. Xu et al. (2021) introduce a machine learning model based on the Abstract Syntax Tree (AST) of smart contracts, utilizing shared child nodes for feature extraction. Their KNN-based model achieved high accuracy in detecting vulnerabilities like reentrancy and front-running. Ashizawa et al. (2021) propose Eth2Vec, a neural network-based static analysis tool for vulnerability detection in smart contracts, focusing on code similarity through embeddings. Eth2Vec showed strong performance in detecting reentrancy vulnerabilities. Yang et al. (2022) propose a vulnerability detection technique for smart contracts using Abstract Syntax Tree (AST) representation. They extract features based on sub-ASTs and use preorder traversal with word embeddings, achieving an accuracy of 98.7% in detecting vulnerabilities like reentrancy and unchecked calls. Eshghie et al. (2021) present Dynamit, a framework for dynamically detecting vulnerabilities, particularly reentrancy, by analyzing Ethereum transaction traces. Using machine learning with transaction metadata, their Random Forest model achieved 94% accuracy. Li et al.

(2024) introduce a machine learning-based method to detect unknown (zero-day) vulnerabilities in smart contracts using opcode sequences. They employ an n-gram model and vector weight penalty mechanism, with the SVM model achieving 96% accuracy and an F1-score of 95%. Momeni et al. (2019) propose a machine learning model for smart contract security analysis based on static code analysis using Abstract Syntax Tree (AST) and Control Flow Graph (CFG). Their model predicted vulnerabilities with an average accuracy of 95% and an F1-score of 79%. Summary of all traditional machine learning models are formulated in table 7. Fig 4, shows machine learning based smart contract vulnerability detection.

Figure 4. Machine learning based smart contract vulnerability detection

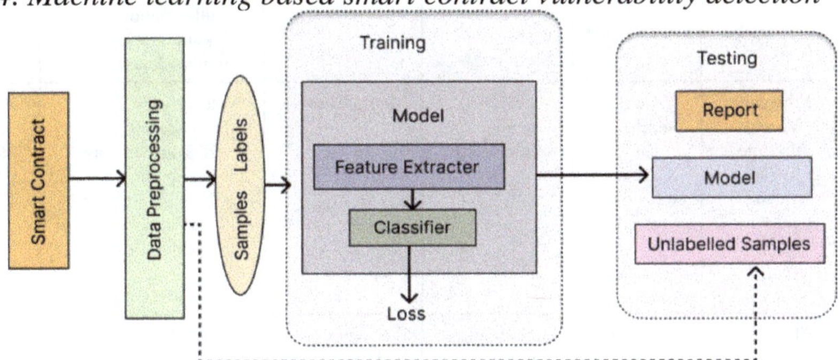

Table 7. Traditional machine learning methods

Author, Year	Input	Features	Dataset used & balanced	Model	Vulnerability type	Evaluation measures
Momeni et al., 2021	AST and CFG	common Solidity code structures (execution path, control flow graph)	13,745 from Etherscan 1 and unbalanced	*SVM*, DT, *NN*, RF	Integer underflow, Re-entrancy vulnerability	Accuracy-90% Precision-69% Recall- 79% F1-score-73%
Li et al., 2024	opcode sequences	vector weight penalty And n-gram model	12,246 smart contract from Ethereum mainnet and unbalanced dataset	KNN,SVM, LR, DT	function invocation, re-entrancy, unexpected, strict check for balance, missing the transfer event, incorrect check for authorisation, and timestamp and block number dependency	Accuracy-96%, Precision-91%, Recall -100%, F1-score- 95%
Ashizawa et al., 2021	Ethereum Virtual Machine (EVM) bytecode	Code similarity using Eth2Vec embeddings	95,152 contracts from Etherscan1	Neural Network	Reentrancy, Time Dependency, ERC-20 Transfer, Gas Consumption, Implicit Visibility, Integer Overflow, Integer Underflow	Precision-77.0% Recall - 50.7%, F1-score-57.5% ***1.2 seconds***
Xu et al., 2021	AST(Abstract Syntax tree)	Shared child nodes, Structural similarity	13241 smart contracts From Smartbugs, SolidiFi—benchmark, Smartbugs—wilds	KNN, SGD(Stochastic Gradient Descent)	Denial of service, Arithmetic, Access control, Re-entrancy, Bad randomness, Unchecked low level, Short address, Front running	KNN Recall-95.45% Accuracy-95.45% Precision-95.86% SGD Recall-68.18% Accuracy-95.45% Precision-70.83%
Yang et al., 2021	AST	Shared child nodes, Structural similarity	3000 smart contracts from EtherScan1	Random Forest	Unchecked Low-Level Calls, Reentrancy, Bad Randomness	Accuracy-98.7%, Recall-81.4%, Precision-97.2%, F1-score-88.5%
Xing et al., 2020	Bytecode	Opcode sequence, Slicing matrix	NNBOOF, CNNBOSM, *RFBOOF*	*Random Forest*, Neural Network	Has_short_address, is_greedy, has_flow	RF Recall-94%, Precision-96%, F_score-95%

3.5.2 Deep Learning Models

Expanding on the significant advancements in deep learning across different fields, researchers have started applying deep neural networks to identify weaknesses in smart contracts [,,*,*,]. These models take advantage of their capability to learn complex features and patterns from data automatically, removing the necessity for manual feature extraction. Deep learning models can identify possible vulnerabilities in smart contracts by analyzing large datasets, which helps to improve generalizability and effectiveness by decreasing the need for manual labeling and expert-defined rules.

Qian et al. (2020) propose a sequential model using BLSTM-ATT for reentrancy detection, achieving 88.47% accuracy on a large real-world dataset of smart contracts. *Xingxin Yu et al. (2021)* develop DeeSCVHunter, a deep learning framework with a Vulnerability Candidate Slice (VCS) concept to improve vulnerability detection performance, particularly for reentrancy and time dependency vulnerabilities. Mi et al. (2021) propose VSCL, a deep learning framework for smart contract vulnerability detection, using metric learning-based DNN on bytecode to detect vulnerabilities like reentrancy and timestamp dependency. Deng et al. (2023) propose a deep learning-based multimodal decision fusion framework for smart contract vulnerability detection, achieving 91.6% accuracy for arithmetic vulnerabilities and 90.9% accuracy for reentrancy vulnerabilities on a dataset of 10,000 Ethereum smart contracts. Zhang et al. (2023) propose a novel deep learning-based model, BiGAS, combining BiGRU, attention mechanism, and SVM for reentrancy vulnerability detection. Their model achieves 93.24% accuracy and an F1-score of 93.17% on a dataset of 2,000 Ethereum smart contracts. Gupta et al. (2022) propose a deep learning-based scheme for detecting malicious smart contracts. Their approach leverages LSTM, ANN, and GRU models, which are trained on a comprehensive Google BigQuery dataset comprising 7,000 smart contracts. The study highlights the effectiveness of these models in identifying logical and structural vulnerabilities in smart contracts. Summary of all deep learning models are formulated in table 8.

Table 8. Deep Learning methods

Author, year	Input type	Feature representation	Dataset	Model used	Performance	Type of vulnerability detected
Qian et al., 2020	Source Code	Contract Snippet Representation	42,000 contracts	BLSTM-ATT	Accuracy-88.47% Recall-88.48% Precision-88.50%F1_score-88.26%	Reentrancy
Yu et al., 2021	Bytecode	Vulnerability Candidate Slice (VCS)	40932 (Code and label pair)	Bi-LSTM	Accuracy-93.02% Recall- 83.46% Precision- 90.70% F1_score-86.87%	Reentrancy, Time Dependency
Mi et al., 2021	Bytecode	CFG, N-gram, TF-IDF	205,848 contracts	VSCL	VSCL A-0.89 P- 0.87 R- 0.68 F1-0.76	-
Luo et al., 2022	Bytecode	Bytecode Sequences	34822 contracts	*variant LSTM* general LSTM BiLSTM	A-90.22% P-91.34% R-90.08% F1-90.14%	-
Deng et al., 2023	Bytecode, Source Code, Control Flow Graph (CFG)	Multimodal Fusion	Ethereum Contracts (10,000 contracts)	*Deep Learning with Multimodal Decision Fusion*	A-91.6%	Arithmetic, Re-entrant, transaction-ordering dependence locked-ether
Zhang et al., 2023	Bytecode	Word Embeddings	9,250 (SmartBugs Dataset-Wild)	BiGRU + SVM	Accuracy: 93%, F1-score: 93%	Reentrancy
Liu et al., 2024	Opcode	Word Embeddings, Positional Encoding	-	Transformer + CNN	-	Reentrancy, Arithmetic, Timestamp
Jain et al., 2024	Opcode Sequences	Text-CNN and spatial attention, transformer	49,552 real-world smart contracts	Bi-GRU	A-96.1% P- 95.1% R-97.8% F1-96.5%	13 types vulnerabilities

Graph Neural Network

The application of Graph Neural Networks (GNNs) for smart contract vulnerability detection presents a highly effective approach, leveraging the structural characteristics of the code to accurately identify potential security vulnerabilities.

Smart contracts, typically written in languages like Solidity, possess a natural graph-like structure, where nodes represent entities such as functions or variables, and edges capture relationships like function calls and data dependencies. These interactions can be effectively modeled using Graph Neural Networks (GNNs), which are adept at learning from graph-structured data. GNNs provide a means to capture complex dependencies within the smart contract's code, allowing for more efficient detection of vulnerabilities. Unlike traditional neural networks, GNNs can exploit the structural relationships within the code to improve analysis accuracy. Thus, GNNs are a promising approach for smart contract vulnerability detection.

Zhuang et al. (2020) introduce a degree-free GCN and temporal message propagation (TMP) to normalize contract graphs and detect vulnerabilities in over 300,000 real-world smart contracts, achieving a significant improvement in F1-score and precision. Liu et al. (2021) propose a hybrid approach combining GNNs and expert-defined security patterns for detecting infinite loop, timestamp, reentrancy and vulnerabilities in Ethereum and VNTChain smart contracts, achieving an accuracy of over 89%. Han et al. (2022) propose a GNN-based vulnerability detection model using graph embedding from CFG and CNN, improving accuracy and F1-score for detecting vulnerabilities like reentrancy and integer overflow. Cao et al. (2022) develop EA-RGCN, a model that leverages residual GCN and edge attention to capture syntax and semantic features, improving precision in detecting vulnerabilities such as timestamp issues and reentrancy in the SmartBugs dataset. Nguyen et al. (2022) propose MANDO, a multi-level heterogeneous graph embedding model that detects vulnerabilities at both the line and contract levels, significantly improving performance on a mixed dataset of 493 contracts.

Cai et al. (2023) develop a Bidirectional Gated GNN model for smart contract vulnerability detection, achieving high precision and recall with a joint graph construction method that removes irrelevant information. Wang et al. (2023) apply a GCN model to detect vulnerabilities in educational blockchains, using CFG bytecode analysis to demonstrate superior performance with fewer GCN layers. Zhen et al. (2024) introduce DA-GNN, a dual-attention graph neural network model, to detect multiple vulnerabilities with precise control flow and opcode feature representation. Gupta et al. (2024) use GNN and degree-free GCN to detect smart contract vulnerabilities, focusing on infinite loop, timestamp dependency, and reentrancy with improved accuracy over traditional methods. Summary of all GCN models are formulated in table 9.

Table 9. GCN based methods for smart contract vulnerability detection

Author, year	Input type	Graph construction, node and edge features	GNN model	Performance	Type of vulnerability	Dataset size
Zhuang et al., 2020	Source Code	Control and Data Flow Graph(Function invocations, critical variables, execution traces)	Degree-Free GCN + Temporal Message Propagation (TMP)	TMP A-84.48% R-82.63% P-74.06% F1-78.11%	Reentrancy, Timestamp, Infinite Loop	307, 396 functions
Liu et al., 2021	Source Code	Control Flow Graph (CFG), Data Flow Graph(Expert-defined security patterns, critical nodes and variables)	Temporal Message Propagation Network + Expert Knowledge	A- 89.15% R- 87.62% P- 85.24% F1- 86.41%	Reentrancy, Timestamp dependence, Infinite Loop	307,396 smart contract functions
Han et al., 2022	Source code	Opcode sequences, control dependencies	GCN + CNN	A-94.33% P- 89.24% R- 85.41% F1-87.28%	Integer Overflow, Integer Underflow,ERC-20 Transfer, Implicit Visibility,	5000 smart contracts
Cao et al., 2022	Source Code	Semantic Graph (SG) (Data-data, instruction-instruction, instruction-data relationships)	Residual GCN with Edge Attention (EA-RGCN)			
Nguyen et al., 2022	Source Code	Heterogeneous Contract Graph(control-flow and call relations)	Multi-Level Heterogeneous Graph Embeddings (MANDO)	Buggy-F1- 88.66% ,Macro-F1- 88.96	Unchecked Low Level Calls, Front Running, Denial of Service, Arithmetic, Access Control, Reentrancy, Time Manipulation	SolidiFI-Benchmark, Smartbugs Wild, Smartbugs Curated
Cai et al., 2023	Source code	Combined AST, CFG, PDG(Syntactic and semantic features)	Bidirectional Gated Graph Neural Network(Bi-GGNN) Hybrid attention	A-90.2% P-89.2% R-92.9% F1-91.1%	9 types of vulnerabilities	SmartBugs Curated + 7000 smart contracts
Wang et al., 2023	Bytecode	Control Flow Graph (CFG)(Opcode execution logic)	GCN	A-53.44% R- 46.53% P- 26.12% F1-27.87%	-	1420 bytecodes
Zhen et al., 2024	Bytecode	Control Flow Graph (CFG) + Opcode sequence(Semantic features of opcodes and relationships between nodes)	Graph attention network(GAT)	P- 72.17% R- 71.54% F1-71.85%	Integer overflow, Transaction order dependency, Self-destruct	17,968 smart contracts
Gupta et al., 2024	Source code	Contract Graphs	GNN + GCN	A-92.92% P- 91.64% R-86.83% F1-88.72%	reentrancy, timestamp and infinite loop	40,731 smart contracts

3.5.3 Ensemble Learning Models

Ensemble learning is a machine learning strategy that combines multiple models, known as "weak learners," to achieve more accurate and reliable predictions than what a single model can provide on its own. The core idea is that by aggregating the outputs of diverse models, the ensemble can correct individual errors, reduce overfitting, and enhance generalization.

Wang et al. (2020) propose ContractWard, an ensemble-based machine learning system that detects six common smart contract vulnerabilities with high F1-scores and efficient runtime performance. Lohith et al. (2024) develop a digital forensic framework using Random Forest for vulnerability detection in Ethereum smart contracts, achieving 90% accuracy and efficient classification performance. Ma et al. (2023) introduce HGAT, a hierarchical graph attention network model, enhancing the accuracy of smart contract vulnerability detection by using multi-level feature extraction from code graphs. Summary of all ensemble models are listed in table 10.

Table 10. Ensemble models for smart contract vulnerability detection

Author, Year	Input	Features	Methods used	Performance Metrics	Vulnerability detected	Dataset size
Wang et al., 2020	Bytecode/ Opcode	Feature extraction from operation codes	XGBoost, AdaBoost, RF, SVM, KNN	Micro-F1-97.98% Macro-F1-9618%	Reentrancy, Timestamp, Integer Overflow	49502 smart contracts
Lohith et al., 2024	Bytecode	Vector space models, word embedding model	Random Forest	-	Bad randomness, access control, arithmetic, re-entrancy, DoS, unchecked low-level calls	SmartBugs
Ma et al., 2023	Source Code (AST, CFG)	Hierarchical feature extraction	Hierarchical Graph Attention Network (HGAT)	A-86.62% P-82.69% R-89.62% F1-88.31%	Reentrancy, Timestamp, Integer Overflow, Integer Underflow	SmartBugs Wild dataset

4. CHALLENGES

Based on the above observations, several challenges emerge that highlight the limitations of existing tools and approaches.

1. Data Collection Challenge: Limited availability of public smart contract data and large bytecode size require significant computational resources, making direct analysis of source code impractical.
2. A significant challenge lies in the constrained scope and suboptimal performance of existing tools. There is a pressing need to enhance and expand these tools

to detect a broader spectrum of vulnerabilities with greater precision while minimizing false positives.

3. Class Imbalance: Smart contract datasets often suffer from class imbalance, where vulnerable contracts are significantly less prevalent than non-vulnerable ones, affecting model training and accuracy.
4. Challenges in Traditional Methods: Traditional methods like formal verification and fuzz testing rely on expert-defined rules, which become impractical with the rapid growth of blockchain technology and result in high false positive rates.
5. Benchmark Dataset Issues: The lack of reliable benchmark datasets, such as limitations in Smartbugs Wild, poses challenges in vulnerability labeling and property definition.
6. Deep Learning Limitations: While deep learning improves detection accuracy, it struggles to identify the exact location of vulnerabilities and lacks comprehensive research on reentrancy vulnerability patterns.
7. Only a limited number of research efforts have expanded their focus to include vulnerability detection across multiple smart contract languages. The majority of existing tools are tailored to a single language, with Solidity being the primary focus.

5. FUTURE DIRECTIONS

Building on the above observations, the following outlines the potential future directions for advancing smart contract vulnerability detection.

1. Anomaly Detection for Unknown Vulnerabilities: Develop anomaly detection techniques to identify new and previously unknown vulnerabilities.
2. Global and Local Feature Integration: Explore the combination of global and local features to enhance smart contract vulnerability detection.
3. Cross-Platform Expansion: Extend vulnerability detection models to support additional blockchain platforms like Hyperledger Fabric, EOSIO, and Solana.
4. Alternative Feature Representation: Investigate different feature representation methods to increase the model's performance across multiple platforms.
5. Cross-Platform Integration: Broaden the model's utility by integrating support for various smart contract languages and blockchain platforms.
6. Adapt to Emerging Threats: Continuously update the model to detect new and evolving smart contract vulnerabilities.
7. Improving Model Interpretability: Develop visualization tools to help developers understand the model's decision-making process, improving the detection and resolution of vulnerabilities.

This summary reflects the key research directions highlighted in the documents, expanding platform compatibility, and addressing emerging threats.

6. CONCLUSION

In this chapter, we presented a comprehensive review of smart contract vulnerability detection using AI-based approaches. The concept of smart contracts is introduced with a focus on vulnerabilities that may lead to financial losses. Various types of these vulnerabilities are examined, along with methods for their detection and analysis. Detection techniques include conventional methods such as formal verification, static analysis, dynamic analysis, and fuzz testing. These approaches are instrumental in identifying previously unknown vulnerabilities; however, they often require substantial time to detect and address these security gaps. Traditional machine learning methods, including Decision Trees (DT), Support Vector Machines (SVM), Neural Networks (NN), and Random Forests (RF), are employed to classify vulnerabilities in smart contracts. However, these methods encounter significant challenges due to the limited availability of labeled datasets, which hinders their effectiveness and accuracy in vulnerability detection. Deep learning and graph neural network approaches detect vulnerabilities with high accuracy and reduced detection time, offering an efficient solution for identifying security risks in smart contracts. Notably, AI-driven methods deep learning and GCN highlighted for their enhanced accuracy and capacity to identify previously undiscovered vulnerabilities. Finally, key challenges and future directions for addressing vulnerabilities in smart contracts are outlined.

REFERENCES

Albert, E., Contro, F., Gordillo, P., & Puebla, G. (2019). Static resource analysis for Ethereum bytecode. In *Proceedings of the 20th International Symposium on Principles and Practice of Declarative Programming (PPDP).*

Amani, S., Bégel, M., Bortin, M., & Staples, M. (2018). Towards verifying Ethereum smart contract bytecode in Isabelle/HOL. In *Proceedings of the 7th ACM SIGPLAN International Conference on Certified Programs and Proofs* (pp. 66–77). https://doi.org/10.1145/3167084

Ashizawa, N., Yamamoto, K., & Takahashi, Y. (2021). Eth2Vec: Learning code similarity for Ethereum smart contract vulnerability detection using neural network embeddings. *IEEE Access : Practical Innovations, Open Solutions*, *9*, 138573–138586. DOI: 10.1109/ACCESS.2021.3118456

Bhargavan, K., Delignat-Lavaud, A., Fournet, C., Gollamudi, A., Gonthier, G., Kobeissi, N., Kulatova, N., Rastogi, A., Sibut-Pinote, T., & Swamy, N. (2016). Formal verification of smart contracts. In *Proceedings of the 2016 ACM Workshop on Programming Languages and Analysis for Security* (pp. 91–96). https://doi.org/10.1145/2993600.2993611

Bigi, G., Bracciali, A., Meacci, G., & Zaccaria, G. (2016). Validation of decentralized smart contracts through game theory and formal verification. In *Proceedings of the 2nd International Workshop on Emerging Trends in Software Engineering for Blockchain.*

Cai, J., Zhao, Y., Zhang, Y., & Liu, S. (2023). Bidirectional gated graph neural network with hybrid attention for smart contract vulnerability detection. *Expert Systems with Applications*, *219*, 119611. https://doi.org/10.1016/j.eswa.2023.119611

Cao, J., Li, Y., Wang, H., & Zhang, L. (2022). EA-RGCN: Residual graph convolutional network with edge attention for smart contract vulnerability detection. *Applied Soft Computing*, *124*, 109052. https://doi.org/10.1016/j.asoc.2022.109052

Dannen, C. (2017). *Introducing Ethereum and Solidity: Foundations of Cryptocurrency and Blockchain Programming for Beginners.* Apress., DOI: 10.1007/978-1-4842-2535-6

Deng, W., Li, Y., Zhang, Z., & Chen, H. (2023). A multimodal deep learning framework for smart contract vulnerability detection. *Computers & Security*, *124*, 102979. https://doi.org/10.1016/j.cose.2023.102979

Eshghie, M., Zolfaghari, B., Alizadeh, M., & Jalili, R. (2021). Dynamit: Dynamic vulnerability detection framework for Ethereum smart contracts using transaction trace analysis and machine learning. *Computers & Security, 110*, 102442. https://doi.org/10.1016/j.cose.2021.102442

Farao, A., Paparis, G., Panda, S., Panaousis, E., Zarras, A., & Xenakis, C. (2024). INCHAIN: A cyber insurance architecture with smart contracts and self-sovereign identity on top of blockchain. *International Journal of Information Security, 23*(1), 347–371. DOI: 10.1007/s10207-023-00741-8

Grieco, G., Groce, A., & Feist, J. (2020). Echidna: Effective, usable, and fast smart contract fuzzing. In *Proceedings of the 29th ACM SIGSOFT International Symposium on Software Testing and Analysis (ISSTA)* (pp. 557–560). https://doi.org/10.1145/3395363.3404366

Grossman, S., Gorbunov, S., & Stoica, I. (2018). Online detection of effectively callback-free objects with applications to smart contracts. Proceedings of the ACM on Programming Languages, 2(OOPSLA), Article 135. https://doi.org/10.1145/3276515

Gupta, N. A., Sharma, P., & Verma, R. (2024). Smart contract vulnerability detection using graph neural networks and degree-free graph convolutional networks. *Journal of Information Security and Applications, 82*, 103653. https://doi.org/10.1016/j.jisa.2024.103653

Gupta, R., Sharma, N., & Verma, A. (2022). Malicious smart contract detection using deep learning models. *Journal of Information Security and Applications, 67*, 103189.

Han, D., Li, Y., Wang, Z., & Chen, J. (2022). Smart contract vulnerability detection based on graph neural networks and convolutional neural networks. *Computers & Security, 118*, 102730. https://doi.org/10.1016/j.cose.2022.102730

He, J., Balunović, M., Ambroladze, N., Tsankov, P., & Vechev, M. (2019). Learning to fuzz from symbolic execution with application to smart contracts. In *Proceedings of the 2019 ACM SIGSAC Conference on Computer and Communications Security (CCS)* (pp. 531–548). https://doi.org/10.1145/3319535.3354247

Jain, V. K., Kumar, R., & Singh, P. (2024). Smart contract vulnerability detection using Bi-GRU and transformer models. *IEEE Access : Practical Innovations, Open Solutions, 12*, 55432–55445.

Jiang, B., Liu, Y., & Chan, W. K. (2018). ContractFuzzer: Fuzzing smart contracts for vulnerability detection. In *Proceedings of the 33rd ACM/IEEE International Conference on Automated Software Engineering (ASE)* (pp. 259–269). https://doi.org/10.1145/3238147.3238177

Jiao, J., Zhao, X., & Wang, Y. (2019). Formal verification of Ethereum smart contracts based on the K framework. *IEEE Access : Practical Innovations, Open Solutions*, *7*, 123–135.

Kalra, S., Goel, S., Dhawan, M., & Sharma, S. (2018). ZEUS: Analyzing safety of smart contracts. In *Proceedings of the 25th Annual Network and Distributed System Security Symposium (NDSS).*

Li, P., Wang, J., Zhang, Y., & Chen, X. (2024). Detecting zero-day smart contract vulnerabilities using opcode sequence analysis with n-gram and vector weight penalty mechanisms. *Computer Standards & Interfaces*, *84*, 103694. https://doi.org/10.1016/j.csi.2023.103694

Liu, C., Liu, H., Cao, Z., Chen, Z., & Zhang, X. (2018). ReGuard: Finding reentrancy bugs in smart contracts. In Proceedings of the 40th International Conference on Software Engineering: Companion Proceedings (ICSE-Companion) (pp. 65–68). https://doi.org/10.1145/3183440.3183491

Liu, H., Liu, C., Zhao, H., & Zhang, X. (2021). Detecting smart contract vulnerabilities using graph neural networks and expert-defined security patterns. *Future Generation Computer Systems*, *124*, 33–45. https://doi.org/10.1016/j.future.2021.05.018

Liu, Y., Chen, X., & Zhang, Z. (2024). Transformer-based vulnerability detection for smart contracts. *Future Generation Computer Systems*. Advance online publication.

Lohith, J. J., Prasad, M. V. N., & Rao, K. R. (2024). A digital forensic framework for vulnerability detection in Ethereum smart contracts using machine learning techniques. *Journal of Information Security and Applications*, *80*, 103612. https://doi.org/10.1016/j.jisa.2024.103612

Luo, R., Wang, Y., & Chen, H. (2022). Deep learning-based vulnerability detection for Ethereum smart contracts. *Security and Communication Networks*, *2022*, 3948721. Advance online publication. https://doi.org/10.1155/2022/3948721

Ma, C., Liu, S., & Xu, G. (2023). HGAT: Smart contract vulnerability detection method based on hierarchical graph attention network. *Journal of Cloud Computing (Heidelberg, Germany)*, *12*(1), 93. DOI: 10.1186/s13677-023-00459-x

Marchuk, G., Levkivskyi, V., Kuzmenko, A., Marchuk, D., & Levchenko, A. (2023). METHODS AND MEANS OF CREATING A PLATFORM BASED ON BLOCKCHAIN TECHNOLOGY. *Transactions of Kremenchuk Mykhailo Ostrohradskyi National University*, *3*(3), 36–43. DOI: 10.32782/1995-0519.2023.3.5

Mi, F., Zhang, Y., & Chen, Z. (2021). VSCL: A deep learning framework for smart contract vulnerability detection. *Applied Sciences (Basel, Switzerland), 11*(12), 5630. https://doi.org/10.3390/app11125630

Momeni, P., Rahmani, A. M., & Javidan, R. (2021). Smart contract vulnerability detection using machine learning techniques based on abstract syntax tree and control flow graph. *Journal of Systems Architecture, 117*, 102143. https://doi.org/10.1016/j.sysarc.2021.102143

Neloy, M. N., Wahab, M., Wasif, S., All Noman, A., Rahaman, M., Pranto, T. H., Haque, A. K. M. B., & Rahman, R. M. (2023). A remote and cost-optimized voting system using blockchain and smart contract. *IET Blockchain, 3*(1), 1–17. DOI: 10.1049/blc2.12021

Nguyen, T., Tran, H., Nguyen, K., & Kim, H. (2022). MANDO: Multi-level heterogeneous graph embedding for smart contract vulnerability detection. *IEEE Transactions on Dependable and Secure Computing*. Advance online publication. https://doi.org/10.1109/TDSC.2022.3156743

Nikolić, I., Kolluri, A., Sergey, I., Saxena, P., & Hobor, A. (2018). Finding the greedy, prodigal, and suicidal contracts at scale. In *Proceedings of the 34th Annual Computer Security Applications Conference (ACSAC)* (pp. 653–663). https://doi.org/10.1145/3274694.3274743

Qian, P., Liu, X., He, J., & Zhang, Z. (2020). BLSTM-ATT: A deep learning approach for reentrancy vulnerability detection in smart contracts. *IEEE Access : Practical Innovations, Open Solutions, 8*, 109042–109054. https://doi.org/10.1109/ACCESS.2020.3001785

Raj, A., & Prakash, S. (2022). Smart Contract-Based Secure Decentralized Smart Healthcare System. *International Journal of Software Innovation, 11*(1), 1–20. DOI: 10.4018/ijsi.315742

Rawashdeh, A. (2024). Bridging the trust gap in financial reporting: The impact of blockchain technology and smart contracts. *Journal of Financial Reporting and Accounting*. DOI: 10.1108/JFRA-08-2023-0494

Sun, X., Tu, L., Zhang, J., Cai, J., Li, B., & Wang, Y. (2023). ASSBert: Active and semi-supervised bert for smart contract vulnerability detection. *Journal of Information Security and Applications, 73*, 103423. DOI: 10.1016/j.jisa.2023.103423

Tang, W., Tang, M., Ban, M., Zhao, Z., & Feng, M. (2023). CSGVD: A deep learning approach combining sequence and graph embedding for source code vulnerability detection. *Journal of Systems and Software*, *199*, 111623. DOI: 10.1016/j.jss.2023.111623

Ullah, F., & Al-Turjman, F. (2023). A conceptual framework for blockchain smart contract adoption to manage real estate deals in smart cities. *Neural Computing & Applications*, *35*(7), 5033–5054. DOI: 10.1007/s00521-021-05800-6

Valencia-Payan, C., Griol, D., & Carlos Corrales, J. (2024). Blockchain self-update smart contract for supply chain traceability with data validation. *Logic Journal of the IGPL*, *33*(5), jzae047. Advance online publication. DOI: 10.1093/jigpal/jzae047

Wang, W., Song, J., Xu, G., Li, Y., & Wang, H. (2020). ContractWard: Automated vulnerability detection models for Ethereum smart contracts. *IEEE Transactions on Network Science and Engineering*, *8*(2), 1133–1144. https://doi.org/10.1109/TNSE.2020.2988429

Wang, Z., Li, Q., Zhang, X., & Chen, Y. (2023). Smart contract vulnerability detection based on graph convolutional networks and control flow graph analysis. *Security and Communication Networks*, *2023*, 6653127. Advance online publication. https://doi.org/10.1155/2023/6653127

Wu, Z., Li, S., Wang, B., Liu, T., Zhu, Y., Zhu, C., & Hu, M. (2022). Detecting Vulnerabilities in Ethereum Smart Contracts with Deep Learning. *2022 4th International Conference on Data Intelligence and Security (ICDIS)*, 55–60. DOI: 10.1109/ICDIS55630.2022.00016

Xing, C., Xie, Y., & Zhang, L. (2020). Vulnerability detection of smart contracts using slicing matrix and machine learning models. *Security and Communication Networks*, *2020*, 8844935. Advance online publication. https://doi.org/10.1155/2020/8844935

Xu, Y., Chen, Z., Li, Z., & Zhao, Y. (2021). Smart contract vulnerability detection based on abstract syntax tree structure and machine learning. *IEEE Access : Practical Innovations, Open Solutions*, *9*, 160953–160965. https://doi.org/10.1109/ACCESS.2021.3131649

Yang, H., Chen, Z., Zhang, X., & Liu, Y. (2021). Smart contract vulnerability detection using abstract syntax tree and random forest classification. *Applied Sciences (Basel, Switzerland)*, *11*(18), 8507. https://doi.org/10.3390/app11188507

Yu, X., Zhao, H., & Zhang, Y. (2021). DeeSCVHunter: A deep learning-based framework for smart contract vulnerability detection. *IEEE Access : Practical Innovations, Open Solutions*, *9*, 150730–150742. https://doi.org/10.1109/ACCESS.2021.3126267

Zhang, L., Zhao, Y., & Liu, S. (2023). BiGAS: BiGRU and attention-based smart contract vulnerability detection model. *Expert Systems with Applications*, *213*, 119094. https://doi.org/10.1016/j.eswa.2022.119094

Zhen, Z., Zhao, X., Zhang, J., Wang, Y., & Chen, H. (2024). DA-GNN: A smart contract vulnerability detection method based on Dual Attention Graph Neural Network. *Computer Networks*, *242*, 110238. DOI: 10.1016/j.comnet.2024.110238

Zhuang, Z., Liu, Y., & Zhang, C. (2020). Smart contract vulnerability detection using degree-free graph convolutional networks with temporal message propagation. *IEEE Access : Practical Innovations, Open Solutions*, *8*, 211176–211187. https://doi.org/10.1109/ACCESS.2020.3040092

Compilation of References

Aamir, M., Rahman, Z., Dayo, Z. A., Abro, W. A., Uddin, M. I., Khan, I., Imran, A. S., Ali, Z., Ishfaq, M., Guan, Y., & Hu, Z. (2022). A deep learning approach for brain tumor classification using MRI images. *Computers & Electrical Engineering*, *101*, 108105. DOI: 10.1016/j.compeleceng.2022.108105

Abbas, B. (2024). Elevating Realism: Cutting-Edge AI NPCs and Environments Transform Gaming in'VirtualEra.'.

Abdusalomov, A. B., Mukhiddinov, M., & Whangbo, T. K. (2023). Brain tumor detection based on deep learning approaches and magnetic resonance imaging. *Cancers (Basel)*, *15*(16), 4172. DOI: 10.3390/cancers15164172 PMID: 37627200

Abu Adla, Y., Raydan, D., Charaf, M.-Z. J., Saad, R. A., Nasreddine, J., & Diab, M. O. (2021). Automated Detection of Polycystic Ovary Syndrome Using Machine Learning Techniques, *Sixth International Conference on Advances in Biomedical Engineering*, 1-5. DOI: 10.1109/ICABME53305.2021.9604905

Ahmad, F., Ansari, M. Z., Anwar, R., Shahzad, B., & Ikram, A. (2024). Deep learning based classification of underwater acoustic signals. *Procedia Computer Science*, *235*, 1115–1124. DOI: 10.1016/j.procs.2024.04.106

Alamoudi, A., Khan, I., Aslam, N., Alqahtani, N., Alsaif, H., Al Dandan, M., Al Gadeeb, M., & Al Bahrani, R. (2023). A Deep Learning Fusion Approach to Diagnosis the Polycystic Ovary Syndrome. *Applied Computational Intelligence and Soft Computing*, *2023*, 1–15. DOI: 10.1155/2023/9686697

Albert, E., Contro, F., Gordillo, P., & Puebla, G. (2019). Static resource analysis for Ethereum bytecode. In *Proceedings of the 20th International Symposium on Principles and Practice of Declarative Programming (PPDP).*

AlKhonaini, A., Sheltami, T., Mahmoud, A., & Imam, M. (2024). UAV Detection Using Reinforcement Learning. *Sensors (Basel)*, *24*(6), 1870. DOI: 10.3390/s24061870 PMID: 38544131

Altay, N., Heaslip, G., Kovács, G., Spens, K., Tatham, P., & Vaillancourt, A. (2024). Innovation in humanitarian logistics and supply chain management: A systematic review. *Annals of Operations Research, 335*(3), 965–987. DOI: 10.1007/s10479-023-05208-6 PMID: 36777409

Amani, S., Bégel, M., Bortin, M., & Staples, M. (2018). Towards verifying Ethereum smart contract bytecode in Isabelle/HOL. In *Proceedings of the 7th ACM SIGPLAN International Conference on Certified Programs and Proofs* (pp. 66–77). https://doi.org/10.1145/3167084

Ashizawa, N., Yamamoto, K., & Takahashi, Y. (2021). Eth2Vec: Learning code similarity for Ethereum smart contract vulnerability detection using neural network embeddings. *IEEE Access : Practical Innovations, Open Solutions, 9*, 138573–138586. DOI: 10.1109/ACCESS.2021.3118456

Ashok, P., & Latha, B. (2023). Absorption of echo signal for underwater acoustic signal target system using hybrid of ensemble empirical mode with machine learning techniques. *Multimedia Tools and Applications, 82*(30), 47291–47311. DOI: 10.1007/s11042-023-15543-2

Aurna, N. F., Yousuf, M. A., Taher, K. A., Azad, A. K. M., & Moni, M. A. (2022). A classification of MRI brain tumor based on two stage feature level ensemble of deep CNN models. *Computers in Biology and Medicine, 146*, 105539. DOI: 10.1016/j.compbiomed.2022.105539 PMID: 35483227

Bach, N. H., Vu, L. H., & Nguyen, V. D. (2021). Classification of surface vehicle propeller cavitation noise using spectrogram processing in combination with convolution neural network. *Sensors (Basel), 21*(10), 3353. DOI: 10.3390/s21103353 PMID: 34065910

Balasubramanian, S., Raghavan, V. V., Selvaraj, R., & Geetha, M. (2021). Effect of big data analytics capability on firm performance: Mediating role of competitive strategy. *Journal of Business Research, 131*, 113–131. DOI: 10.1016/j.jbusres.2021.03.023

Basingab, M. S., Bukhari, H., Serbaya, S. H., Fotis, G., Vita, V., Pappas, S., & Rizwan, A. (2024). AI-Based Decision Support System Optimizing Wireless Sensor Networks for Consumer Electronics in E-Commerce. *Applied Sciences (Basel, Switzerland), 14*(12), 4960. DOI: 10.3390/app14124960

Batool, A., Zowghi, D., & Bano, M. (2025). AI governance: A systematic literature review. *AI and Ethics*, •••, 1–15.

Bhargavan, K., Delignat-Lavaud, A., Fournet, C., Gollamudi, A., Gonthier, G., Kobeissi, N., Kulatova, N., Rastogi, A., Sibut-Pinote, T., & Swamy, N. (2016). Formal verification of smart contracts. In *Proceedings of the 2016 ACM Workshop on Programming Languages and Analysis for Security* (pp. 91–96). https://doi.org/10.1145/2993600.2993611

Bian, S. (2023). Research on the Application of VR in Games. *Highlights in Science, Engineering and Technology*, *39*, 389–394. DOI: 10.54097/hset.v39i.6558

Bigi, G., Bracciali, A., Meacci, G., & Zaccaria, G. (2016). Validation of decentralized smart contracts through game theory and formal verification. In *Proceedings of the 2nd International Workshop on Emerging Trends in Software Engineering for Blockchain.*

Blei, D. M., Ng, A. Y., & Jordan, M. I. (2003). Latent Dirichlet Allocation. *Journal of Machine Learning Research*, *3*, 993–1022.

Cai, J., Zhao, Y., Zhang, Y., & Liu, S. (2023). Bidirectional gated graph neural network with hybrid attention for smart contract vulnerability detection. *Expert Systems with Applications*, *219*, 119611. https://doi.org/10.1016/j.eswa.2023.119611

Cao, J., Li, Y., Wang, H., & Zhang, L. (2022). EA-RGCN: Residual graph convolutional network with edge attention for smart contract vulnerability detection. *Applied Soft Computing*, *124*, 109052. https://doi.org/10.1016/j.asoc.2022.109052

Cao, X., Zhang, X., Togneri, R., & Yu, Y. (2019). Underwater target classification at greater depths using deep neural network with joint multiple-domain feature. *IET Radar, Sonar & Navigation*, *13*(3), 484–491. DOI: 10.1049/iet-rsn.2018.5279

Castelli, T., Sharghi, A., Harper, D., Tremeau, A., & Shah, M. (2016). *Autonomous navigation for low-altitude UAVs in urban areas.* In arXiv preprint (arXiv:1602.08141).

Celik, M., & Inik, O. (2024). Development of hybrid models based on deep learning and optimized machine learning algorithms for brain tumor Multi-Classification. *Expert Systems with Applications*, *238*, 122159. DOI: 10.1016/j.eswa.2023.122159

Chawla, M., Panda, S. N., Khullar, V., Garg, K. D., & Angurala, M. (2024). Deep learning based next word prediction aided assistive gaming technology for people with limited vocabulary. *Entertainment Computing*, *50*, 100661. DOI: 10.1016/j.entcom.2024.100661

Cheah, J. H., Kersten, W., Ringle, C. M., & Wallenburg, C. (2023). Guest editorial: Predictive modeling in logistics and supply chain management research using partial least squares structural equation modeling. *International Journal of Physical Distribution & Logistics Management*, *53*(7/8), 709–717. DOI: 10.1108/IJPDLM-08-2023-552

Cheiran, J. F. P., Bandeira, D. R., & Pimenta, M. S. (2025). Measuring the key components of the user experience in immersive virtual reality environments. *Frontiers in Virtual Reality*, *6*, 1585614. DOI: 10.3389/frvir.2025.1585614

Chen, M., Mao, S., & Liu, Y. (2014). Big Data: A Survey. *Mobile Networks and Applications*, *19*(2), 171–209. DOI: 10.1007/s11036-013-0489-0

Creed, C., Al-Kalbani, M., Theil, A., Sarcar, S., & Williams, I. (2024). Inclusive AR/VR: Accessibility barriers for immersive technologies. *Universal Access in the Information Society*, *23*(1), 59–73. DOI: 10.1007/s10209-023-00969-0

Dannen, C. (2017). *Introducing Ethereum and Solidity: Foundations of Cryptocurrency and Blockchain Programming for Beginners*. Apress., DOI: 10.1007/978-1-4842-2535-6

Deepak, S., & Ameer, P. M. (2019). Brain tumor classification using deep CNN features via transfer learning. *Computers in Biology and Medicine*, *111*, 103345. DOI: 10.1016/j.compbiomed.2019.103345 PMID: 31279167

Deng, W., Li, Y., Zhang, Z., & Chen, H. (2023). A multimodal deep learning framework for smart contract vulnerability detection. *Computers & Security*, *124*, 102979. https://doi.org/10.1016/j.cose.2023.102979

Deraj, R., Kumar, R. S., Alam, M. S., & Somayajula, A. (2023). Deep reinforcement learning-based controller for ship navigation. *Ocean Engineering*, *273*, 113937. DOI: 10.1016/j.oceaneng.2023.113937

Doan, V.-S., Huynh-The, T., & Kim, D.-S. (2022). Underwater Acoustic Target Classification Based on Dense Convolutional Neural Network. *IEEE Geoscience and Remote Sensing Letters*, *19*, 1–5. DOI: 10.1109/LGRS.2020.3029584

Dong, X., Hu, W., Xu, W., & He, T. (2025, July). Sata: A paradigm for llm jailbreak via simple assistive task linkage. In Findings of the Association for Computational Linguistics: ACL 2025 (pp. 1952-1987).

Duhr, P., Buccheri, D., Balerna, C., Cerofolini, A., & Onder, C. H. (2023). Minimum-race-time energy allocation strategies for the hybrid-electric formula 1 power unit. *IEEE Transactions on Vehicular Technology*, *72*(6), 7035–7050. DOI: 10.1109/TVT.2023.3237388

Dwivedi, D. N. (2024). The use of artificial intelligence in supply chain management and logistics. In *Leveraging AI and Emotional Intelligence in Contemporary Business Organizations* (pp. 306–313). IGI Global.

Ergin, P. (2024). Are video streaming services offering incomplete entertainment? *Media Culture & Society*, *46*(2), 414–424. DOI: 10.1177/01634437231216443

Eshghie, M., Zolfaghari, B., Alizadeh, M., & Jalili, R. (2021). Dynamit: Dynamic vulnerability detection framework for Ethereum smart contracts using transaction trace analysis and machine learning. *Computers & Security*, *110*, 102442. https://doi.org/10.1016/j.cose.2021.102442

Farao, A., Paparis, G., Panda, S., Panaousis, E., Zarras, A., & Xenakis, C. (2024). INCHAIN: A cyber insurance architecture with smart contracts and self-sovereign identity on top of blockchain. *International Journal of Information Security*, *23*(1), 347–371. DOI: 10.1007/s10207-023-00741-8

Faruk, L. I. D., Pal, D., Funilkul, S., Perumal, T., & Mongkolnam, P. (2025). Introducing CASUX: A standardized scale for measuring the user experience of artificial intelligence based conversational agents. *International Journal of Human-Computer Interaction*, *41*(9), 5274–5298. DOI: 10.1080/10447318.2024.2359206

Fowler, S. J., & Fowler, J. J. (2011). A quantitative analysis of entertainment consumption: 1984-2009. *MEIEA Journal*, *11*(1), 39–61. DOI: 10.25101/11.2

Gammelgaard, B. (2023). Systems approaches are still providing new avenues for research as the foundation of logistics and supply chain management. *International Journal of Logistics Management*, *34*(1), 1–4. DOI: 10.1108/IJLM-01-2023-601

Geng, X., & Hui, X. (2024). Power allocation based on multi-agent deep deterministic policy gradient for underwater acoustic communication networks. *Electronics (Basel)*, *13*(2), 295. DOI: 10.3390/electronics13020295

Ghassemi, N., Shoeibi, A., & Rouhani, M. (2020). Deep neural network with generative adversarial networks pre-training for brain tumor classification based on MR images. *Biomedical Signal Processing and Control*, *57*, 101678. DOI: 10.1016/j.bspc.2019.101678

Grieco, G., Groce, A., & Feist, J. (2020). Echidna: Effective, usable, and fast smart contract fuzzing. In *Proceedings of the 29th ACM SIGSOFT International Symposium on Software Testing and Analysis (ISSTA)* (pp. 557–560). https://doi.org/10.1145/3395363.3404366

Grossman, S., Gorbunov, S., & Stoica, I. (2018). Online detection of effectively callback-free objects with applications to smart contracts. Proceedings of the ACM on Programming Languages, 2(OOPSLA), Article 135. https://doi.org/10.1145/3276515

Gumusel, E. (2025). A literature review of user privacy concerns in conversational chatbots: A social informatics approach: An Annual Review of Information Science and Technology (ARIST) paper. *Journal of the Association for Information Science and Technology*, *76*(1), 121–154. DOI: 10.1002/asi.24898

Gupta, N. A., Sharma, P., & Verma, R. (2024). Smart contract vulnerability detection using graph neural networks and degree-free graph convolutional networks. *Journal of Information Security and Applications*, *82*, 103653. https://doi.org/10.1016/j.jisa.2024.103653

Gupta, R., Sharma, N., & Verma, A. (2022). Malicious smart contract detection using deep learning models. *Journal of Information Security and Applications*, *67*, 103189.

Hadi, B., Khosravi, A., & Sarhadi, P. (2023). *Adaptive formation motion planning and control of autonomous underwater vehicles using deep reinforcement learning*. In IEEE Journal of Oceanic Engineering.

Ha, N. T., Akbari, M., & Au, B. (2023). Last mile delivery in logistics and supply chain management: A bibliometric analysis and future directions. *Benchmarking*, *30*(4), 1137–1170. DOI: 10.1108/BIJ-07-2021-0409

Han, D., Li, Y., Wang, Z., & Chen, J. (2022). Smart contract vulnerability detection based on graph neural networks and convolutional neural networks. *Computers & Security*, *118*, 102730. https://doi.org/10.1016/j.cose.2022.102730

Haq, A., Li, J. P., Khan, S., Alshara, M. A., Alotaibi, R. M., & Mawuli, C. B. (2022). DACBT: Deep learning approach for classification of brain tumors using MRI data in IoT healthcare environment. *Scientific Reports*, *12*(1), 15331. DOI: 10.1038/s41598-022-19465-1 PMID: 36097024

Heilmeier, A., Graf, M., & Lienkamp, M. (2018). A race simulation for strategy decisions in circuit motorsports. 2018 21st International Conference on Intelligent Transportation Systems (ITSC), 2351-2356.

He, J., Balunović, M., Ambroladze, N., Tsankov, P., & Vechev, M. (2019). Learning to fuzz from symbolic execution with application to smart contracts. In *Proceedings of the 2019 ACM SIGSAC Conference on Computer and Communications Security (CCS)* (pp. 531–548). https://doi.org/10.1145/3319535.3354247

Herbe, A., Estermann, Z., Holzwarth, V., & vom Brocke, J. (2024). How to effectively use distributed ledger technology in supply chain management? *International Journal of Production Research, 62*(7), 2522–2547. DOI: 10.1080/00207543.2023.2218947

Hirschberg, J., & Manning, C. D. (2015). Advances in Natural Language Processing. *Science, 349*(6245), 261–266. DOI: 10.1126/science.aaa8685 PMID: 26185244

Hong, S. H. (2007). The recent growth of the internet and changes in household-level demand for entertainment. *Information Economics and Policy, 19*(3-4), 304–318.

Hu, X. (2024). Analysing the new marketing model for entertainment companies: A case study of SM. entertainment. In SHS Web of Conferences (Vol. 181, p. 01007). EDP Sciences.

Huang, K. H., & Chiu, C. J. (2021). Integrating measurement of sentiments and social network measurement to explore customer-brand associations. *Industrial Management & Data Systems, 121*(2), 296–316. DOI: 10.1108/IMDS-05-2020-0258

Huang, M. H., & Rust, R. T. (2021). A strategic framework for artificial intelligence in marketing. *Journal of the Academy of Marketing Science, 49*(1), 30–50. DOI: 10.1007/s11747-020-00749-9

Hu, G., Wang, K., Peng, Y., Qiu, M., Shi, J., & Liu, L. (2018). Deep Learning Methods for Underwater Target Feature Extraction and Recognition. *Computational Intelligence and Neuroscience, 2018*, 1–10. DOI: 10.1155/2018/1214301 PMID: 29780407

Ikram, N., & Mahajan, S. (2016, March). Road accidents: Overview of its causes, avoidance scheme and a new proposed technique for avoidance. In 2016 3rd International Conference on Computing for Sustainable Global Development (INDIACom) (pp. 497-499). IEEE.

Jafari, H., Sheikhi, A., & Fathi, M. R. (2021). The impact of digital transformation on customer experience and business performance. *Journal of Enterprise Information Management, 34*(3), 768–789. DOI: 10.1108/JEIM-09-2020-0377

Jaferian, G., Ramezani, D., Polyak, E., & Wagner, M. (2024). Exploring blockchain's horizons in educational gaming. Inted2024 Proceedings, 5050-5058.

Jain, V. K., Kumar, R., & Singh, P. (2024). Smart contract vulnerability detection using Bi-GRU and transformer models. *IEEE Access : Practical Innovations, Open Solutions, 12*, 55432–55445.

Jiang, B., Liu, Y., & Chan, W. K. (2018). ContractFuzzer: Fuzzing smart contracts for vulnerability detection. In *Proceedings of the 33rd ACM/IEEE International Conference on Automated Software Engineering (ASE)* (pp. 259–269). https://doi.org/10.1145/3238147.3238177

Jiang, Y., & Zhao, Q. (2021). The impact of online brand community engagement on brand loyalty: The mediating role of brand trust and brand affect. *Journal of Product and Brand Management, 30*(4), 562–576. DOI: 10.1108/JPBM-03-2020-2822

Jiao, J., Zhao, X., & Wang, Y. (2019). Formal verification of Ethereum smart contracts based on the K framework. *IEEE Access : Practical Innovations, Open Solutions, 7*, 123–135.

Joulin, A., Mikolov, T., Grave, E., Bojanowski, P., Mikolov, T., & Grave, E. (2017). Bag of Tricks for Efficient Text Classification. *arXiv preprint arXiv:1607.01759*. DOI: 10.18653/v1/E17-2068

Juliet, A. H. (2025, June). AI-Driven Smart Logistics Route Optimization Using IoT and Machine Learning for Efficient Supply Chain Management. In 2025 11th International Conference on Communication and Signal Processing (ICCSP) (pp. 925-930). IEEE.

Kalaiarasan, S. M.. (2024). Can we engage players with extended reality in gaming applications? A Stimulus-Organism-Response framework. *Entertainment Computing, 50*, 100651. DOI: 10.1016/j.entcom.2024.100651

Kalra, S., Goel, S., Dhawan, M., & Sharma, S. (2018). ZEUS: Analyzing safety of smart contracts. In *Proceedings of the 25th Annual Network and Distributed System Security Symposium (NDSS).*

Kamal, R., & Malhan, S. (2024). Synchronizing Senses: Neuromarketing Techniques and the Marketing Mix. In *Sensible Selling Through Sensory Neuromarketing* (pp. 107-126). IGI Global.

Kamal, R., Kaur, M., Kaur, J., & Malhan, S. (2024). Artificial Intelligence-Powered Political Advertising: Harnessing Data-Driven Insights for Campaign Strategies. In *The Ethical Frontier of AI and Data Analysis* (pp. 100-109). IGI Global.

Kamal, R., & Sofat, Y. (2024). Neurological Pathways to Impulse Buying in Virtual Reality. In *Sensible Selling Through Sensory Neuromarketing* (pp. 287–307). IGI Global. DOI: 10.4018/979-8-3693-4236-7.ch014

Kamal, S., Chandran, C. S., & Supriya, M. H. (2021). Passive sonar automated target classifier for shallow waters using end-to-end learnable deep convolutional LSTMs. *Engineering Science and Technology, an International Journal*, *24*(4), 860–871. DOI: 10.1016/j.jestch.2021.01.014

Kaur, M., & Vijay, S. (2023). Deep learning with invariant feature-based species classification in underwater environments. *Multimedia Tools and Applications*, *83*(7), 19587–19608. DOI: 10.1007/s11042-023-15896-8

Kehrle, F., Frasch, J. V., Kirches, C., & Sager, S. (2011). Optimal control of formula 1 race cars in a VDrift based virtual environment. IFAC Proceedings Volumes, 44(1), 10062-10067. DOI: 10.3182/20110828-6-IT-1002.02954

Kesuma, A. E., & Princes, E. (2024). Antecedents of Gacha gaming intention: Extending UTAUT2 with structural video game characteristics. *Computers in Human Behavior Reports*, *14*, 100405. DOI: 10.1016/j.chbr.2024.100405

Khanna, V., Chadaga, K., Sampathila, N., Prabhu, S., Bhandage, V., & Hegde, G. (2023). A Distinctive Explainable Machine Learning Framework for Detection of Polycystic Ovary Syndrome. *Applied System Innovation*, *6*(2), 1–26. DOI: 10.3390/asi6020032

Khishe, M., & Mohammadi, H. (2019). Passive sonar target classification using multi-layer perceptron trained by salp swarm algorithm. *Ocean Engineering*, *181*, 98–108. DOI: 10.1016/j.oceaneng.2019.04.013

Korkmaz, B. N., Diamant, R., Danino, G., & Testolin, A. (2023). Automated detection of dolphin whistles with convolutional networks and transfer learning. *Frontiers in Artificial Intelligence*, *6*, 1099022. DOI: 10.3389/frai.2023.1099022 PMID: 36776422

Kreps, J., Narkhede, N., & Rao, J. (2011). Kafka: A Distributed Messaging System for Log Processing. *Proceedings of the NetDB Conference*.

Kumar, K. A., Prasad, A. Y., & Metan, J. (2022). A hybrid deep CNN-Cov-19-Res-Net Transfer learning architype for an enhanced Brain tumor Detection and Classification scheme in medical image processing. *Biomedical Signal Processing and Control*, *76*, 103631. DOI: 10.1016/j.bspc.2022.103631

Kumar, K., Bhaumik, S., & Arulampalam, S. (2022). Tracking an underwater object with unknown sensor noise covariance using orthogonal polynomial filters. *Sensors (Basel)*, *22*(13), 4970. DOI: 10.3390/s22134970 PMID: 35808465

Li, P., Wang, J., Zhang, Y., & Chen, X. (2024). Detecting zero-day smart contract vulnerabilities using opcode sequence analysis with n-gram and vector weight penalty mechanisms. *Computer Standards & Interfaces*, *84*, 103694. https://doi.org/10.1016/j.csi.2023.103694

Liu, C., Liu, H., Cao, Z., Chen, Z., & Zhang, X. (2018). ReGuard: Finding reentrancy bugs in smart contracts. In Proceedings of the 40th International Conference on Software Engineering: Companion Proceedings (ICSE-Companion) (pp. 65–68). https://doi.org/10.1145/3183440.3183491

Liu, H., Liu, C., Zhao, H., & Zhang, X. (2021). Detecting smart contract vulnerabilities using graph neural networks and expert-defined security patterns. *Future Generation Computer Systems*, *124*, 33–45. https://doi.org/10.1016/j.future.2021.05.018

Liu, X., & Fotouhi, A. (2020). Formula-E race strategy development using artificial neural networks and Monte Carlo tree search. *Neural Computing & Applications*, *32*(18), 14525–14539. DOI: 10.1007/s00521-020-04871-1

Liu, Y., Chen, X., & Zhang, Z. (2024). Transformer-based vulnerability detection for smart contracts. *Future Generation Computer Systems*. Advance online publication.

Lohith, J. J., Prasad, M. V. N., & Rao, K. R. (2024). A digital forensic framework for vulnerability detection in Ethereum smart contracts using machine learning techniques. *Journal of Information Security and Applications*, *80*, 103612. https://doi.org/10.1016/j.jisa.2024.103612

Luo, R., Wang, Y., & Chen, H. (2022). Deep learning-based vulnerability detection for Ethereum smart contracts. *Security and Communication Networks*, *2022*, 3948721. Advance online publication. https://doi.org/10.1155/2022/3948721

Luo, X., Feng, Y., & Zhang, M. (2021). An underwater acoustic target recognition method based on combined feature with automatic coding and reconstruction. *IEEE Access : Practical Innovations, Open Solutions*, *9*, 63841–63854. DOI: 10.1109/ACCESS.2021.3075344

Luo, X., Zhang, M., Liu, T., Huang, M., & Xu, X. (2021). An Underwater Acoustic Target Recognition Method Based on Spectrograms with Different Resolutions. *Journal of Marine Science and Engineering*, *9*(11), 1246. DOI: 10.3390/jmse9111246

Luo, Y., Pu, L., Zuba, M., Peng, Z., & Cui, J.-H. (2014). Challenges and opportunities of underwater cognitive acoustic networks. *IEEE Transactions on Emerging Topics in Computing*, *2*(2), 198–211. DOI: 10.1109/TETC.2014.2310457

Ma, C., Liu, S., & Xu, G. (2023). HGAT: Smart contract vulnerability detection method based on hierarchical graph attention network. *Journal of Cloud Computing (Heidelberg, Germany)*, *12*(1), 93. DOI: 10.1186/s13677-023-00459-x

Mahajan, S. (2023). Phishing uniform resource locator detection using machine learning: A step towards secure system. *Security and Privacy*, *6*(6), e311. DOI: 10.1002/spy2.311

Mahajan, S., & Ikram, N. (2019). An android-based hardware system for accident avoidance and detection on sharp turns. *International Journal of Computer Aided Engineering and Technology*, *11*(4-5), 543–560. DOI: 10.1504/IJCAET.2019.100450

Manning, C. D., Raghavan, P., & Schütze, H. (2008). *Introduction to Information Retrieval*. Cambridge University Press. DOI: 10.1017/CBO9780511809071

Marchuk, G., Levkivskyi, V., Kuzmenko, A., Marchuk, D., & Levchenko, A. (2023). METHODS AND MEANS OF CREATING A PLATFORM BASED ON BLOCKCHAIN TECHNOLOGY. *Transactions of Kremenchuk Mykhailo Ostrohradskyi National University*, *3*(3), 36–43. DOI: 10.32782/1995-0519.2023.3.5

Mathivanan, S. K., Sonaimuthu, S., Murugesan, S., Rajadurai, H., Shivahare, B. D., & Shah, M. A. (2024). Employing deep learning and transfer learning for accurate brain tumor detection. *Scientific Reports*, *14*(1), 7232. DOI: 10.1038/s41598-024-57970-7 PMID: 38538708

Mehrotra, P., Chatterjee, J., Chakraborty, C., Ghoshdastidar, B., & Ghoshdastidar, S. (2011). Automated screening of Polycystic Ovary Syndrome using machine learning techniques, *2011 Annual IEEE India Conference*, 1-5. DOI: 10.1109/INDCON.2011.6139331

Menard, P., & Bott, G. J. (2025). Artificial intelligence misuse and concern for information privacy: New construct validation and future directions. *Information Systems Journal*, *35*(1), 322–367. DOI: 10.1111/isj.12544

Miao, C., Humphrey, R. H., & Qian, S. (2021). A meta-measurement of emotional intelligence and work attitudes. *Journal of Occupational and Organizational Psychology*, *94*(1), 78–112. DOI: 10.1111/joop.12297

Miao, Y., Zakharov, Y. V., Sun, H., Li, J., & Wang, J. (2021). Underwater acoustic signal classification based on sparse time–frequency representation and deep learning. *IEEE Journal of Oceanic Engineering*, *46*(3), 952–962. DOI: 10.1109/JOE.2020.3039037

Mi, F., Zhang, Y., & Chen, Z. (2021). VSCL: A deep learning framework for smart contract vulnerability detection. *Applied Sciences (Basel, Switzerland)*, *11*(12), 5630. https://doi.org/10.3390/app11125630

Mohsen, H., El-Dahshan, E. S. A., El-Horbaty, E. S. M., & Salem, A. B. M. (2018). Classification using deep learning neural networks for brain tumors. *Future Computing and Informatics Journal*, *3*(1), 68–71. DOI: 10.1016/j.fcij.2017.12.001

Molina-Castillo, F. J., Rodríguez-Escudero, A. I., Munuera-Aleman, J. L., & Marks, M. (2021). The role of internal dynamics and external mechanisms in the success of new product launches. *Industrial Marketing Management*, *92*, 128–140. DOI: 10.1016/j.indmarman.2020.11.013

Momeni, P., Rahmani, A. M., & Javidan, R. (2021). Smart contract vulnerability detection using machine learning techniques based on abstract syntax tree and control flow graph. *Journal of Systems Architecture*, *117*, 102143. https://doi.org/10.1016/j.sysarc.2021.102143

Montoya-Torres, J. R., Muñoz-Villamizar, A., & Mejia-Argueta, C. (2023). Mapping research in logistics and supply chain management during COVID-19 pandemic. *International Journal of Logistics*, *26*(4), 421–441. DOI: 10.1080/13675567.2021.1958768

Nayak, S., & Ravindran, B. (2020). Reinforcement Learning for Improving Object Detection. arXiv:2008.08005.

Neloy, M. N., Wahab, M., Wasif, S., All Noman, A., Rahaman, M., Pranto, T. H., Haque, A. K. M. B., & Rahman, R. M. (2023). A remote and cost-optimized voting system using blockchain and smart contract. *IET Blockchain*, *3*(1), 1–17. DOI: 10.1049/blc2.12021

Nenkova, A., & McKeown, K. R. (2011). Automatic Summarization. *Foundations and Trends® in Information Retrieval, 5*(2), 103-233.

Nguyen, T., Tran, H., Nguyen, K., & Kim, H. (2022). MANDO: Multi-level heterogeneous graph embedding for smart contract vulnerability detection. *IEEE Transactions on Dependable and Secure Computing*. Advance online publication. https://doi.org/10.1109/TDSC.2022.3156743

Nicoletti, B. (2025). AI Transformation of Logistics. In *Artificial Intelligence for Logistics 5.0: From Foundation Models to Agentic AI* (pp. 107–131). Springer Nature Switzerland. DOI: 10.1007/978-3-031-94046-0_4

Nikolić, I., Kolluri, A., Sergey, I., Saxena, P., & Hobor, A. (2018). Finding the greedy, prodigal, and suicidal contracts at scale. In *Proceedings of the 34th Annual Computer Security Applications Conference (ACSAC)* (pp. 653–663). https://doi.org/10.1145/3274694.3274743

Nsalo Kong, D. F., Shen, C., Tian, C., & Zhang, S. R. (2024). *Underwater acoustic monitoring: A comprehensive approach to enhance MFCC robustness and classification accuracy. Preprints.*

Oriekhoe, O. I., Ashiwaju, B. I., Ihemereze, K. C., Ikwue, U., & Udeh, C. A. (2024). Blockchain technology in supply chain management: A comprehensive review. *International Journal of Management & Entrepreneurship Research*, *6*(1), 150–166. DOI: 10.51594/ijmer.v6i1.714

Oriekhoe, O. I., Omotoye, G. B., Oyeyemi, O. P., Tula, S. T., Daraojimba, A. I., & Adefemi, A. (2024). Blockchain in supply chain management: a systematic review: evaluating the implementation, challenges, and future prospects of blockchain technology in supply chains. *Engineering Science & Technology Journal*, *5*(1), 128–151. DOI: 10.51594/estj.v5i1.732

Pailhas, Y., Petillot, Y., & Capus, C. (2010). High-resolution sonars: What resolution do we need for target recognition? *EURASIP Journal on Advances in Signal Processing*, *2010*(1), 205095. DOI: 10.1155/2010/205095

Pang, B., & Lee, L. (2008). Opinion mining and sentiment analysis. Foundations and Trends® in information retrieval, 2(1–2), 1-135.

Partarakis, N., & Zabulis, X. (2024). A review of immersive technologies, knowledge representation, and AI for human-centered digital experiences. *Electronics (Basel)*, *13*(2), 269.

Peng, B., Li, J., Akkas, S., & Araki, T. (2021). Rank position forecasting in car racing. *2021 IEEE International Conference on Data Mining (ICDM)*, 919-924.

Pushpa Mala, S., Prajwal Raju, P., Poojashree, B., Hebbar, R., Bedre, V., & Manasa, K. R. (2024). *Underwater fleck detection using convolutional neural network.* Journal of The Institution of Engineers (India): Series B, 105(2), 365–373.

Qian, P., Liu, X., He, J., & Zhang, Z. (2020). BLSTM-ATT: A deep learning approach for reentrancy vulnerability detection in smart contracts. *IEEE Access : Practical Innovations, Open Solutions*, *8*, 109042–109054. https://doi.org/10.1109/ACCESS.2020.3001785

Rahman, M. L., Reza, A. W., & Shabuj, S. I. (2022). An internet of things-based automatic brain tumor detection system. *Indonesian Journal of Electrical Engineering and Computer Science*, *25*(1), 214–222. DOI: 10.11591/ijeecs.v25.i1.pp214-222

Raj, A., & Prakash, S. (2022). Smart Contract-Based Secure Decentralized Smart Healthcare System. *International Journal of Software Innovation*, *11*(1), 1–20. DOI: 10.4018/ijsi.315742

Rani, R., Hajam, Y., Kumar, R., Bhat, R., Rai, S., & Rather, M. (2021). A Landscape Analysis of the Potential Role of Polyphenols for the Treatment of Polycystic Ovarian Syndrome. *Phytomedicine Plus : International Journal of Phytotherapy and Phytopharmacology*, *2*(1), 1–21.

Rawashdeh, A. (2024). Bridging the trust gap in financial reporting: The impact of blockchain technology and smart contracts. *Journal of Financial Reporting and Accounting*. DOI: 10.1108/JFRA-08-2023-0494

Roy, P., Podder, A., & Roy, S. (2023). A Voting classification approach for Sentiment Extraction from Bengali text. *International Journal of Emerging Trends in Engineering Research*, *11*(5), 132–136. DOI: 10.30534/ijeter/2023/021152023

Rupp, M. A. (2024). Is it getting hot in here? The effects of VR headset microclimate temperature on perceived thermal discomfort, VR sickness, and skin temperature. *Applied Ergonomics*, *114*, 104128. DOI: 10.1016/j.apergo.2023.104128 PMID: 37708655

Salazar, M., Balerna, C., & Elbert, P. (2017). Real-time control algorithms for a hybrid electric race car using a two-level model predictive control scheme. *IEEE Transactions on Intelligent Transportation Systems*, *18*(12), 3308–3319.

Selvaraj, S., Nidhyananthan, S. S., Vanmathi, R., & Ramya, M. (2022). Diet Recommendation for Poly Cystic Ovarian Syndrome of Indian Patients Using Multi-Attribute and Multi-Labeling Classifier. *Journal of Pharmaceutical Negative Results*, •••, 13.

Shahzad, K., Zhang, Q., Ashfaq, M., Zafar, A. U., & Ahmad, B. (2024). Pre-to post-adoption of blockchain technology in supply chain management: Influencing factors and the role of firm size. *Technological Forecasting and Social Change*, *198*, 122989. DOI: 10.1016/j.techfore.2023.122989

Sicoie, H. (2022). Machine Learning framework for Formula 1 race winner and championship standings predictor. Bachelor's thesis, Tilburg University, School of Humanities and Digital Sciences.

Siddhartha, J. B., Jaya, T., & Rajendran, V. (2023). RDNN for classification and prediction of rock/mine in underwater acoustics. *Materials Today: Proceedings, 80*, 3221–3228. DOI: 10.1016/j.matpr.2021.07.216

Singh, S., Debata, I., Behera, A. A., Panda, P. S., Samantaray, A., & Behera, B. K. (2025). Over-the-top (OTT) entertainment viewership addiction among the undergraduates of a medical college in Bhubaneswar, Odisha. *Journal of Family Medicine and Primary Care, 14*(3), 1110–1115.

Sohn, S. Y., & Ju, Y. H. (2021). Identifying potential causes of customer churn in the mobile communication industry using decision tree measurement. *Expert Systems with Applications, 163*, 113794. DOI: 10.1016/j.eswa.2020.113794

Somani, P. P.. (2024). *"The Rise of OTT: A Dynamic Shift Towards Binge Watching, an Increase for On-Demand Entertainment." The Rise of Over-the-Top (OTT) Media and Implications for Media Consumption and Production*. IGI Global. DOI: 10.4018/979-8-3693-0116-6.ch012

Soni, P., & Vashisht, S. (2018). Exploration on Polycystic Ovarian Syndrome and Data Mining Techniques, *Proceedings of the International Conference on Communication and Electronics Systems*. DOI: 10.1109/CESYS.2018.8724087

Srisawatsakul, C., & Jermsittiparsert, K. (2021). The impact of big data analytics capability on firm performance: Moderating role of organizational culture. The Journal of Asian Finance. *Monetarys and Business, 8*(1), 475–487. DOI: 10.13106/jafeb.2021.vol8.no1.475

Steiniger, Y., Groen, J., Stoppe, J., Kraus, D., & Meisen, T. (2021). *A study on modern deep learning detection algorithms for automatic target recognition in sidescan sonar images.* In Proceedings of the 6th Underwater Acoustics Conference and Exhibition (Virtual Meeting, p. 070010). DOI: 10.1121/2.0001470

Steiniger, Y., Kraus, D., & Meisen, T. (2022). Survey on deep learning based computer vision for sonar imagery. *Engineering Applications of Artificial Intelligence, 114*, 105157.

Stoppels, E. (2017). Predicting race results using artificial neural networks. Master's thesis, University of Twente.

Sumitha, R., Dhanalakshmi, R., & Senthamaraikannan, K. (2022). Evaluating the impact of measurement of sentiments in services of customers interactions. *International Journal of Speech Technology, 24*(1), 125–138. DOI: 10.1007/s10772-020-09747-x

Sung, M., Kim, J., Kim, J., & Yu, S.-C. (2019). Realistic sonar image simulation using generative adversarial network. *IFAC-PapersOnLine*, *52*(21), 291–296. DOI: 10.1016/j.ifacol.2019.12.322

Sun, X., Tu, L., Zhang, J., Cai, J., Li, B., & Wang, Y. (2023). ASSBert: Active and semi-supervised bert for smart contract vulnerability detection. *Journal of Information Security and Applications*, *73*, 103423. DOI: 10.1016/j.jisa.2023.103423

Surabhi, S. N. R. D., & Buvvaji, H. V. (2024). The AI-Driven Supply Chain: Optimizing Engine Part Logistics For Maximum Efficiency. *Educational Administration: Theory and Practice*, *30*(5), 8601–8608.

Tang, C., Wang, Z., Sima, X., & Zhang, L. (2020, October). Research on artificial intelligence algorithm and its application in games. In 2020 2nd International Conference on Artificial Intelligence and Advanced Manufacture (AIAM) (pp. 386-389). IEEE.

Tang, W., Tang, M., Ban, M., Zhao, Z., & Feng, M. (2023). CSGVD: A deep learning approach combining sequence and graph embedding for source code vulnerability detection. *Journal of Systems and Software*, *199*, 111623. DOI: 10.1016/j.jss.2023.111623

Thakur, R., & Srivastava, M. (2023). Linking brand engagement to loyalty: Role of perceived risk and relative advantage. *International Journal of Retail & Distribution Management*, *49*(2), 193–212. DOI: 10.1108/IJRDM-06-2020-0220

Thomas, N., & Kavitha, A. (2020). Prediction of polycystic ovarian syndrome with clinical dataset using a novel hybrid data mining classification technique. [IJARET]. *Int J Adv Res Eng Technol*, *11*(11), 1872–1881.

Tian, S., Chen, D., Wang, H., & Liu, J. (2021). Deep convolution stack for waveform in underwater acoustic target recognition. *Scientific Reports*, *11*(1), 9614. DOI: 10.1038/s41598-021-88799-z PMID: 33953232

Tiwari, S., Kane, L., Koundal, D., Jain, A., Alhudhaif, A., Pola, K., Zaguia, A., Alenezi, F., & Althubiti, S. (2022). SPOSDS: A Smart Polycystic Ovary Syndrome Diagnostic System Using Machine Learning. *Expert Systems with Applications*, *203*, 203. DOI: 10.1016/j.eswa.2022.117592

Tseng, F. C., Wu, H. H., & Wu, M. C. (2021). Manifesting the impact of artificial intelligence on individual employees. *Internet Research*, *31*(1), 311–331. DOI: 10.1108/INTR-06-2019-0236

Tuan, L. T. (2021). Drivers of customer engagement and customer loyalty in retail fintech. *Journal of Retailing and Consumer Services*, *59*, 102372. DOI: 10.1016/j.jretconser.2020.102372

Tulabandhula, T., & Rudin, C. (2014). Tire changes, fresh air, and yellow flags: Challenges in predictive analytics for professional racing. *Big Data*, *2*(2), 97–112. DOI: 10.1089/big.2014.0018 PMID: 27442303

Turkyilmaz, A., & Ozkan, C. (2021). The impact of employee engagement and knowledge sharing on service innovation performance. *Journal of Business Research*, *125*, 679–689. DOI: 10.1016/j.jbusres.2020.01.012

Ugwu, A. O., Gao, X., Ugwu, J. O., & Chang, V. (2022, September). Ethical implications of AI in healthcare data: a case study using healthcare data breaches from the US department of health and human services breach portal between 2009-2021. In *2022 International Conference on Industrial IoT, Big Data and Supply Chain (IIoTBDSC)* (pp. 343-349). IEEE.

Ukato, A., Sofoluwe, O. O., Jambol, D. D., & Ochulor, O. J. (2024). Optimizing maintenance logistics on offshore platforms with AI: Current strategies and future innovations. *World Journal of Advanced Research and Reviews*, *22*(1), 1920–1929. DOI: 10.30574/wjarr.2024.22.1.1315

Ullah, F., & Al-Turjman, F. (2023). A conceptual framework for blockchain smart contract adoption to manage real estate deals in smart cities. *Neural Computing & Applications*, *35*(7), 5033–5054. DOI: 10.1007/s00521-021-05800-6

Valencia-Payan, C., Griol, D., & Carlos Corrales, J. (2024). Blockchain self-update smart contract for supply chain traceability with data validation. *Logic Journal of the IGPL*, *33*(5), jzae047. Advance online publication. DOI: 10.1093/jigpal/jzae047

Van Eck, P. S., Jager, W., Leeflang, P. S., & Wieringa, J. E. (2021). Chasing the tail: When do cumulative advantage processes drive Internet markets and when do they not? *Journal of Interactive Marketing*, *53*, 100–116. DOI: 10.1016/j.intmar.2020.08.004

Van Kesteren, E. J., & Bergkamp, T. (2023). Bayesian analysis of Formula One race results: Disentangling driver skill and constructor advantage. *Journal of Quantitative Analysis in Sports*, *19*(4), 273–293. DOI: 10.1515/jqas-2022-0021 PMID: 38020583

Vedpathak, S., & Thakre, V. S. (2020). Pcocare: PCOS Detection and Prediction Using Machine Learning Algorithms. *Bioscience Biotechnology Research Communications*, •••, 240–244.

Vergari, M. (2025). User experience for public usage of extended reality (Doctoral dissertation, Technische Universität Berlin).

Verhoef, P. C., Broekhuizen, T., Bart, Y., Bhattacharya, A., Dong, J. Q., Fabian, N., & Haenlein, M. (2021). Digital transformation: A multidisciplinary reflection and research agenda. *Journal of Business Research*, *122*, 889–901. DOI: 10.1016/j.jbusres.2019.09.022

Walia, J. S., & K, P. L. (2024). Deep Learning Innovations for Underwater Waste Detection: An In-Depth Analysis. arXiv:2405.18299.

Wang, H., Li, H., Zhu, J., Wang, X., Pan, C., Huang, M., & Sha, L. (2025, November). Diffusionattacker: Diffusion-driven prompt manipulation for llm jailbreak. In *Proceedings of the 2025 Conference on Empirical Methods in Natural Language Processing* (pp. 22193-22205).

Wang, W. A. N. G., Zhou, Z. H. U., Zhou, Z. H. O. U., & Tang, T. A. N. G. (2024). Deep-reinforcement-learning-based UAV autonomous navigation and collision avoidance in unknown environments. *Chinese Journal of Aeronautics*, *37*(3), 237–257. DOI: 10.1016/j.cja.2023.09.033

Wang, W., Song, J., Xu, G., Li, Y., & Wang, H. (2020). ContractWard: Automated vulnerability detection models for Ethereum smart contracts. *IEEE Transactions on Network Science and Engineering*, *8*(2), 1133–1144. https://doi.org/10.1109/TNSE.2020.2988429

Wang, X., Liu, A., Zhang, Y., & Xue, F. (2019). Underwater Acoustic Target Recognition: A Combination of Multi-Dimensional Fusion Features and Modified Deep Neural Network. *Remote Sensing (Basel)*, *11*(16), 1888. DOI: 10.3390/rs11161888

Wang, Y., Xiao, J., Cheng, X., Wei, Q., & Tang, N. (2024). Underwater acoustic signal classification based on a spatial–temporal fusion neural network. *Frontiers in Marine Science*, *11*, 1331717. DOI: 10.3389/fmars.2024.1331717

Wang, Z., Li, Q., Zhang, X., & Chen, Y. (2023). Smart contract vulnerability detection based on graph convolutional networks and control flow graph analysis. *Security and Communication Networks*, *2023*, 6653127. Advance online publication. https://doi.org/10.1155/2023/6653127

Weng, Y., Chun, S., Ohashi, M., Matsuda, T., Sekimori, Y., Pajarinen, J., Peters, J., & Maki, T. (2024). *Autonomous underwater vehicle link alignment control in unknown environments using reinforcement learning*. In Journal of Field Robotics. DOI: 10.1002/rob.22348

Widjaja, A. E., Chen, C. H., & Hsu, J. S. C. (2021). Manifesting the role of text analytics in improving services of customers quality. *Information & Management*, *58*(1), 103273. DOI: 10.1016/j.im.2020.103273

Wischnewski, A., Euler, M., Gümüs, S., & Lohmann, B. (2022). Tube model predictive control for an autonomous race car. *Vehicle System Dynamics*, *60*(1), 26–44. DOI: 10.1080/00423114.2021.1943461

Woo, J., Kim, D., Lee, J., & Jang, S. (2024, January). Enhancing Viewer Experience: Combining TV and Projector Technologies for a New Era of Entertainment. In *2024 IEEE International Conference on Consumer Electronics (ICCE)* (pp. 1-3). IEEE.

Wu, Z., Li, S., Wang, B., Liu, T., Zhu, Y., Zhu, C., & Hu, M. (2022). Detecting Vulnerabilities in Ethereum Smart Contracts with Deep Learning. *2022 4th International Conference on Data Intelligence and Security (ICDIS)*, 55–60. DOI: 10.1109/ICDIS55630.2022.00016

Wu, C. H., Kao, S. C., & Shih, Y. W. (2022). Linking transformational leadership and knowledge sharing: The mediating effects of perceived intrinsic and extrinsic rewards. *Leadership & Organization Sustainability Journal*, *42*(2), 275–291. DOI: 10.1108/LODJ-05-2020-0184

Xiao, X., Wang, W., Ren, Q., Gerstoft, P., & Ma, L. (2021). Underwater acoustic target recognition using attention-based deep neural network. *JASA Express Letters*, *1*(10), 106001. DOI: 10.1121/10.0006299 PMID: 36154215

Xi, N., Buruk, O. O., Chen, J., Jabari, S., & Hamari, J. (2024). Wearable gaming technology: A study on the relationships between wearable features and gameful experiences. *International Journal of Human-Computer Studies*, *181*, 103157. DOI: 10.1016/j.ijhcs.2023.103157

Xing, C., Xie, Y., & Zhang, L. (2020). Vulnerability detection of smart contracts using slicing matrix and machine learning models. *Security and Communication Networks*, *2020*, 8844935. Advance online publication. https://doi.org/10.1155/2020/8844935

Xue, L., Zeng, X., & Jin, A. (2022). A novel deep-learning method with channel attention mechanism for underwater target recognition. *Sensors (Basel)*, *22*(15), 5492. DOI: 10.3390/s22155492 PMID: 35897996

Xu, Q., Jiang, J., Xu, K., Dou, Y., Gao, C., Zhu, B., You, K., & Zhu, Q. (2024). Self-supervised learning for underwater acoustic signal classification with mixup. *IEEE Journal of Selected Topics in Applied Earth Observations and Remote Sensing*, *17*, 3530–3542. DOI: 10.1109/JSTARS.2023.3325921

Xu, Y., Chen, Z., Li, Z., & Zhao, Y. (2021). Smart contract vulnerability detection based on abstract syntax tree structure and machine learning. *IEEE Access : Practical Innovations, Open Solutions*, *9*, 160953–160965. https://doi.org/10.1109/ACCESS.2021.3131649

Xu, Z., Guo, L., Zhou, S., Song, R., & Niu, K. (2024). Enterprise supply chain risk management and decision support driven by large language models. *Applied Science and Engineering Journal for Advanced Research*, *3*(4), 1–7.

Yaiprasert, C., & Hidayanto, A. N. (2024). AI-powered ensemble machine learning to optimize cost strategies in logistics business. *International Journal of Information Management Data Insights*, *4*(1), 100209. DOI: 10.1016/j.jjimei.2023.100209

Yang, H., Chen, Z., Zhang, X., & Liu, Y. (2021). Smart contract vulnerability detection using abstract syntax tree and random forest classification. *Applied Sciences (Basel, Switzerland)*, *11*(18), 8507. https://doi.org/10.3390/app11188507

Yang, H., Li, J., Shen, S., & Xu, G. (2019). A Deep Convolutional Neural Network Inspired by Auditory Perception for Underwater Acoustic Target Recognition. *Sensors (Basel)*, *19*(5), 1104. DOI: 10.3390/s19051104 PMID: 30836716

Yang, Y., Yan, L. F., Zhang, X., Han, Y., Nan, H. Y., Hu, Y. C., Hu, B., Yan, S.-L., Zhang, J., Cheng, D.-L., Ge, X.-W., Cui, G.-B., Zhao, D., & Wang, W. (2018). Glioma grading on conventional MR images: A deep learning study with transfer learning. *Frontiers in Neuroscience*, *12*, 804. DOI: 10.3389/fnins.2018.00804 PMID: 30498429

Yao, Q., Wang, Y., & Yang, Y. (2023). Underwater acoustic target recognition based on data augmentation and residual CNN. *Electronics (Basel)*, *12*(5), 1206. DOI: 10.3390/electronics12051206

Yu, X., Zhao, H., & Zhang, Y. (2021). DeeSCVHunter: A deep learning-based framework for smart contract vulnerability detection. *IEEE Access : Practical Innovations, Open Solutions*, *9*, 150730–150742. https://doi.org/10.1109/ACCESS.2021.3126267

ZainEldin, H., Gamel, S. A., El-Kenawy, E.-S. M., Alharbi, A. H., Khafaga, D. S., Ibrahim, A., & Talaat, F. M.ZainEldin. (2022). Brain tumor detection and classification using deep learning and sine-cosine fitness grey wolf optimization. *Bioengineering (Basel, Switzerland)*, *10*(1), 18. DOI: 10.3390/bioengineering10010018 PMID: 36671591

Zhang, L., Zhao, Y., & Liu, S. (2023). BiGAS: BiGRU and attention-based smart contract vulnerability detection model. *Expert Systems with Applications*, *213*, 119094. https://doi.org/10.1016/j.eswa.2022.119094

Zhang, Y., Dong, Z., Wu, L., & Wang, S. (2011). A hybrid method for MRI brain image classification. *Expert Systems with Applications*, *38*(8), 10049–10053. DOI: 10.1016/j.eswa.2011.02.012

Zhang, Z. L., Li, X. Y., Cao, X. H., Liu, Y., & Liu, J. (2024). Determinants of customer satisfaction and customer loyalty in social commerce. *Industrial Management & Data Systems*, *121*(3), 678–703. DOI: 10.1108/IMDS-06-2020-0319

Zhao, S., Wang, W., Li, J., Huang, S., & Liu, S. (2023). Autonomous navigation of the UAV through deep reinforcement learning with sensor perception enhancement. *Mathematical Problems in Engineering*, *2023*(1), 3837615. DOI: 10.1155/2023/3837615

Zhen, Z., Zhao, X., Zhang, J., Wang, Y., & Chen, H. (2024). DA-GNN: A smart contract vulnerability detection method based on Dual Attention Graph Neural Network. *Computer Networks*, *242*, 110238. DOI: 10.1016/j.comnet.2024.110238

Zhuang, Z., Liu, Y., & Zhang, C. (2020). Smart contract vulnerability detection using degree-free graph convolutional networks with temporal message propagation. *IEEE Access : Practical Innovations, Open Solutions*, *8*, 211176–211187. https://doi.org/10.1109/ACCESS.2020.3040092

Zhufeng, L., Xiaofang, L., Na, W., & Qingyang, Z. (2022). Present status and challenges of underwater acoustic target recognition technology: A review. *Frontiers in Physics (Lausanne)*, *10*, 1044890. DOI: 10.3389/fphy.2022.1044890

Zhu, Q., Wang, T., & Pourhejazy, P. (2024). The effect of data-driven innovation on firm performance: The mediating role of business model innovation. *Journal of Business Research*, *126*, 110–120. DOI: 10.1016/j.jbusres.2020.12.058

About the Contributors

Mohit Mittal is a Senior AI Data Scientist at Smart Labs AI GmbH (Karlsruhe, Germany), with over 14 years of experience in applied AI, focusing on Machine Learning, Deep Learning, and Explainable AI (XAI). He has hands-on expertise in NLP, Large Language Models (LLMs), and Computer Vision, including LLM fine-tuning and cloud-oriented AI development.Previously, he worked as a Data Scientist at Knowtion GmbH (Oct 2022–Jun 2025) and held postdoctoral research positions at Inria (Lille, France; Oct 2020–Sep 2022) and Kyoto Sangyo University (Kyoto, Japan; Mar 2019–Sep 2020).He earned his PhD in Computer Science (2012–2018) from Gurukul Kangri University, and completed his M.Tech (2010–2011) and B.Tech (2006–2010) in Computer Science. He is a published researcher with 1500+ citations, bridging research and real-world AI impact.

Swadha Gupta is a Chief Data Scientist at CAI GmbH in Germany. She has previously worked at Shiratech Knowtion.She completed her doctorate degree at Thapar Institute of Engineering and Technology in India in 2023. Swadha received her Bachelor's degree in Computer Science and Engineering from Shri Mata Vaishno Devi University (SMVDU) in India in 2013 and her Master's degree from Chandigarh University India in 2015. She has authored numerous papers published in prestigious journals and top-tier conferences, focusing on research areas such as face recognition, Online learning, Machine Learning, and Deep Learning

***

Arivarasi A is currently employed at Vellore Institute of Technology (VIT), Chennai as Assistant Professor Senior Grade 2. She has three and half years of teaching experience, eight years of research experience (inclusive of her Ph.D.), and over 13 years of experience in the IT industry. Her current areas of expertise include micro - nanotechnology and materials engineering, along with emerging digital transformation technologies, such as 3D printing, artificial intelligence, robotic process automation (RPA), sensor applications along with IOT. She has 5 design patents granted/filed and 2 utility patents. Her work focuses on digital solutions based on nanotechnology, material engineering, 3D printing, IoT solutions, micro–nano sensors, environmental research, rehabilitation areas and a number of interdisciplinary research areas along with AI and data science. Having 20+ numbers of publications including journals, conference proceedings and book chapters, she is a reviewer for several leading journals, including Rapid Prototyping, AIP advances and Micro Systems. Having a patent filed on sensor area, she handles electronics and computer-based courses at VIT Chennai, along with project implementations under VIT RGEMS SEED GRANT on medical rehabilitation areas, including consulting work for industry, and predominantly involved in product development.

G. Ananthi obtained her ME (Computer Science and Engineering) from Mepco Schlenk Engineering College, Sivakasi in 2010. She is currently working as Associate Professor in the Department of Computer Science and Engineering, Mepco Schlenk Engineering College, Sivakasi. She is in the teaching profession for the past 21 years. She has published 23 technical papers in International, National journals and Conferences. Her research interests are biometrics, machine learning, image processing and pattern recognition. She is a Life Member in Indian Society for Technical Education (ISTE) and Computer Society of India (CSI)

G. Shankar is a dedicated Research Scholar in the Department of Computer Science at Pondicherry University, India. My current research is keenly focused on the critical area of blockchain security, with a particular emphasis on developing innovative methods for smart contract vulnerability detection.

Roop Kamal <roope7606@cumail.in> Thu, Apr 11, 1:36 PM to me Dr. Roop Kamal is currently working as an Assistant Professor in University Business School,Chandigarh University,Mohali,Punjab.She is a post graduate (M.com) from Panjab University,Chandigarh.She has also qualified UGC NET in Commerce and comleted PhD in Commerce from RIMT University,Mandi Gobindgarh. She has over 9 years of experience in academics. Her research interests include Green marketing, Digital Marketing and Consumer Buying behaviour. She has published several research papers and articles in reputed international and national journals and has presented papers in various national and international conferences.

Soham Kapur is an engineering student of Vellore Institute of Technology Chennai, who is an eager enthusiast of electronics, digital systems and computer science. He has worked on a variety of projects in this field, related to aerial robotics, algorithm design and VLSI.

M. Nandhini is Professor of Computer Science at Pondicherry University. She holds B.Sc. (Mathematics), MCA, M.Phil., Ph.D., and UGC-NET qualified. With 28 years teaching and 22 years research, she specializes in Soft Computing, Evolutionary Optimization and Data Mining. Recipient of Best Paper awards, she holds DST-SERB-CRG (2472008 for 3 yrs) and CPRHE-NIEPA (335000 for 2 yrs) grants and has numerous publications.

Shilpa Mahajan, a distinguished Certified Ethical Hacker (CEHv11) and CISCO Certified Instructor with a notable career spanning over 16 years in research and education. Currently serving as an Associate Professor at the NorthCap University. Dr. Mahajan holds a Ph.D. in Wireless Sensor Networks from Guru Nanak Dev University, Amritsar, and graduated with distinction from Punjab Engineering College, Chandigarh. Her extensive contributions include authoring numerous papers published in prestigious international journals, books, conferences, and holding patents. In her current role, she guides doctoral scholars and successfully supervises M. Tech and B. Tech projects. Dr. Mahajan has designed courses focusing on Computer Networks, Network Security, and Cryptography. She actively participates in various academic activities, serving as a resource person for Faculty Development Programs (FDPs), workshops, guest lectures, invited talks, and panel discussions. Dr. Mahajan's expertise is underscored by her proactive involvement in chairing sessions at conferences, highlighting her standing within the academic community. Notably, she coordinated the ATAL FDP on Web Security in 2022 and or

Rashid Nadeem is currently pursuing a Ph.D. from the Department of Computer Science at Pondicherry University, Puducherry, India. His research interests are Deep Reinforcement Learning, Deep Learning, and Digital Signal Processing.

Selva Nidhyananthan S received his PhD Degree from Anna University, Chennai, Tamil Nadu, India. He is currently working as Associate Professor, Senior Grade with the Department of Electronics and Communication Engineering. His current research interest includes Signal, Speech Processing, Image Processing, and IoT.

Amitava Podder is an Assistant Professor of Computer Science and Engineering at Brainware University and a Ph.D. scholar with a focus on AI, cybersecurity, and optical networks. He holds a B.Tech and M.Tech in CSE, has published extensively in reputed journals, and holds multiple patents. Amitava is also a reviewer for IGI Global and actively contributes to academic research and innovation.

Piyal Roy is an accomplished academician in the field of Computer Science & Engineering. He has completed his BSc in Computer Science, MSc in Computer

Science and MTech in Computer Science & Engineering. Currently, he is working as an Assistant Professor at Computer Science & Engineering-AI department at Brainware University, India.

Santhi S received her post graduate from Anna University, Chennai, Tamil Nadu, India. She is currently working as Assistant Professor, Selection Grade with the Department of Computer Science and Engineering. Her current research interest includes Text Mining, Sentiment Analysis, and Recommendation Systems

V. Uma received the M.Tech, and PhD degrees in computer science from Pondicherry University in 2007 and 2014 respectively. She was awarded the Pondicherry University gold medal for M.Tech. degree in Distributed Computing Systems. She has more than 10 years of teaching experience at PG level. Her research interest includes Data mining, knowledge representation and reasoning (spatial and temporal knowledge),Machine Learning and sentiment analysis. She has authored and co-authored more than 20 peer-reviewed journal papers, which includes publications in Elsevier, IGI, Springer and Inderscience. She has also authored 8 chapters in various books published by IGI Global. She has also authored books on temporal knowledge representation and reasoning, Python Programming and Data Analysis and Programming in C++- A Hands on approach. She received the Best Paper Award in International Conference on Digital Factory in the year 2008 and also in IEEE sponsored International Conference on Smart Structures and Systems in 2019.

Meenu Vijarania received her B.Tech degree in Information Technology from MDU university, Haryana in 2005 and M.Tech(I.T) degree from GGSIPU, New Delhi in 2007. She is currently working with K R Mangalam University Gurugram, Haryana since 2021. She has 15 years of experience in teaching. She has worked at Amity University Haryana as faculty in Computer Science Department for 10.4 years and Completed PhD in the field of Wireless Ad-hoc Network. Her research area include topics of Wireless Networks and Genetic Algorithm .

Index

N

P

R

S

T

U

V

W

www.ingramcontent.com/pod-product-compliance
Lightning Source LLC
LaVergne TN
LVHW080855300926
849162LV00003B/422
* 9 7 9 8 3 6 9 3 8 3 2 7 8 *